The Spirit of Wisdom in

UNDERSTANDING PRAYER AND FAITH

Dynamic Spiritual Revelations
for
Developing Faith and Prayer

Carmelita Cartwright

xulon
PRESS

"Give instruction to a wise man, and he will be yet wiser: teach a just man, and he will increase in learning. The fear of the LORD is the beginning of wisdom: and the knowledge of the holy is understanding" (Proverbs 9:9–10).

"Thus saith the LORD, Let not the wise man glory in his wisdom, neither let the mighty man glory in his might, let not the rich man glory in his riches: But let him that glorieth glory in this, that he understandeth and knoweth me, that I am the LORD which exercise lovingkindness, judgment, and righteousness, in the earth: for in these things I delight, saith the LORD" (Jeremiah 9:23-24).

Contents

Preface

We pray ...

That the God of our Lord Jesus Christ, the Father of glory, may give unto you the spirit of wisdom and revelation in the knowledge of him. The eyes of your understanding being enlightened; that ye may know what is the hope of his calling, and what the riches of the glory of his inheritance in the saints, And what is the exceeding greatness of his power to us-ward who believe, according to the working of his mighty power. (Ephesians 1:17–19)

That he would grant you, according to the riches of his glory, to be strengthened with might by his Spirit in the inner man; That Christ may dwell in your hearts by faith; that ye, being rooted and grounded in love, May be able to comprehend with all saints what is the breadth, and length, and depth, and height; And to know the love of Christ, which passeth knowledge, that ye might be filled with all the fullness of God. (Ephesians 3:16-19)

"Wisdom is the principal thing; therefore get wisdom: and with all thy getting get understanding" (Proverbs 4:7).

Prayer works, prayer is powerful, and prayer changes things. So then, why is prayer effective for some, and others do not see tangible results? Are your prayers being answered? Do you doubt your prayers are heard? Have you lost faith? Do you want to learn how to pray effectively? If you answered yes to any of these questions, this book is for you.

There is not a magic formula in the process and development of prayer, but many facets that comprise and encompass a whole in making prayer powerful and effective. So as we begin our journey on the path of enlightenment and revelation based only on biblical based Scriptures, we will pull the pieces together, dismiss the fallacies, and provide pragmatic, step-by-step guidelines and keys to unlocking and discovering the power of prayer and how to pray for results.

For the Christian believer, some, or most of these Scriptures, may be familiar; however, you are still not experiencing the manifestation of your petitions and prayer requests. Do not dismiss the familiarity or the simplicity of the approach of this perspective outline. However, herein the importance of the approach is to commit, meditate on, and apply each one of these precious pearls of wisdom so that they penetrate your mind, your spirit, and your lifestyle daily. We really don't know it until we are living it.

We have a propensity when we are in trouble, unfortunately, and usually only in that dire time of the need, to call on God in prayer, a source of power greater than ourselves. Whether it is facing an insurmountable challenge, hopelessness, an illness, a loss of a loved one, or at the onset of facing death, we then call on a power higher than that of ourselves. But the Bible calls for us to, "pray without ceasing."

The atheist does not believe there is anyone or anything listening.

The doubter or skeptic believes that God has no intervention or role in the manifestation of answering prayers, because if He did, why is it that so many suffer, and why would He answer some prayers and not all prayers? This would mean that God is discriminatory. Well, He is not, for Romans 2:11 declares, "For there is no respect of persons with God."

A large number of Christians or faith-based believers believe that it is all God's doing and do not acknowledge that the person praying plays the most important role in having prayer answered.

Our prayers are the method by which we commune with the Spirit of God. It is the medium through which our spirit is purposed to affect, and be affected, by God. Answered prayer is predicated on both the person praying doing their part, and God intervening and doing His part through the spiritual laws that are in operation.

More than not, many are disillusioned, disappointed, tired, and discouraged because prayers appear to go unanswered. Well, change is coming ... and if change doesn't come, it's not God's fault!

We will address wisdom, faith, the Holy Spirit, and our relationship with God and Jesus Christ, which are the cornerstones and the fundamental elements for developing a powerful and effective prayer life. This book takes you step by step into a fuller understanding in what makes prayer work, how it works, why it works, how to make it work for you, why prayer is not answered, and how to develop your God-given divine potential, power, and authority to get results.

The Bible is the source of all wisdom. It teaches one how to think, believe, speak, and act so that you can manifest your dreams, turn despair into hope, fear and worry into faith, defeat into victory, sickness into healing, and prayer into power. By applying this knowledge, you can change every aspect of your life and positively impact the lives of others!

So, let's start our journey in *The Spirit Of Wisdom In Understanding Prayer And Faith* ...

Introduction

Returning to the Bible

Millions of books, doctrines, and philosophies have been written on positive thinking, spirituality, new age transformation, theoretics, and yet, the Bible states, "The thing that hath been, it is that which shall be; and that which is done is that which shall be done: and there is no new thing under the sun" (Ecclesiastes 1:9).

Spiritual books are good, but a large majority of people go from one book to another, seeking truths but never searching the Holy Bible for that truth. Scripture states that this person is, "Ever learning, and never able to come to the knowledge of the truth" (2 Timothy 3:7).

Perhaps our first choice of preference in ascertaining truth and knowledge should be from the Holy Bible, for the most worthy and moral books allude to the Bible anyway, because "Godliness is profitable unto all things, having promise of the life that now is, and of that which is to come" (1 Timothy 4:8). "Blessed are those who hear the word of God, and keep it" (Luke 11:28).

God has provided the answers and the know-how for us through His Word to live an abundant life. "All scripture is given by inspiration of God, and is profitable for doctrine, for reproof, for correction, for instruction in righteousness" (2 Timothy 3:16).

In order to understand how prayer works, we must first understand our relationship with God and how we interact with Him, His authority, our authority on Earth, and how He interacts with us.

Our Heavenly Creator

"In the beginning God created the heaven and the earth" (Genesis 1:1) and "there are three that bear record in heaven, the **Father**, the **Word**, and the **Holy Ghost**: and these three are one" (1 John 5:7, emphasis added).

The first body of evidence to support the spiritual realm is the world and our mere existence. The very existence of the universe, its power, order, and complexity, illustrate that a power All-Knowing to create it, in other words, God, must be behind it. The power of the unseen realm (the spiritual) is the origin and the root of all that is seen and experienced in our physical realm, and it is governed by God's principles. "For the invisible things of him from the creation of the world are clearly seen, being understood by the things that are made, even his eternal power and Godhead; so that they are without excuse" (Romans 1:20).

> "God [The Father] is a Spirit: and they that worship him must worship him in spirit and in truth" (John 4:24).

> "I am Alpha and Omega, the beginning and the ending, saith the Lord, which is, and which was, and which is to come, the Almighty" (Revelation 1:8). "I AM THAT I AM" (Exodus 3:14). Whatever is man-made can change; whatever is from God is eternal. "For I am the LORD, I change not" (Malachi 3:6). "Your word, O LORD, is eternal; it stands firm in the heavens. Your faithfulness continues through all generations; you established the earth, and it endures" (Psalm 119:89-90 -NIV). "For the things

which are seen are temporal; but the things which are not seen are eternal" (2 Corinthians 4:18).

The **Word**. We know from Scripture that the worlds were spoken into existence. "In the beginning was the Word, and the Word was with God, and the Word was God" (John 1:1). The power of the Word is stated in Isaiah 55:11, "So shall my word be that goeth forth out of my mouth: it shall not return unto me void, but it shall accomplish that which I please, and it shall prosper in the thing whereto I sent it."

Jesus Emmanuel (God with us). "And the **Word was made flesh**, and dwelt among us (and we beheld his glory, the glory as of the only begotten of the Father), full of grace and truth" (John 1:14, emphasis added).

The Holy Ghost. In God's creative process, the Holy Spirit performed a role in the creation of Earth, "And the earth was without form, and void; and darkness was upon the face of the deep. And the Spirit of God moved upon the face of the waters" (Genesis 1:2); and in the creation of the Son of God. To the Virgin Mary at Nazareth, the angel Gabriel came with the message, "The Holy Ghost shall come upon thee, and the power of the Highest shall overshadow thee: therefore also that holy thing which shall be born of thee shall be called the Son of God" (Luke 1:35).

And the angel of the Lord told Joseph in a dream, "Joseph, thou son of David, fear not to take unto thee Mary thy wife: for that which is conceived in her is of the Holy Ghost. And she shall bring forth a son, and thou shalt call his name JESUS: for he shall save his people from their sins" (Matthew 1:20–21).

> Now all this was done, that it might be fulfilled which was spoken of the Lord by the prophet, saying, Behold, a virgin shall be with child, and shall bring forth a son, and they shall call his name Emmanuel, which being interpreted is, **God with us**. (Matthew 1:23, emphasis added)

The Holy Ghost is also the channel of the Spirit of truth. "For the prophecy came not in old time by the will of man: but holy men of God spake as they were moved by the Holy Ghost" (2 Peter 1:21).

The Holy Spirit plays a vital role in God's plan of redemption from creation to eternity. The Holy Spirit was in the beginning; He was involved in the creation; and He is involved in spiritual regeneration of redemption, transformation, salvation, glorification, and sanctification (to purify from sin, and to make holy).

The Father (God), the Word (Son), and the Holy Ghost (Holy Spirit) are the divine omnipotent, omnipresent, omniscient, and omnificent powers that we operate in; they are the powers that affect humanity and the powers that channel through us to present an affect to Heaven. Let us hear from Heaven, and Heaven will hear us.

Our Earthly Relationship with Our Heavenly Creator

Since God is the Creator and Sustainer of all life, our life independent, non-connected, and severed from God is one of inadequate potential, power and authority. It is exemplified in the parable Jesus quoted in John 15:4, "As the branch cannot bear fruit of itself, except it abide in the vine; no more can ye, except ye abide in me." And that navigates us to the Bible.

The Bible is a book of covenant. A covenant deals with the conditional promises made to man by God as revealed in Scripture. The Bible is the Word of God and is a representation of God's love, law, order, and principles; it is a revelation of Him. God *is faithful in His promises when we are faithful to operate within His order, laws, principles, and code of ethics.*

We are spiritual beings undergoing physical experiences. We are a spirit being residing in a physical form (the body). "We have this treasure in earthen vessels, that the excellency of the power may be of God, and not of us" (2 Corinthians 4:7). We are a physical and spiritual being that have a soul (the mind, the will, and emotions), "And the LORD God formed man of the dust of the ground, and breathed into his nostrils the breath of life; and man became a living soul" (Genesis 2:7). We are spirit, soul, and body. It was the prayer of the Apostle Paul that, "the very God of peace sanctify you wholly; and I pray God your whole spirit and soul and body be preserved blameless unto the coming of our Lord Jesus Christ" (1 Thessalonians 5:23).

It is through our spirit by the Holy Spirit that we commune and worship with God. Scripture tells us in Galatians 5:25, "If we live in the Spirit, let us also walk in the Spirit." To walk in the Spirit is a way of thinking, acting, and living predicated in godly wisdom and being led of the Holy Spirit; consequently, it is living a lifestyle based on God's Word, order, code of ethics, and principles.

There is an earthly wisdom and a heavenly spiritual wisdom. The continuing progression on our path of spiritual enlightenment, spiritual maturity, and spiritual development determines the degree of interaction, the degree of power, and the degree of results between the realm of Heaven and Earth, the spiritual and the physical, between our prayers and our answers. "It is sown a natural body; it is raised a spiritual body. There is a natural body and there is a spiritual body" (1 Corinthians 15:44).

"As is the earthy, such are they also that are earthy: and as is the heavenly, such are they also that are heavenly. And as we have borne the image of the earthy, we shall also bear the image of the heavenly" (1 Corinthians 15:48–49). We are God's creation, His offspring, and we were created to fellowship with Him. Scripture tells us in John 4:23–24 that, "true worshippers shall worship the Father in spirit and in truth: for the Father seeketh such to worship him. God is a Spirit: and they that worship him must worship him in spirit and in truth."

Humanity was intended to be a reflection of the nature of God on Earth; however, the Fall of man brought about by the disobedience of the first man, Adam, and first woman, Eve, severed our communion and fellowship with God. God's plan to restore humanity to His intended divine nature was perfected in Christ Jesus. "Therefore as by the offence of one judgment came upon all men to condemnation; even so by the righteousness of one the free gift came upon all men unto justification of life. For as by one man's disobedience many were made sinners, so by the obedience of one shall many be made righteous" (Romans 5:18–19).

In Romans 8:15 Christ tells believers, "You have received the Spirit of adoption, whereby we cry, Abba, Father"; and the Apostle Paul in Romans 8:16 tells us, "The Spirit itself beareth witness with our spirit, that we are the children of God." When we pray, we should do as Christ instructed us, "After this manner therefore pray ye: Our Father which art in heaven, Hallowed be thy name. Thy kingdom come, Thy will be done in earth, as it is in heaven" (Matthew 6:9–10).

"Our Father which art in heaven" establishes our relationship with God. When we pray "Thy kingdom come, Thy will be done in earth, as it is in heaven," we are praying for the fulfillment of God working through us to fulfill His purpose of heavenly manifestation in earthly matters. "Thy will be done" is frequently interpreted as a sense of deference to what has already happened; however, its full significance is that it is a creative and faith-filled operative to the manifestation of an act that we also participate in. We are to pray according to the authority of God's Word, based on the promise of His Word and His purpose, through the instrument of faith, in expectation and thanksgiving. Faith, by its very nature, begins in the realm of the unseen (the spiritual) and ends in what is seen (the physical).

The Spirit of God is our sustaining life force. "There is no man that hath power over the spirit to retain the spirit; neither hath he power in the day of death" (Ecclesiastes 8:8). Mankind was created out of the essence of God, yet is always dependent on God as his or her source of existence. "Thou hidest thy face, they are troubled: thou takest away their breath, they die, and return to their dust. Thou sendest forth thy spirit, they are created" (Psalm 104:29–30).

God is the source of all that is as Acts 17:24–28 poignantly illustrates, "God that made the world and all things therein, seeing that he is Lord of heaven and earth, dwelleth not in temples made with hands; Neither is worshipped with men's hands, as though he needed any thing, seeing he giveth to all life, and breath, and all things; And hath made of one blood all nations of men for to dwell on all the face of the earth, and hath determined the times before appointed, and the bounds of their habitation; That they should seek the Lord, if haply they might feel after him, and find him, though he be not far from every one of us: For in him we live, and move, and have our being; as certain also of your own poets have said, For we are also his offspring." "Not that we are sufficient of ourselves to think any thing as of ourselves; but our sufficiency is of God" (2 Corinthians 3:5). Therefore, nothing in and of itself is of ourself, but it is His power, His gifts and talents in us, and His sustenance through us. Glory to His holy name, He is worthy to be exalted and praised!

We were created and intended to reflect God's nature on Earth in the context of being continually connected to Him in fellowship. "Know ye not that ye are the temple of God, and that the Spirit of God dwelleth in you" (1 Corinthians 3:16). This is how God expresses Himself on the Earth, and the Holy Spirit has the expression on Earth through us.

Mankind has been created in the image and likeness of God with inherent power and authority. "So God created man in his own image, in the image of God created he him; male and female created he them" (Genesis 1:27). "And God said, Let us make man in our image, after our likeness ... and let them have dominion over all the earth" (Genesis 1:26). This delegation of our authority in the earthly realm is established when God said, "let them have dominion over all the earth" and again when it is stated in Hebrews 2:6–8, "What is man, that thou art mindful of him? or the son of man that thou visitest him? Thou madest him a little lower than the angels; thou crownedst him with glory and honour, and didst set him over the works of thy hands: Thou hast put all things in subjection under his feet. For in that he put all in subjection under him, he left nothing that is not put under him."

God's intent for creation was that God rules the unseen realm in Heaven, and man has been commissioned to rule as stewards, the visible realm on Earth in communion with Him. "The heaven, even the heavens, are the LORD's: but the earth hath he given to the children of men" (Psalm 115:16). We are His offspring, and Scripture has referred to humanity as "little gods." Psalm 82:6 states, "Ye are gods; and all of you are children of the most High"; and in John 10:34, "Jesus answered them, Is it not written in your law, I said, Ye are gods?"

This does not mean that we are equal to God or that we are deity, nor can we create universes, but it does illustrate our authority in the earthly realm in relationship with our God. This authority was declared by Christ in Matthew 16:19, "I will give unto thee the keys of the kingdom of heaven: and whatsoever thou shalt bind on earth shall be bound in heaven: and whatsoever thou shalt loose on earth shall be loosed in heaven." The "*keys*" are spiritual principles and insight that have been disclosed so we can live a powerful and liberated life in Christ; for "the Lord is that Spirit: and where the Spirit of the Lord is, there is liberty" (2 Corinthians 3:17).

The Greek word for keys is *kleis*, and it is defined as that which "locks and unlocks." The spiritual keys represent the ability to enter and have authority. These keys must be used with wisdom and anointing. We must have the strategies, words of knowledge, power and spiritual wisdom of the Holy Ghost to use the keys that Jesus has given us.

The spiritual system of binding and loosing must operate in accordance with the plan of God to produce its full potential. To bind is *deo* in the Greek. *Deo* has several definitions; one meaning "is to put under obligation, of the law" and "to tie." The word loose in the Greek is *luo*, and means to "break the barrier or to lacerate" (to make an opening). *Luo* also means to "cause a release that gives room to a breaking forth."

Spiritual loosing does not only consist of a "sending forth"; it also entails tearing down the strongholds that Satan puts between our promise and us. After we have bound these operations, we must release the promise. The keys are unique; they give us authority and power in spiritual warfare, because the spirit realm is as much a reality as the natural realm.

When you "send forth" you speak the Word of God. When God delegates authority, there is accountability. We must not be conformed to the sinful nature of this world and grieve the Holy Spirit. We cannot come against Satan and be in agreement with him at the same time. Jesus declared in Mark 3:23-27, "How can

Satan cast out Satan? And if a kingdom be divided against itself, that kingdom cannot stand. And if a house be divided against itself, that house cannot stand. And if Satan rise up against himself, and be divided, he cannot stand, but hath an end."

In Luke 10:19 Christ said, "I give unto you power to tread on serpents and scorpions, and over all the power of the enemy: and nothing shall by any means hurt you." Also in Matthew 18:19–20, Christ declared, "I say unto you, That if two of you shall agree on earth as touching any thing that they shall ask, it shall be done for them of my Father which is in heaven. For where two or three are gathered together in my name, there am I in the midst of them."

Christ delegated and commissioned believers to have the spiritual authority (influence) and the right of (privilege) to act in the authority of His name. "For at the name of Jesus every knee should bow, of things in heaven, and things in earth, and things under the earth" (Philippians 2:10).

These Scriptures clearly illustrate our authority in interacting within the earthly realm and the spiritual realm in a reciprocal relationship. Our heavenly connection is to affect earthly matters, so God can work on the Earth through us. This promise of power in the name of Jesus is available to all born-again Christians *that are obedient to the Scriptures of the living Word*. Christ declared in Mark 16:17–18, "And these signs shall follow them that believe; In my name shall they cast out devils; they shall speak with new tongues; They shall take up serpents; and if they drink any deadly thing, it shall not hurt them; they shall lay hands on the sick, and they shall recover."

Through Christ with the power of the Holy Spirit, we can perform miracles, heal, cast out demons, pray for our personal needs to be met, and attain powerful prayers (as we are led of the Holy Spirit). Let us hear from Heaven, and Heaven will hear us.

Our spirit and **the Holy Spirit** are the vehicles by which we are meant to commune with the Spirit of God. It is the medium through which our spirit is intended to affect and be affected by God. The Holy Spirit is the function of God's voice to mediate between the realms of Heaven and Earth to communicate with us. The wind, like the Spirit of God, is an unseen manifestation in the world. The invisible working of the Holy Spirit resembles the wind that cannot be seen, but the evidence of it is manifested by the result of what is seen, what is heard, and what is felt, which is evident in John 3:8, "The wind bloweth where it listeth, and thou hearest the sound thereof, but canst not tell whence it cometh, and whither it goeth: so is every one that is born of the Spirit."

This powerful presence is key to the awakening and revelation in our spiritual transformation in wisdom, relationship, and fellowship with God to experience a powerful prayer life with the manifestation of results. Nothing is more invincible than a conscience that acknowledges the sovereignty of the Holy Spirit. But, in order to experience this divine gift, we must "be not conformed to this world: but be ye transformed by the renewing of your mind, that ye may prove what is that good, and acceptable, and perfect, will of God" (Romans 12:2). In John 3:5, "Jesus said … Except a man be born of water and of the Spirit, he cannot enter into the kingdom of God."

To be born of the Spirit is a new mind-set in living, thinking, and acting in the precepts of God's standards as it is written in His Word. Yet we should know that our faith is not just a "mind thing"—as anyone can come to a "mental ascent" of Jesus, acknowledging the existence and historical life of the Messiah, or decide that he or she will "not sin" or "start doing good things" or even "keep God's laws." Rather, repentance is a matter of the heart, one's innermost being.

To be born of the Spirit is, "… that ye put on the new man, which after God is created in righteousness and true holiness" (Ephesians 4:24). In order to walk in kingdom authority and to exercise our divine authority with power, we must be born-again of the Spirit, "Because it is written, Be ye holy; for I am holy" (1 Peter 1:16).

To accept Jesus Christ as your Lord and Savoir is to invite, and surrender to, the Holy Spirit to reside and operate within your heart and thoughts. As instructed in Acts 2:38, the Apostle, Paul tells us to, "repent, and be baptized every one of you in the name of Jesus Christ for the remission of sins, and ye shall receive the gift of the Holy Ghost." Repent in Greek is *metanoeō* meaning, "to change one's mind for better and to amend with abhorrence of one's past sins."

Christ is recorded telling the disciples in John 16:7-11, "... the Comforter [Holy Spirit]...when he is come, he will reprove the world of sin, and of righteousness, and of judgment: Of sin, because they believe not on me; Of righteousness, because I go to my Father, and ye see me no more; Of judgment, because the prince of this world is judged."

As stated in Matthew 4:4, "It is written, Man shall not live by bread alone, but by every word that proceedeth out of the mouth of God"; and the impartation of the spiritual life is, "... given unto us exceeding great and precious promises: that by these ye might be partakers of the divine nature" (2 Peter 1:4). The Holy Spirit, the Word, and wisdom of God enlighten the natural man's conscience; it is motivated and empowered by the Word of God, which is conveyed by Scripture.

The Word of God is not just the law for man, for it is also the Law of God. In Hebrews 11:3 we see that, "Through faith we understand that the worlds were framed by the word of God, so that things which are seen were not made of things which do appear."

The Word of God has inherent power in it, and it contains the power and Spirit of God. The Bible is God-breathed, authoritative, alive, and powerful, and each word and sentence has a purpose and function. Scripture tells us in Hebrews 4:12, "For the word of God is quick, and powerful, and sharper than any two edged sword, piercing even to the dividing asunder of soul and spirit, and of the joints and marrow, and is a discerner of the thoughts and intents of the heart."

There are earthly laws and spiritual laws that govern our existence, which are always in operation. Romans 7:14 affirms, "that the law is spiritual." The blessings and promises of God, as well as the consequences that are a result of sin and disobedience in the transgression of the law, are subject to these spiritual laws, which are subject to kingdom principles and the Word of God. What will be released in your life, whether blessings or cursing, will be determined by the extent of your ability to trust, believe and walk in the precepts of God's Word and the extent of authority you exercise. "For to be carnally minded is death [spiritual death]; but to be spiritually minded is life and peace" (Romans 8:6).

A revelation of God's character, Jesus Christ was the demonstration of the laws living out God's commandments. Our real source of power for prayer is from our Creator, God, and through the name and NATURE of Jesus Christ, our example, and the Holy Spirit that will dwell within us. The power and authority that will be manifested through prayer by the born-again Christian is **commissioned** by **Christ's prayer** in John 17:15-23:

> I pray not that thou shouldest take them out of the world, but that thou shouldest keep them from the evil. They are not of the world, even as I am not of the world. Sanctify them through thy truth: thy word is truth. As thou hast sent me into the world, even so have I also sent them into the world. And for their sakes I sanctify myself, that they also might be sanctified through the truth.
>
> Neither pray I for these alone [the disciples], but for them also which shall believe on me through their word; That they all may be one; as thou, Father, art in me, and I in thee, that they also may be one in us: that the world may believe that thou hast sent me. And the glory which thou gavest me I have given them; that they may be one, even as we are one: I in them, and thou in me, that they may be made perfect in one; and that the world may know that thou hast sent me, and hast loved them, as thou hast loved me.

As we develop in our faith and our spirituality by living in the Spirit, Scripture states, "For as many as are led by the Spirit of God, they are the sons of God" (Romans 8:14). In order to be led of the Holy Spirit, Jesus said, "If a man love me, he will keep my words: and my Father will love him, and we will come unto him, and make our abode with him. He that loveth me not keepeth not my sayings: and the word which ye hear is not mine, but the Father's which sent me. These things have I spoken unto you, being yet present with you. But the Comforter, which is the Holy Ghost, whom the Father will send in my name, he shall teach you all things" (John 14:23–27).

We know that we are created in His image and His likeness; therefore, we have authority and power through His Word. The fundamental concept is that we are not God, but we are like Him once we have taken on the likeness, the attributes, and the divine nature of Jesus Christ, our example. Then we also can operate in His authority and power. "But as many as received him, to them gave he power to become the sons of God, even to them that believe on his name" (John 1:12). "For through him we both have access by one Spirit unto the Father" (Ephesians 2:18).

The power of Jesus Christ is given to all who are believers that have accepted Christ as their Lord and Savior, and who have relationship with the Holy Spirit living within them. John 14:12–14 states, "He that believeth on me, the works that I do shall he do also; and greater works than these shall he do; because I go unto my Father. And whatsoever ye shall ask in my name, that will I do, that the Father may be glorified in the Son. If ye shall ask any thing in my name, I will do it."

In Luke 17:20-21 the Pharisees asked Jesus, when the Kingdom of God should come, He answered them and said, "The kingdom of God cometh not with observation: Neither shall they say, Lo here! or, lo there! for, behold, the kingdom of God is within you."

The Greek word for kingdom is *basileia* meaning, "royal power, kingship, dominion, and rule." *Basileia* "is not to be confused with an actual kingdom but rather the right or authority to rule over kingdom-of the royal power of Jesus as the triumphant Messiah-and of the royal power and dignity conferred on Christians in the Messiah's kingdom."

Prayer should be a lifestyle as a means to commune with God that can, and should, be used daily to strengthen, enlighten, and to build a intimate relationship and a fellowship with God; and through this relationship, to do what some would think as the impossible.

Most miracles in the earthly realm were manifested through humanity uniting our earthly relationship with the heavenly. In the parting of the Red Sea, Moses was the instrument that was utilized to carry out the miraculous marvels. It was not in and of himself, but God's power through him that was operating. So it is with prayer through faith, the Word, and the Holy Spirit. It is submission to God's will and obedience to His laws and our ability to let the divine work in and through us. Simply put, miracles are God's divine intervention (His Super) on (Our Natural) which equates to The Supernatural. The union of the divine with our human conscience brings power—invincible power; as Acts 1:8 declares, "Ye shall receive power, after that the Holy Ghost is come upon you."

In the physical world, in order to know how something works, you need a manual; to build a house, you need a blueprint; to learn a trade, you acquire knowledge. "For we know that the law is spiritual" (Romans 7:14), and in the spiritual world, the Bible is the manual-the blueprint-the knowledge; the truth and the wisdom. The Holy Spirit is the power. Faith is the seed for miracles, and prayer is the vehicle as an act of faith. Certain components, concepts, and principles must be understood, exercised, and executed to achieve effective prayer power.

The principles outlined in this book are illustrated first in an in-depth analogy of spiritual wisdom, the Holy Spirit, our authority and power through Jesus Christ, prayer, and faith. Second, Scriptures are outlined for biblical meditation in biblical truths; a question and answer format is given, a summary format is presented, and finally, compiling and formatting the principles of Scriptures in a step-by-step life application for us to learn how to be led and empowered by the Holy Spirit, we learn how to walk in faith, how to think with wisdom, and how to have a *powerful, result-orientated prayer life.*

CHAPTER 1

How Do We Start—First Things First

⟶⌣⟵

"All scripture is given by inspiration of God, and is profitable for doctrine, for reproof, for correction, for instruction in righteousness" (2 Timothy 3:16).

The First Steps: The Word of God is the foundation. "For the LORD giveth wisdom: out of his mouth cometh knowledge and understanding" (Proverbs 2:6). The Bible was not merely written for our information, but for our transformation. The discipline of studying the Holy Bible is vital to the process of "renewing the mind" and fostering an intimate relationship with the Lord. The study of Scripture involves, not only, reading but also interpreting, understanding, revelation and active involvement in applying the wisdom of its contents in our life daily.

King Solomon said in Proverbs 25:2, " It is the glory of God to conceal a thing: but the honour of kings is to search out a matter." God has graciously chosen to reveal Himself to those that seek after Him.

Discipleship

Christ calls for us to, "Take my yoke upon you, and **learn** of me; for I am meek and lowly [humble] in heart: and ye shall find rest unto your souls" (Matthew 11:29, emphasis added). "Then said Jesus to those Jews which believed on him, **If ye continue in my word, then are ye my disciples** indeed; And ye shall know the truth, and the truth shall make you free" (John 8:31-32, emphasis added). The word disciple means "a pupil, a learner," which is a continual discipline and process of "renewing the mind" in transforming from the inside, out.

To learn, obviously, requires knowledge and pristine knowledge requires disciplined study. Studying the Bible helps us to know the truth. As students of the Bible, we must search the Scriptures personally, first hand, to see what God says. Pastoral ministry is important, however, our due diligence is of equal importance. We see the practice in Acts 17:1, "These were more noble than those in Thessalonica, in that they received the word with all readiness of mind, and searched the scriptures daily, whether those things were so."

Many Christians have only a secondhand knowledge of the Bible and rely almost exclusively on the input of pastoral ministry. While this may be the norm, however, there should be a responsibility to individually study the Bible with diligence, prayer, commitment, and spiritual discernment. Truth is important; Scripture calls for the believer to "worship God in spirit and in **truth**." When we study God's Word, we will know His truth and we will be able to recognize a lie or a half-truth when we hear one, as well as worship Him effectively.

Biblical truths in the Bible are not always disclosed by subject context all in one book or chapter; instead, bits and pieces are given here and there; the dots need to be connected... "Precept upon precept; line upon line" (Isaiah 28:10). Verses should be interpreted in the context of the verses that come before and after them, the whole passage, the chapter, the book and even the whole Bible. Bible scholars affirm that every verse in the Bible has only one interpretation, although that verse may have several principles of applications. The best way to grasp a subject thoroughly is to study, take notes, read (and re-read) the Bible from Genesis to Revelation with guidance and impartation from the Holy Spirit, in addition, to pastoral ministry.

When we study the Bible let Scripture interpret Scripture. The primary rule of biblical interpretation is this; we must interpret Scripture with other Scriptures. This means that by referring to other verses about the same subject, we can get a complete picture of that subject. We use cross-references to consult with other verses, which deal with the same subject matter in a simpler way. The science of interpretation is called hermeneutics from the Greek word *hermēneuō,* which means, "to interpret, explain or expound." This is where a concordance can be a great study tool, as well as a Hebrew and Greek Lexicon will also bring more clarity and understanding.

Scholars attest that the Old Testament of the Bible was originally written in the Hebrew language with a few sections written in the Aramaic language. The New Testament, however, was written in Greek. Since no language exactly mirrors the vocabulary and grammar of biblical Hebrew and Greek, the actual Hebrew or Greek definition will occasionally bring into focus a clearer meaning of the translated word.

Understanding Knowledge: Scriptures states in Hosea 4:6, "My people are destroyed for lack of knowledge: because thou hast rejected knowledge, I will also reject thee, that thou shalt be no priest to me: seeing thou hast forgotten the law of thy God, I will also forget thy children." Isaiah 5:13 quoted, "Therefore my people are gone into captivity, because they have no knowledge." Proverbs 24:14 says, "So shall the knowledge of wisdom be unto thy soul: when thou hast found it, then there shall be a reward, and thy expectation shall not be cut off."

Knowing of knowledge does not entitle you to its rewards; you must first, thoroughly, understand the principles and then apply and commit to the principles to reap the results. Knowing is easy, but placing those beliefs into execution requires discipline, commitment, and strength. Praying without understanding and applying the principles of prayer is usually ineffective. James

1:22 tells us, "But be ye doers of the word, and not hearers only, deceiving your own selves."

Wisdom: Scripture states in Proverbs 9:9–10, "Give instruction to a wise man, and he will be yet wiser: teach a just man, and he will increase in learning. The fear [reverence] of the LORD is the beginning of wisdom: and the knowledge of the holy is understanding."

Knowledge, understanding of knowledge, and the application of knowledge are power. Knowledge is the accumulation of facts and information. Understanding is the knowledge of arranging the information and wisdom is applying the knowledge.

Revelation: Revelation is the process by which God makes truth about Himself or instructions known to man. Revelation leads us to a deeper understanding with wisdom and application in knowing. Revelation leads us to know about God's ways, His nature, His character, His will, His purpose and ultimately His salvation. We see throughout the Bible that God gave divine revelations through visions, prophetic dreams, ministering spirits-angels, unexplainable circumstances, and audible voices from heavenly realms. The Greek word translated revelation is *apokalypsis*, which means "an unveiling, a disclosure of truth, or instruction."

In Matthew 13:35 Jesus tells us, "I will utter things which have been kept secret from the foundation of the world," and in Mark 4:11 Jesus says, "Unto you it is given to know the mystery of the kingdom of God: but unto them that are without, all these things are done in parables."

The word "mystery" is synonymous to "secret," a thing hidden or something impossible to understand. A mystery is no longer a mystery when you have knowledge, understanding, and revelation of a given thing, and no longer a secret when it is brought to the surface. "For there is nothing hid, which shall not be manifested; neither was any thing kept secret, but that it should come abroad" (Mark 4:22).

The word Bible comes from the Egyptian word for "parchment," *byblos.* The Greek word *biblios* means "books" or "scrolls." Later, it was translated into Latin, *biblia*, meaning "book." The

Bible is more than a single book, it is a library (of sixty-six books)—*ta biblia*, which means "the books." The Bible is also called *Scripture*, a word meaning "something written."

There are two primary Greek words that describe Scripture which are translated in the New Testament. The first, *Logos*, refers principally to the total inspired, written Word of God and to Jesus, who is the Living *Logos*. The second primary Greek word that describes Scripture is *rhema*, which refers to a word that is spoken and means "an utterance." A rhema is a verse or portion of Scripture that the Holy Spirit brings to our attention by revelation with application to a current situation or need for direction. The word *testament* is from the Latin word *testamentum*, which translates the Hebrew word for "covenant," *berith*.

The Bible is a book of covenant. A covenant deals with the conditional promises made to man by God as revealed in Scripture. The Bible is a representation of God's love, law, order, nature, and principles. God is faithful in His promises when we are faithful to operate within His love, order, laws, and principles.

The Bible is our road map and the Holy Spirit is our guide like a GPS (global positioning system). The scale of the map is so vast that we need the guide (Holy Spirit) for direction. The voice and promptings of the Holy Spirit are so softly spoken that we need both to confirm that we have chosen the right path. Without close attention to both sources of wisdom, we can easily be set off course and inevitably lost.

God, the Father, the author of the Bible wants us to come to know His Word, not just to read the Word to learn head knowledge; rather in contrast, God longs for us to turn it into prayer so that the Word speaks to our spirit through the Holy Spirit, and thereby, converting knowledge to understanding, understanding to wisdom, wisdom to revelation, and revelation to *execution with consistency, resulting in manifestation.*

Oftentimes, we are presented and focus only on the historical contents of the Bible and what Christ and His disciples were able to do. Not realizing, however, the same life empowering principles are given to us through the blood of Jesus in relationship with the Father. Both are true and both are equally required to be reunited to produce, and execute, the whole message, for our intended purpose, that will become life changing, powerful, and dynamic. "Herein is my Father glorified, that ye bear much fruit; so shall ye be my disciples" (John 15:8).

What Having a Relationship with God Provides

We are God's creation. We were created to fellowship with Him. John 4:23–24 tells us that, "true worshippers shall worship the Father in spirit and in truth: for the Father seeketh such to worship him."

The Bible when properly understood is wisdom; the Words, "are spirit, and they are life" (John 6:63). Studying knowledge with understanding, wisdom, and revelation are the perquisites in bridging the gap between the earthly and the divine.

Scripture is indeed, "profitable for reproof, for correction, and for instruction," however, its profit does not stop on the level of doctrine; it must move from the head to the heart to accomplish the purpose for which it is intended.

In order for prayer to be effective, you must first learn about God and commune with God to build a personal relationship. Relationship with God imparts wisdom. Similarly, one must grow in this relationship to increase their capacity to understand Scripture, as well as apply and execute the principles.

You cannot have a relationship with anyone if you don't know him or her. This is why Scripture says, "But seek ye first the kingdom of God, and his righteousness; and all these things shall be added unto you" (Matthew 6:33). The Kingdom of God is doing it God's way; His love, principles, order, wisdom, commandments, code of ethics, and laws. God's love and commands can be compared to parents' rules for their children. Parents guide their children not only so they can be good—but also for their own good—for the benefit of their well being because they love them; and like a loving parent, God has instituted certain rules, commands and principles for the benefit of our well being, our protection, and our "wholeness."

Our fellowship with the Lord and the Holy Spirit is dependent upon obedience to God's principles. The Lord constantly speaks to us and gives us His direction. However, it's never the Lord who is not speaking, but it is us who are not hearing. Christ tells us in Revelation 3:20, "Behold, I stand at the door, and knock: if any man hear my voice, and open the door, I will come in to him, and will sup with him, and he with me." Worship and fellowship imparts relationship and thereby, "My sheep hear my voice, and I know them, and they follow me" (John 10:27).

As humbling as it may seem, we cannot run this race in our own merits. Eventually our human fragility will reveal our dependence for our Maker. In the Book of Micah 6:8 the prophet said, "What doth the LORD require of thee, but to do justly, and to love mercy, and to walk humbly with thy God?"

Admitting you can't do it all yourself is not a weakness, it is a strength! Tragedy, desperation, loss, brokenness, depression, hopelessness, and fear, these too, can serve a purpose, because they have a tendency to direct our attention and draw us closer to God. The Psalmist wrote in Psalm 119:71, "It is good for me that I have been afflicted; that I might learn thy statutes."

However, God wants us to acknowledge Him every day, commune with Him every day, that's what a relationship is all about. You know how you feel when you only hear from a friend or relative when they need something. Fellowship with God should be a way of life and a lifestyle. God is worthy of our praise, reverence, worship, fellowship, and our time for, "The Spirit of God hath made me, and the breath of the Almighty hath given me life" (Job 33:4).

The Old Testament of the Bible starts with the creation of the universe and the human race, the generation of all things. The Old Testament depicts the trials, tribulations, victories, mistakes, and the life experiences of the Jewish people, which we learn from, the foundation of the laws, statues, commandments, and the prophetic coming of the Messiah. The New Testament tells the life, death, and Resurrection of Jesus Christ, the Messiah, the beginning of the Christian Church, prophecies of the end times, the Second Coming of Jesus Christ, the Messiah, and "a new Heaven and a new Earth." The New Testament also reflects the teachings to the Gentiles and the Jewish people outlining a blueprint, a road map, and instructions on how to live life abundantly in mind, in body, and in spirit.

The essence of it all is that God loves us. As truly as God's unconditional love reflects the glory of the morning sun, the unfolding of nature, the majestic beauty, and splendor, of our world, as well as the sacrifice of "His only begotten Son," so the Bible reflects God's unconditional love for us through His statues, code of ethics, commandments, and promises. God wants us to be happy, healthy, prosperous, blessed, and whole in all areas of our lives. He has made provisions for every good thing we should ever want for. "God is love" (1 John 4:8) and God speaks to us through His Word. The goal of the written Word is to restore us to a place of wholeness and completion in every area of our lives, to maximize the purpose of our creation.

There are earthly laws and spiritual laws that govern our existence which are always in operation, and the blessings and promises of God, as well as the consequences that are a result of sin and disobedience in the transgression of the law, are subject to these spiritual laws. "There is no respect of persons with God" (Romans 2:11), "for he maketh his sun to rise on the evil and on the good, and sendeth rain on the just and on the unjust" (Matthew 5:45). Therefore, it is our responsibility to be knowledgeable, disciplined, and committed based on our choices. Your commitment to action requires taking responsibility for your choices, your actions, and your thoughts. "For to be carnally minded is death [spiritual death]; but to be spiritually minded is life and peace" (Romans 8:6).

The living Word cleanses you from sin, sanctifies you with truth, and imparts wisdom; it is the seed for faith and the sword of the Spirit. Knowing, understanding, and "being doers of the Word" creates, and maintains, an intimate relationship with the Lord.

We are to pray to God on the basis of His Word—the revelation of who He is, what His will is, and what He has promised through the Word (Scripture) of the Bible. The Word of God is our spiritual nutrition. Just as you eat every day—feed your spirit every day.

In hearing, reading, meditating, and in speaking (the living Word—Scripture), it will provide the following:

Feeds Your Inner Man
- "It is written, Man shall not live by bread alone, but by every word that proceedeth out of the mouth of God" (Matthew 4:4).
- "It is the spirit that quickeneth; the flesh profiteth nothing: the words that I speak unto you, they are spirit, and they are life" (John 6:63).
- "For to be carnally minded is death; but to be spiritually minded is life and peace" (Romans 8:6).

Willpower to Overcome Sin
- "Submit yourselves therefore to God. Resist the devil, and he will flee from you" (James 4:7).
- "There hath no temptation taken you but such as is common to man: but God is faithful, who will not suffer you to be tempted above that ye are able; but will with the temptation also make a way to escape, that ye may be able to bear it" (1 Corinthians 10:13).
- "The Lord knoweth how to deliver the godly out of temptations" (2 Peter 2:9).

Increases Your Faith
- "So then faith cometh by hearing, and hearing by the word of God" (Romans 10:17).

Power
- "For the word of God is quick, and powerful, and sharper than any two edged sword, piercing even to the dividing asunder of soul and spirit, and of the joints and marrow, and is a discerner of the thoughts and intents of the heart" (Hebrews 4:12).

- "For the kingdom of God is not in word, but in power" (1 Corinthians 4:20).
- "Ye shall receive power, after that the Holy Ghost is come upon you" (Acts 1:8).
- "Fear thou not; for I am with thee: be not dismayed; for I am thy God: I will strengthen thee; yea, I will help thee; yea, I will uphold thee with the right hand of my righteousness" (Isaiah 41:10).
- "Call unto me, and I will answer thee, and show thee great and mighty things, which thou knowest not" (Jeremiah 33:3).
- "He giveth power to the faint; and to them that have no might he increaseth strength... But they that wait [hope] upon the LORD shall renew their strength; they shall mount up with wings as eagles; they shall run, and not be weary; and they shall walk, and not faint" (Isaiah 40:29, 31).
- "Trust ye in the LORD for ever: for in the LORD JEHOVAH is everlasting strength" (Isaiah 26:4).
- "I can do all things through Christ which strengtheneth me" (Philippians 4:13).
- "Ye are of God, little children, and have overcome them: because greater is he that is in you, than he that is in the world" (1 John 4:4).
- "Behold, I give unto you power to tread on serpents and scorpions, and over all the power of the enemy: and nothing shall by any means hurt you" (Luke 10:19).
- "And I will give unto thee the keys of the kingdom of heaven: and whatsoever thou shalt bind on earth shall be bound in heaven: and whatsoever thou shalt loose on earth shall be loosed in heaven" (Matthew 16:19).

Protection against Spiritual Warfare
- "Put on the whole armour of God, that ye may be able to stand against the wiles of the devil. For we wrestle not against flesh and blood, but against principalities, against powers, against the rulers of the darkness of this world,

against spiritual wickedness in high places...And take the helmet of salvation, and the sword of the Spirit, which is the word of God" (Ephesians 6:11–12, 17).

- "Every word of God is pure: he is a shield unto them that put their trust in him" (Proverbs 30:5).
- "No weapon that is formed against thee shall prosper; and every tongue that shall rise against thee in judgment thou shalt condemn. This is the heritage of the servants of the LORD, and their righteousness is of me, saith the LORD" (Isaiah 54:17).
- "When the enemy shall come in like a flood, the Spirit of the LORD shall lift up a standard against him" (Isaiah 59:19).
- "And the Lord shall deliver me from every evil work, and will preserve me unto his heavenly kingdom: to whom be glory for ever and ever" (2 Timothy 4:18).

The Assistance of Angels
- "Bless the LORD, ye his angels, that excel in strength, that do his commandments, hearkening unto the voice of his word" (Psalm 103:20).
- "For he shall give his angels charge over thee, to keep thee in all thy ways. They shall bear thee up in their hands, lest thou dash thy foot against a stone" (Psalm 91:11–12).

Peace
- "Thou wilt keep him in perfect peace, whose mind is stayed on thee: because he trusteth in thee" (Isaiah 26:3).
- "For the kingdom of God is not meat and drink; but righteousness, and peace, and joy in the Holy Ghost" (Romans 14:17).

Answered Prayer
- "And whatsoever we ask, we receive of him, because we keep his commandments, and do those things that are pleasing in his sight" (1 John 3:22).

- "That if two of you shall agree on earth as touching any thing that they shall ask, it shall be done for them of my Father which is in heaven" (Matthew 18:19).
- "The LORD is far from the wicked: but he heareth the prayer of the righteous" (Proverbs 15:29).

Produces Results

- For my thoughts are not your thoughts, neither are your ways my ways, saith the LORD. For as the heavens are higher than the earth, so are my ways higher than your ways, and my thoughts than your thoughts. For as the rain cometh down, and the snow from heaven, and returneth not thither, but watereth the earth, and maketh it bring forth and bud, that it may give seed to the sower, and bread to the eater: So shall my word be that goeth forth out of my mouth: it shall not return unto me void, but it shall accomplish that which I please, and it shall prosper in the thing whereto I sent it. (Isaiah 55:8–11)

Kingdom Principles

- When any one heareth the word of the kingdom, and understandeth it not, then cometh the wicked one, and catcheth away that which was sown in his heart. This is he which received seed by the way side. But he that received the seed into stony places, the same is he that heareth the word, and anon with joy receiveth it; Yet hath he not root in himself, but dureth for a while: for when tribulation or persecution ariseth because of the word, by and by he is offended. He also that received seed among the thorns is he that heareth the word; and the care of this world, and the deceitfulness of riches, choke the word, and he becometh unfruitful.

  But he that received seed into the good ground is he that heareth the word, and understandeth it; which also beareth fruit, and bringeth forth, some an hundredfold, some sixty, some thirty. (Matthew 13:19–23)

Universal Laws Are Unchangeable
- "My covenant will I not break, nor alter the thing that is gone out of my lips. It shall be established for ever as the moon, and as a faithful witness in heaven. Selah" (Psalm 89:34, 37).
- "Being born again, not of corruptible seed, but of incorruptible, by the word of God, which liveth and abideth for ever. For all flesh is as grass, and all the glory of man as the flower of grass. The grass withereth, and the flower thereof falleth away: But the word of the Lord endureth forever. And this is the word which by the gospel is preached unto you" (1 Peter 1:23–25).
- "Jesus Christ the same yesterday, and to day, and for ever" (Hebrews 13:8).
- "For the things which are seen are temporal; but the things which are not seen are eternal" (2 Corinthians 4:18).

Health
- "My son, forget not my law; but let thine heart keep my commandments: For length of days, and long life, and peace, shall they add to thee" (Proverbs 3:1–2).
- "Be not wise in thine own eyes: fear the LORD, and depart from evil. It shall be health to thy navel, and marrow to thy bones" (Proverbs 3:7–8).

Healing
- "I am the LORD that healeth thee" (Exodus 15:26).
- "Bless the LORD, O my soul, and forget not all His benefits: Who forgiveth all thine iniquities; who healeth all thine diseases" (Psalm 103:2–3).
- "But he was wounded for our transgressions, he was bruised for our iniquities: the chastisement of our peace was upon him; and with his stripes we are healed" (Isaiah 53:5).
- "And these signs shall follow them that believe; In my name shall they cast out devils; they shall speak with new tongues; They shall take up serpents; and if they drink any

deadly thing, it shall not hurt them; they shall lay hands on the sick, and they shall recover" (Mark 16:17–18).

- "Then they cry unto the LORD in their trouble, and he saveth them out of their distresses. He sent his word, and healed them, and delivered them from their destructions" (Psalm 107:19–20).
- "Heal me, O LORD, and I shall be healed; save me, and I shall be saved: for thou art my praise" (Jeremiah 17:14).
- "The prayer of faith shall save the sick, and the Lord shall raise him up; and if he have committed sins, they shall be forgiven him" (James 5:15).

Victory

- "For whatsoever is born of God overcometh the world: and this is the victory that overcometh the world, even our faith" (1 John 5:4).
- "God shall supply all your need according to his riches in glory by Christ Jesus" (Philippians 4:19).

Favor

- "God is our refuge and strength, a very present help in trouble" (Psalm 46:1).
- "The LORD will not suffer the soul of the righteous to famish: but he casteth away the substance of the wicked" (Proverbs 10:3).
- "Rejoice not against me, O mine enemy: when I fall, I shall arise; when I sit in darkness, the LORD shall be a light unto me" (Micah 7:8).
- "If ye abide in me, and my words abide in you, ye shall ask what ye will, and it shall be done unto you" (John 15:7).
- "Neither death, nor life, nor angels, nor principalities, nor powers, nor things present, nor things to come, Nor height, nor depth, nor any other creature, shall be able to separate us from the love of God, which is in Christ Jesus our Lord" (Romans 8:38–39).
- "But as it is written, Eye hath not seen, nor ear heard, neither have entered into the heart of man, the things which

God hath prepared for them that love him" (1 Corinthians 2:9).

- "And we have known and believed the love that God hath to us. God is love; and he that dwelleth in love dwelleth in God, and God in him" (1 John 4:16).
- "For the LORD God is a sun and shield: the LORD will give grace and glory: no good thing will he withhold from them that walk uprightly" (Psalm 84:11).

Mercy

- "It is of the LORD's mercies that we are not consumed, because his compassions fail not. They are new every morning: great is thy faithfulness" (Lamentations 3:22–23).
- "O give thanks unto the LORD; for he is good: for his mercy endureth for ever. O give thanks unto the God of gods: for his mercy endureth for ever. O give thanks to the Lord of lords: for his mercy endureth for ever. To him who alone doeth great wonders: for his mercy endureth for ever. To him that by wisdom made the heavens: for his mercy endureth for ever. To him that made great lights: for his mercy endureth for ever: The sun to rule by day: for his mercy endureth for ever: The moon and stars to rule by night: for his mercy endureth for ever" (Psalm 136:1-9).

Saving Grace

- "For by grace are ye saved through faith; and that not of yourselves: it is the gift of God" (Ephesians 2:8).
- "Moreover the law entered, that the offence might abound. But where sin abounded, grace did much more abound" (Romans 5:20).
- "God is able to make all grace abound toward you; that ye, always having all sufficiency in all things, may abound to every good work" (2 Corinthians 9:8).
- "My grace is sufficient for thee: for my strength is made perfect in weakness" (2 Corinthians 12:9).

The Joy of the Lord

- "For the joy of the LORD is your strength" (Nehemiah 8:10).
- "Thy words were found, and I did eat them; and thy word was unto me the joy and rejoicing of mine heart" (Jeremiah 15:16).
- "These things I speak in the world, that they might have my joy fulfilled in themselves" (John 17:13).

Blessings, Wealth, and Riches

- "But thou shalt remember the LORD thy God: for it is he that giveth thee power to get wealth, that he may establish his covenant" (Deuteronomy 8:18).
- "The blessing of the LORD, it maketh rich, and he addeth no sorrow with it" (Proverbs 10:22).
- "Praise ye the LORD. Blessed is the man that feareth the LORD, that delighteth greatly in his commandments. His seed shall be mighty upon earth: the generation of the upright shall be blessed. Wealth and riches shall be in his house: and his righteousness endureth for ever" (Psalm 112:1–3).
- "Blessed is the man that walketh not in the counsel of the ungodly, nor standeth in the way of sinners, nor sitteth in the seat of the scornful. But his delight is in the law of the LORD; and in his law doth he meditate day and night. And he shall be like a tree planted by the rivers of water, that bringeth forth his fruit in his season; his leaf also shall not wither; and whatsoever he doeth shall prosper" (Psalm 1:1-3).
- "Blessed are the undefiled in the way, who walk in the law of the LORD. Blessed are they that keep his testimonies, and that seek him with the whole heart. They also do no iniquity: they walk in his ways. Thou hast commanded us to keep thy precepts diligently" (Psalm 119:1–4).
- "Let the LORD be magnified, which hath pleasure in the prosperity of his servant" (Psalm 35:27).

The Anointing

- "And it shall come to pass in that day, that his burden shall be taken away from off thy shoulder, and his yoke from off thy neck, and the yoke shall be destroyed because of the anointing" (Isaiah 10:27).

The Holy Spirit

- "He that hath my commandments, and keepeth them, he it is that loveth me: and he that loveth me shall be loved of my Father, and I will love him, and will manifest myself to him" (John 14:21).
- "Jesus answered and said unto him, If a man love me, he will keep my words: and my Father will love him, and we will come unto him, and make our abode with him. But the Comforter, which is the Holy Ghost, whom the Father will send in my name, he shall teach you all things, and bring all things to your remembrance, whatsoever I have said unto you" (John 14:23, 26).

Wisdom

- "For the LORD giveth wisdom: out of his mouth cometh knowledge and understanding" (Proverbs 2:6).
- "Behold, thou desirest truth in the inward parts: and in the hidden part thou shalt make me to know wisdom" (Psalm 51:6).
- "Through wisdom is an house builded; and by under-standing it is established" (Proverbs 24:3).
- "How much better is it to get wisdom than gold! and to get understanding rather to be chosen than silver" (Proverbs 16:16)!
- "So shall the knowledge of wisdom be unto thy soul: when thou hast found it, then there shall be a reward, and thy expectation shall not be cut off" (Proverbs 24:14).

CHAPTER 2

The Spirit of Wisdom

"Wisdom is the principal thing; therefore get wisdom: and with all thy getting get understanding" (Proverbs 4:7).

Spiritual Wisdom is the Word of God. The Word of God is the seed that produces Faith. Prayer is an act of Faith. Faith is the seed for Miracles. Miracles are the execution of Spiritual Wisdom through Faith by the Glory of God.

Random House Dictionary's definition of *wisdom*: "the quality or state of being wise; knowledge of what is true or right coupled with good judgment; scholarly knowledge or learning."

Godly Wisdom
Godly wisdom is the perfect wisdom that was and is with God from the beginning. God is, "Alpha and Omega, the beginning and the ending, saith the Lord, which is, and which was, and which is to come, the Almighty" (Revelations 1:8).

"For my thoughts are not your thoughts, neither are your ways my ways, saith the LORD. For as the heavens are higher than the earth, so are my ways higher than your ways, and my thoughts than your thoughts" (Isaiah 55:8–9).

Wisdom is presented as being with God from eternity, as at work in the creation of the world and its inhabitants, in the salvation of man, and as dwelling in man as a gift from God.

The Wisdom of God for Man

Spiritual Wisdom is the **Word of God** and a **Word from God** through the Holy Spirit.

But we speak the wisdom of God in a mystery, even the hidden wisdom, which God ordained before the world unto our glory: Which none of the princes of this world knew: for had they known it, they would not have crucified the Lord of glory. But as it is written,

Eye hath not seen, nor ear heard, neither have entered into the heart of man, the things which God hath prepared for them that love him. But God hath revealed them unto us by his Spirit: for the Spirit searcheth all things, yea, the deep things of God.

For what man knoweth the things of a man, save the spirit of man which is in him? even so the things of God knoweth no man, but the Spirit of God. Now we have received, not the spirit of the world, but the spirit which is of God; that we might know the things that are freely given to us of God. Which things also we speak, not in the words which man's wisdom teacheth, but which the Holy Ghost teacheth; comparing spiritual things with spiritual.

But the natural man receiveth not the things of the Spirit of God: for they are foolishness unto him: neither can he know them, because they are spiritually discerned. But he that is spiritual judgeth all things, yet he himself is judged of no man. For who hath known the mind of the Lord, that he may instruct him? but we have the mind of Christ. (I Corinthians 2:7–19)

The decisions that are influenced by spiritual wisdom involve earthly matters and start with a basis of knowledge, and understanding, of biblical principles that lead to godly decisions, and discernment, resulting in godly action.

Thus saith the LORD, Let not the wise man glory in his wisdom, neither let the mighty man glory in his might, let not the rich man glory in his riches: But let him that glorieth glory in this, that he understandeth and knoweth me, that I am the LORD which exercise lovingkindness, judgment, and righteousness, in the earth: for in these things I delight, saith the LORD. (Jeremiah 9:23-24)

Wisdom that is from above is first pure, then peaceable, gentle, and easy to be intreated, full of mercy and good fruits, without partiality, and without hypocrisy. And the fruit of righteousness is sown in peace of them that make peace. (James 3:17–18)

The wisdom of God for humanity is the knowledge, understanding, skill, and practice of biblical values and principles that are the requisites for godly and upright living of things both earthly and divine.

Spiritual wisdom is also seeking God, being connected to our heavenly Father, hearing from God, obeying and being led by the Holy Spirit. When we are intentionally and consciously seeking a deeper relationship with God, which means, very simply, seeking and making God first, with worship and prayer, with thanksgiving, and reminding ourselves of the reality of God in our daily lives, we will become more sensitive and aware of the presence of the Holy Spirit in our lives, for Scripture says, "Let this mind be in you, which was also in Christ Jesus" (Philippians 2:5).

Spiritual wisdom belongs to the Lord and He imparts it to those who acknowledge Him to be Lord. In other words, God's wisdom comes only to those who confess Jesus as Lord as evident in Mark 9:38–39, "And John answered him, saying, Master, we saw one casting out devils in thy name, and he followeth not us: and we forbad him, because he followeth not us. But Jesus said, Forbid him not: for there is no man which shall do a miracle in my name, that can lightly speak evil of me."

Jesus stated in John 4:23, "If a man love me, he will keep my words: and my Father will love him, and we will come unto him, and make our abode with him." This intimate fellowship forms a bond that imparts the wisdom of the Holy Spirit to nurture, enlighten, comfort, lead, and empower the consciousness.

Jesus also relied on this bond with the Father, as He stated in John 5:30, "I can of mine own self do nothing: as I hear, I judge: and my judgment is just; because I seek not mine own will, but the will of the Father which hath sent me."

The gift of wisdom, an unction or a *rhema Word*, involves having a sense of divine direction, being led by the Holy Spirit to act appropriately in a given set of circumstances, understanding of circumstances, situations, problems, or a body of facts by revelation and rightly applying knowledge. "Ye have an unction from the Holy One, and ye know all things" (1 John 2:20). We are instructed in Matthew 6:33, "to first seek the kingdom of God and his righteousness; and all these things shall be added unto you."

The impartation of divine wisdom is conditional. We cannot live and act any way that is ungodly and then expect the blessings and promises of God. To live in the righteousness of God is simply being in right standing with God. If we hear from Heaven, then Heaven will hear from us. 2 Chronicles 7:14 tells us, "If my people, which are called by my name, shall humble themselves, and pray, and seek my face, and turn from their wicked ways; then will I hear from heaven, and will forgive their sin, and will heal their land." Proverbs 1:23 tells us, "Turn you at my reproof:

behold, I will pour out my spirit unto you, I will make known my words unto you."

Seeking the truth requires committing and setting aside time to study, read Scripture, and meditate in the Word. Luke 11:10 states, "For every one that asketh receiveth; and he that seeketh findeth; and to him that knocketh it shall be opened."

The Bible instructs us in 2 Timothy 2:15, "Study to shew thyself approved unto God, a workman that needeth not to be ashamed, rightly dividing the word of truth." To study God's Word will enable you to use discernment, which will safeguard you from false doctrines. "Beloved, believe not every spirit, but try the spirits whether they are of God: because many false prophets are gone out into the world" (1John 4:1).

Discerning of spirits must be done by the power of the Holy Spirit; He bears witness with our spirit when something is or is not of God. Discerning of spirits is God speaking to our spirit by the Holy Spirit to determine whether the source is holy or unholy, and this impartation will always agree with the written Word.

Knowledge is the first component in acquiring wisdom in the pursuit of seeking the kingdom. Knowledge, understanding, discernment and revelation are the instruments and factors that prepare us to receive the promises in our process of spiritual development and maturity. These functions build on each other as illustrated below:

- Knowledge is that which comes from the ability to see, to hear, and to ascertain through facts, truths, or principles, and experience. Knowledge resides in the intellect.
- Understanding is insight into the nature of a thing, a deeper level of knowing mentally.
- Discernment is the ability to distinguish one thing from another and often involves one's moral sensitivities or feelings about right and wrong. The discerning person not only distinguishes one thing from another but also will normally proceed to make a moral judgment as to which is best.

- Wisdom sheds light on knowledge and goes beyond knowledge, understanding, and discernment. Wisdom is to exercise sound judgment based on these which will enable you to pursue a proper course of action.
- Revelation means an unveiling of something that was once hidden, the mystery removed, or a disclosure or realization. It reveals facts about a person, condition, thoughts, and circumstances that are not possible by our own natural minds. It implies the power of spiritual insight. Revelation knows that you know, that you know; it is sometimes an "Aha!" moment.

Biblical wisdom has its foundation in knowledge and understanding, but it moves beyond that to discernment, revelation, and then, the resulting action. The gift of the Word of wisdom works interactively with understanding, discernment, and revelation, as indicated in Ephesians 1:17, "That the God of our Lord Jesus Christ, the Father of glory, may give unto you the spirit of wisdom and revelation in the knowledge of him." Revelations are always by the Spirit and not by flesh and blood. It is this principle of revelation that Jesus declares in Matthew 16:17-18, "for flesh and blood hath not revealed it unto thee, but my Father which is in heaven. And I say also unto thee...and upon this rock I will build my church [the body of Christ made up of all born-again believers]; and the gates of hell shall not prevail against it."

The Holy Spirit speaks the gift of the Word of wisdom, usually in a soft whisper. This knowing does not only come from study. Instead, it is also nurtured from the revelation of knowing God and the union of our relationship with Christ.

The gift of the Spirit of truth is the application of knowledge that speaks through the Spirit. A word of knowledge is a definite conviction, impression, or knowing that comes to you in a dream, through a vision, or by a Scripture that is quickened to you, or a deep sense of just knowing.

"Howbeit when he, the Spirit of truth, is come, he will guide you into all truth: for he shall not speak of himself; but whatsoever he shall hear, that shall he speak: and he will shew you things to come" (John 16:13).

The degree of time spent in seeking God will determine the degree of God's intervention in our lives. No time, no knowledge; no knowledge, no manifestation. Jeremiah 33:3 says, "Call unto me, and I will answer thee, and show thee great and mighty things, which thou knowest not."

Seeking God is also discerning His will and purpose in our daily lives, which affects our intentions, choices, and decisions. Spiritual wisdom may not always line up with natural understanding. In order, to enter the supernatural you have to be taught kingdom principles. Scripture tells us, "Trust in the LORD with all thine heart; and lean not unto thine own understanding. In all thy ways acknowledge him, and he shall direct thy paths" (Proverbs 3:5–6).

The Natural Man's Intellectual Wisdom

There is an earthly wisdom and a heavenly spiritual wisdom. 1 Corinthians 1:21 makes this distinction, "For after that in the wisdom of God the world by wisdom knew not God, it pleased God by the foolishness of preaching to save them that believe." James 4:4 states, "know ye not that the friendship of the world is enmity with God? whosoever therefore will be a friend of the world is the enemy of God."

The wisdom of earthly values is foolishness to God. 1 Corinthians 3:18–19 tells us, "Let no man deceive himself. If any man among you seemeth to be wise in this world, let him become a fool, that he may be wise. For the wisdom of this world is foolishness with God. For it is written, He taketh the wise in their own craftiness."

Intellectual wisdom is a process of acquiring knowledge, discerning knowledge, applying the knowledge, and incorporating it into life experiences. At one level, it is intelligence or shrewdness. Intellectual wisdom comes from combining what is scholarly known with what is intellectually known. Wisdom is executed from the lessons that are learned from experiencing what is right and what is wrong; what works and what doesn't; life experiences from setbacks, failures, and experiences of accomplishments.

Most earthly wisdom comes out of selfish ambition as recorded in 1 John 2:16, "For all that is in the world, the lust of the flesh, and the lust of the eyes, and the pride of life, is not of the Father, but is of the world." The earthly approach is usually self-centered, driven by selfish desires, overzealous ambition, envy, lust, greed, pride, ego, deceit, self-preservation, and materialism.

Ambition, success, and materialism are not evil or bad in themselves, but to what sacrifice, to what extreme measures of gain, to what extent of infractions against our fellow man, to what quest for power and control, to what pursuit of fame, to what neglect of family values and deprivation of health do we pursue the illusion of the dream?

Wisdom is part of a belief of knowing that everything that happens, or has happened to you, has happened for a reason; and whatever the outcome, there is or has been a lesson learned. It has been said that you will repeat the same circumstances, the same trials, until the lesson is finally learned. You can decide rightly or wrongly, and every decision has consequences— maybe not immediately but eventually, maybe not externally but internally, maybe not mentally or physically but spiritually, maybe not in this life, but the next.

The Holy Spirit's work in convicting of righteousness encompasses more than convicting the sinner that Christ is righteous; it also includes convincing us that we have the same righteousness and power through the Holy Spirit. To believe in Jesus Christ is to invite the Holy Spirit to dwell and operate within our hearts and mind. For, "if Christ be in you, the body is dead because of sin; but the Spirit is life because of righteousness" (Romans 8:10).

The continuing progression on our path of spiritual enlightenment, spiritual maturity, and spiritual development in realizing deeper truths is that we need to learn how to live deeper within the truths and values of who we are in Christ. "Therefore if any man be in Christ, he is a new creature: old things are passed away; behold, all things are become new" (2 Corinthians 5:17).

We cannot of ourselves always cope with the trials of life; but through the power of the Holy Spirit and Christ Jesus, Emmanuel in 1 Corinthians 1:30–31 says, "But of him are ye in Christ Jesus, who of God is made unto us wisdom, and righteousness, and sanctification, and redemption: That, according as it is written, He that glorieth, let him glory in the Lord."

For He is the peace in the middle of the storm—joy in sorrow—courage in the midst of fear—strength in faith—power in prayer—for God is our source. As it is written, "our faith should not stand in the wisdom of men, but in the power of God" (1 Corinthians 2:5).

Some other Scriptures that teach us about God's wisdom, strength, and might can be found in the following:

> "My grace is sufficient for thee: for my strength is made per-fect in weakness" (2 Corinthians 12:9).

> "He giveth power to the faint; and to them that have no might he increaseth strength... But they that wait [hope] upon the LORD shall renew their strength; they shall mount up with wings as eagles; they shall run, and not be weary; and they shall walk, and not faint" (Isaiah 40:29, 31).

> "Call unto me, and I will answer thee, and show thee great and mighty things, which thou knowest not" (Jeremiah 33:3).

The Bible is a manual that gives us godly instructions in all aspects of life, and it clearly states how vital and important the role wisdom plays in our lives. A prayer of Moses the man of God is found in Psalm 90:12, "So teach us to number our days, that we may apply our hearts unto wisdom..."

Hebrews 12:9 states, "Furthermore we have had fathers of our flesh which corrected us, and we gave them reverence: shall we not much rather be in subjection unto the Father of spirits, and live?" Humankind needs God's Spirit to see things from

God's perspective. The role of spiritual wisdom is primary and fundamental in the "renewing of the mind" which is evident in Romans 8:6, "For to be carnally minded is death; but to be spiritually minded is life and peace."

The Proverbs are a library of wisdom instructing young and old alike in the proper conduct of their lives that we might live our best life, governing the practices of the godly to ensure a happy life in the present and a reward in the life to come. Solomon, the son of David, king of Israel, was the primary author of the Proverbs, but maxims from other wise men, both identified and anonymous are also included.

Wisdom is described, expressed, and defined not only as a spirit in Proverbs, but also in the *feminine sense* as it is reflective of a *mother* giving instruction in love and guidance to her children.

According to Proverbs 3:13–35:

Happy is the man that findeth wisdom, and the man that getteth understanding. For the merchandise of it is better than the merchandise of silver, and the gain thereof than fine gold. She is more precious than rubies: and all the things thou canst desire are not to be compared unto her. Length of days is in her right hand; and in her left hand riches and honour. Her ways are ways of pleasantness, and all her paths are peace. She is a tree of life to them that lay hold upon her: and happy is every one that retaineth her.

The LORD by wisdom hath founded the earth; by understanding hath he established the heavens. By his knowledge the depths are broken up, and the clouds drop down the dew.

My son, let not them depart from thine eyes: keep sound wisdom and discretion: So shall they be life unto thy soul, and grace to thy neck. Then shalt thou walk in thy way safely, and thy foot shall not stumble. When thou liest down, thou shalt not be afraid: yea, thou shalt lie down, and thy sleep shall be sweet. Be not afraid of sudden fear, neither of the desolation of the wicked, when it cometh. For the LORD shall be thy confidence, and shall keep thy foot from being taken.

Withhold not good from them to whom it is due, when it is in the power of thine hand to do it. Say not unto thy neighbour, Go, and come again, and to morrow I will give; when thou hast it by thee.

Devise not evil against thy neighbour, seeing he dwelleth securely by thee. Strive not with a man without cause, if he have done thee no harm. Envy thou not the oppressor, and choose none of his ways. For the froward is abomination to the LORD: but his secret is with the righteous. The curse of the LORD is in the house of the wicked: but he blesseth the habitation of the just. Surely he scorneth the scorners: but he giveth grace unto the lowly. The wise shall inherit glory: but shame shall be the promotion of fools.

Listen to the words found in Proverbs 8:1–22:

Doth not wisdom cry? and understanding put forth her voice? She standeth in the top of high places, by the way in the places of the paths. She crieth at the gates, at the entry of the city, at the coming in at the doors. Unto you, O men, I call; and my voice is to the sons of man. O ye simple, understand wisdom: and, ye fools, be ye of an understanding heart. Hear; for I will speak of excellent things; and the opening of my lips shall be right things. For my mouth shall speak truth; and wickedness is an abomination to my lips. All the words of my mouth are in righteousness; there is nothing froward or perverse in them. They are all plain to him that understandeth, and right to them that find knowledge.

Receive my instruction, and not silver; and knowledge rather than choice gold. For wisdom is better than rubies; and all the things that may be desired are not to be compared to it.

I wisdom dwell with prudence, and find out knowledge of witty inventions. The fear of the LORD is to hate evil: pride, and arrogancy, and the evil way, and the froward mouth, do I hate. Counsel is mine, and sound wisdom: I am understanding; I have strength. By me kings reign, and princes decree justice. By me princes rule, and nobles, even all the judges of the earth.

I love them that love me; and those that seek me early shall find me. Riches and honour are with me; yea, durable riches and righteousness. My fruit is better than gold, yea, than fine gold; and my revenue than choice silver. I lead in the way of righteousness, in the midst of the paths of judgment: That I may cause those that love me to inherit substance; and I will fill their treasures. The LORD possessed me in the beginning of his way, before his works of old.

Proverbs 8:31–36 tells us:

Rejoicing in the habitable part of his earth; and my delights were with the sons of men. Now therefore hearken unto me, O ye children: for blessed are they that keep my ways. Hear instruction, and be wise, and refuse it not.

Blessed is the man that heareth me, watching daily at my gates, waiting at the posts of my doors. For whoso findeth me findeth life, and shall obtain favour of the LORD. But he that sinneth against me wrongeth his own soul: all they that hate me love death.

According to Proverbs 4:

Hear, ye children, the instruction of a father, and attend to know understanding. For I give you good doctrine, forsake ye not my law. For I was my father's son, tender and only beloved in the sight of my mother. He taught me also, and said unto me, Let thine heart retain my words: keep my commandments, and live. Get wisdom, get understanding: forget it not; neither decline from the words of my mouth. Forsake her not, and she shall preserve thee: love her, and she shall keep thee.

Wisdom is the principal thing; therefore get wisdom: and with all thy getting get understanding. Exalt her, and she shall promote thee: she shall bring thee to honour, when thou dost embrace her. She shall give to thine head an ornament of grace: a crown of glory shall she deliver to thee. Hear, O my son, and receive my sayings; and the years of thy life shall be many. I have taught thee in the way of wisdom; I have led thee in right paths. When thou goest, thy steps shall not be straitened; and when thou runnest, thou shalt not stumble.

Take fast hold of instruction; let her not go: keep her; for she is thy life. Enter not into the path of the wicked, and go not in the way of evil men. Avoid it, pass not by it, turn from it, and pass away. For they sleep not, except they have done mischief; and their sleep is taken away, unless they cause some to fall. For they eat the bread of wickedness, and drink the wine of violence. But the path of the just is as the shining light, that shineth more and more unto the perfect day. The way of the wicked is as darkness: they know not at what they stumble.

My son, attend to my words; incline thine ear unto my sayings. Let them not depart from thine eyes; keep them in the midst of thine heart. For they are life unto those that find them, and health to all their flesh. Keep thy heart with all diligence; for out of it are the issues of life. Put away from thee a froward mouth, and perverse lips put far from thee. Let thine eyes look right on, and let thine eyelids look straight. Ponder the path of thy feet, and let all thy ways be established. Turn not to the right hand nor to the left: remove thy foot from evil.

Listen to the message of Jesus in Matthew 7:21–27:

Not every one that saith unto me, Lord, Lord, shall enter into the kingdom of heaven; but he that doeth the will of my Father which is in heaven. Many will say to me in that day, Lord, Lord, have we not prophesied in thy name? and in thy name have cast out devils? and in thy name done many wonderful works? And then will I profess unto them, I never knew you: depart from me, ye that work iniquity.

Therefore whosoever heareth these sayings of mine, and doeth them, I will liken him unto a wise man, which built his house upon a rock: And the rain descended, and the floods came, and the winds blew, and beat upon that house; and it fell not: for it was founded upon a rock. And every one that heareth these sayings of mine, and doeth them not, shall be likened unto a foolish man, which built his house upon the sand: And the rain descended, and the floods came, and the winds blew, and beat upon that house; and it fell: and great was the fall of it.

We pray...

"That the God of our Lord Jesus Christ, the Father of glory, may give unto you the spirit of wisdom and revelation in the knowledge of him: The eyes of your understanding being enlightened; that ye may know what is the hope of his calling, and what the riches of the glory of his inheritance in the saints, And what is the exceeding greatness of his power to us-ward who believe, according to the working of his mighty power" (Ephesians 1:17–19).

CHAPTER 3

The Holy Spirit

$$\smile\!\!\!-\!\!\!\frown\!\!\!-\!\!\!\smile$$

"Not by might, nor by power, but by my spirit, saith the LORD of hosts" (Zechariah 4:6).

Spiritual Regeneration

The Bible's Greek definition for regeneration is *paliggenesia* defined as, "hence renovation, the production of a new life consecrated to God, a radical change of mind for the better." "Therefore, if anyone is in Christ, he is a new creation; old things have passed away; behold, all things have become new" (2 Corinthians 5:17).

Humanity apart from God is fallen or morally defective. God did not create man to function independent of Him. Rather, He created man to be in union and to fellowship with Him, and it is only under His anointing and relationship with Him, we reach our full potential. Our relationship and partnership with God is an essential aspect to prayer.

The Jews believed in the Christ who was to come and, "He came unto his own, and his own received him not" (John 1:11). Christians (Gentiles), Christian Jews and Messianic Jews believe in the Christ who has come. The times have changed, but the reality of faith has not changed. There is only one God and one faith, the faith that saves all men, and deliverance from carnal degeneration to spiritual regeneration. God's plan to restore humanity to His intended divine nature was perfected in Christ Jesus. "And so it is written, The first man Adam was made a living soul; the last Adam [Jesus] was made a quickening spirit. Howbeit that was not first which is spiritual, but that which is natural; and afterward that which is spiritual. The first man is of the earth, earthy; the second man is the Lord from heaven. As is the earthy, such are they also that are earthy: and as is the heavenly, such are they also that are heavenly. And as we have borne the image of the earthy, we shall also bear the image of the heavenly" (1 Corinthians 15:45–49).

"The Revelation of Jesus Christ, which God gave unto him, to shew unto his servants things which must shortly come to pass; and he sent and signified it by his angel unto his servant John. Who bare record of the word of God, and of the testimony of Jesus Christ" (Revelation 1:1-2). According to this revelation, hear the Word of Jesus addressing the Church, "So then because thou art lukewarm, and neither cold nor hot, I will spue thee out of my mouth" (Revelation 3:16).

The world consists of three spiritual conditions of man: cold, lukewarm, and hot. Divided into the *once born* and the *reborn*, the earthly and the spiritual, between the persons of the old Adam, and the persons of the new Adam, Christ, between the unregenerate and the regenerate. The basis of distinction is not color, race, nationality, gender, or wealth. Rather, the "hot" person is the anointed one, Christ-like, the "lukewarm" are those who have been called to that superior state but, as yet, have not totally embraced it; and the "cold" are the defiled, rebellious, and unknowing, or knowing and not believing.

Only through Christ are we restored to our purpose in God. Only through a spiritual rebirth can we obtain powerful, effective, and answered prayer. Only through a spiritual rebirth are we redeemed, conformed, transformed, sanctified, and regenerated. "Wherefore, as by one man sin entered into the world, and death by sin; and so death passed upon all men, for that all have sinned: Therefore as by the offence of one judgment came upon all men to condemnation; even so by the righteousness of one the free gift came upon all men unto justification of life. For as by one man's disobedience many were made sinners, so by the obedience of one shall many be made righteous. Moreover the law entered, that the offence might abound. But where sin abounded, grace did much more abound" (Romans 5:12–20).

Regeneration in its most defined sense means to affect a complete moral reform in, to make over, especially in a better form or condition. In theology, its definition is to be born-again spiritually. Regeneration may be compared to the process of a metamorphosis in which the complete change in character or nature of a thing is transformed, which is evident in Romans 12:2, "And be not conformed to this world: but be ye transformed by the renewing of your mind, that ye may prove what is that good, and acceptable, and perfect, will of God." In conversion, the Holy Spirit redefines our nature, attitudes, actions, thoughts, motives, and virtues. The same Holy Spirit that was operative in the creation of mankind and Earth is also operating in the re-creating of our spiritual nature.

Without the Holy Spirit, there can be no rebirth, and without a rebirth, there can be no spiritual life. It is by this rebirth of a new nature, which was exemplified by Christ Jesus and by the sacrifice of Christ for our redemption, and through the gift of the Holy Spirit, that we are regenerated. Titus 3:4–5 makes this clear as stated, "But after that the kindness and love of God our Saviour toward man appeared, Not by works of righteousness which we have done, but according to his mercy he saved us, by the washing of regeneration, and renewing of the Holy Ghost." Christ makes it clear in John 3:5 that, "Except a man be born of water and of the Spirit, he cannot enter into the kingdom of God." If there is no spiritual connection, there is no intervention and; therefore, there is no kingdom authority or power.

"For there are three that bear record in heaven, the Father, the Word, and the Holy Ghost: and these three are one. And there are three that bear witness in earth, the Spirit, and the water, and the blood: and these three agree in one" (1 John 5:7–8).

Who Is the Holy Spirit?

He is our Comforter, Counselor, Helper, Intercessor, Advocate, Strengthener, Wisdom, and our Judge. The Holy Spirit plays a vital role in God's plan of redemption, from creation to eternity. The Holy Spirit was in the beginning; He was involved in the creation; and He is involved in spiritual regeneration of redemption, transformation, salvation, glorification, and sanctification (to purify from sin, and to make holy).

One of several definitions of the term Spirit translates the Hebrew word *Ruach*, which, in its primary sense, means breath, air, and wind. Remember, the wind, like the Spirit of God, is an unseen manifestation in the world. The invisible working of the Holy Spirit resembles the wind that cannot be seen, but the evidence of it is manifested by the result of what is seen, what is heard, and what is felt. John 3:8 illustrates the Spirit as, "The wind bloweth where it listeth, and thou hearest the sound thereof, but canst not tell whence it cometh, and whither it goeth: so is every one that is born of the Spirit."

In the New Testament, the word for Spirit is *Pneuma*, which, like the Hebrew word, also means "the third person of the triune God, the Holy Spirit, coequal, coeternal with the Father and the Son." In John 14:16, the Holy Spirit is also called the Comforter or Helper; translated from the Greek word *Parakletos,* meaning "one who comes alongside to plead the case before the judge."

The word for holy, saint, and sanctify is derived from the Greek word *hagios*, meaning "separated," or "set apart." A person "coming to faith" means God has set that person apart from those in the world. Scripture calls all who are saved as saints, or holy, because they are separated, as evident in Leviticus 20:26, "And ye shall be holy unto me: for I the LORD am holy, and have severed you from other people, that ye should be mine."

Christ states in Matthew 5:13–14 that the righteous, "are the salt of the earth and the light of the world" and shall be distinguished and set apart by their lifestyle. The Apostle Paul preached in 2 Corinthians 6:16–19, "For ye are the temple of the living God; as God hath said, I will dwell in them, and walk in them; and I will be their God, and they shall be my people. Wherefore come out from among them, and be ye separate, saith the Lord, and touch not the unclean thing; and I will receive you. And will be a Father unto you, and ye shall be my sons and daughters, saith the Lord Almighty."

The Ascension of Jesus Christ is the culmination of Christ's glorification after His Resurrection, and was necessary for His heavenly exaltation and the impartation of the Holy Spirit. Christ is recorded telling the disciples in John 16:7-11, "Nevertheless I tell you the truth; It is expedient for you that I go away: for if I go not away, the Comforter will not come unto you; but if I depart, I will send him unto you. And when he is come, he will reprove the world of sin, and of righteousness, and of judgment: Of sin, because they believe not on me; Of righteousness, because I go to my Father, and ye see me no more; Of judgment, because the prince of this world is judged."

> And I will pray the Father, and he shall give you another Comforter, that he may abide with you for ever; ...Even the Spirit of truth; ... whom the world cannot receive, because it seeth him not, neither knoweth him: but ye know him; for he dwelleth with you, and shall be in you. I will not leave you comfortless: I will come to you...The Comforter, which is the Holy Ghost, whom the Father will send in my name, he shall teach you all things, and bring all things to your remembrance, whatsoever I have said unto you. (John 14:16-18, 26)

"Ye shall receive power, after that the Holy Ghost is come upon you: and ye shall be witnesses unto me both in Jerusalem, and in all Judaea, and in Samaria, and unto the uttermost part of the earth. And when he had spoken these things, while they beheld, he was taken up; and a cloud received him out of their sight. And while they looked stedfastly toward heaven as he went up, behold, two men stood by them in white apparel; Which also said, Ye men of Galilee, why stand ye gazing up into heaven? this same Jesus, which is taken up from you into heaven, shall so come in like manner as ye have seen him go into heaven" (Acts 1:8-11).

Ten days after the Ascension of Jesus, on the holy Day of Pentecost, proceeded the promise of the gift of the Holy Spirit, the infilling of the Holy Ghost, on the disciples and worshippers.

> When the day of Pentecost was fully come, they were all with one accord in one place. And suddenly there came a sound from heaven as of a rushing mighty wind, and it filled all the house where they were sitting. And there appeared unto them cloven tongues like as of fire, and it sat upon each of them. And they were all filled with the Holy Ghost, and began to speak with other tongues, as the Spirit gave them utterance. (Acts 2:1-4)

The Purpose of the Holy Spirit

The Holy Spirit is the vehicle by which our spirit is meant to commune with God. It is the medium through which our spirit is intended to affect and be affected by God. "God is a Spirit and they that worship him must worship him in spirit and in truth" (John 4:24). Christ ascended, "into heaven itself, now to appear in the presence of God for us" (Hebrews 9:24). "It is Christ that died, yea rather, that is risen again, who is even at the right hand of God, who also maketh intercession for us" (Romans 8:34); and the Holy Spirit makes intercession through us on earth.

This powerful presence is key to revelation, unwavering faith, spiritual transformation, spiritual wisdom, relationship with God, an empowered love walk, a powerful prayer life, and the power in the manifestation of miracles.

Your Connection to the Holy Spirit is an awareness and sensitivity to the presence of the Holy Spirit. The Holy Spirit takes up residence in us when we accept Christ as our personal

Lord and Savior. Stillness is usually when the Holy Spirit speaks, and the softness of the voice is so soft, that hurriedness, stress, and confusion oftentimes will overshadow the whisper. Psalm 46:10 instructs us to, "Be still, and know that I am God."

It is through the Holy Spirit by prayer that we commune with God, which is both speaking and listening. Seeking the will of God to hear from Him is hearing the voice of the Holy Spirit in an impartation of instruction on what to say, or guidance on what to do, or revelation in understanding. This is "being led of the Spirit." "Howbeit when he, the Spirit of truth, is come, he will guide you into all truth: for he shall not speak of himself; but whatsoever he shall hear, that shall he speak: and he will shew you things to come" (John 16:13).

"For the Holy Ghost shall teach you in the same hour what ye ought to say" (Luke 12:12) and "you have an unction from the Holy One, and ye know all things" (1 John 2:20).

The Holy Spirit empowers us to hear from God, to receive guidance from the word of knowledge and the Spirit of truth, to discern spiritual wisdom, to conquer in spiritual warfare, to fight sin and temptation, and to lead us to redemption.

The Holy Spirit Has a Twofold Part in Redemption. First, the Holy Spirit convicts us of sin, and then the Holy Spirit leads us to repentance of sins. We cannot repent if we do not think we need repenting. In the same vein, we limit the power of the Holy Spirit in our lives once we rely on our own righteousness.

Once we realize we are lost and need redemption, the Holy Spirit leads us to repentance and salvation. Jesus states in John 6:44, "No man can come to me, except the Father which hath sent me draw him." "That if thou shalt confess with thy mouth the Lord Jesus, and shalt believe in thine heart that God hath raised him from the dead, thou shalt be saved. For with the heart man believeth unto righteousness; and with the mouth confession is made unto salvation" (Romans 10:9–10). "Whosoever shall confess that Jesus is the Son of God, God dwelleth in him, and he in God" (1 John 4:15).

Once we have accepted Christ, as Lord and Savior, then the Holy Spirit takes up residence in our spirit, and as an infusion with the Holy Spirit, we become, through obedience and love, the righteousness of Christ. We are then "born-again" of the Spirit.

The result of the transformed life, which is yielded to the Holy Spirit, is a "Spirit-filled" life. The Holy Spirit is given as a gift from God according to Acts 2:38, "Peter said unto them, Repent, and be baptized every one of you in the name of Jesus Christ for the remission of sins, and ye shall receive the gift of the Holy Ghost." In John 3:3, 5, Jesus answered... Verily, verily, I say unto thee, "Except a man be born again, he cannot see the kingdom of God... Except a man be born of water and of the Spirit, he cannot enter into the kingdom of God."

Repentance and baptism are commands that Jesus instructs for His followers recorded in Matthew 28:18–20, known as "The Great Commission" "... All power is given unto me in heaven and in earth. Go ye therefore, and teach all nations, baptizing them in the name of the Father, and of the Son, and of the Holy Ghost: Teaching them to observe all things whatsoever I have commanded you."

Baptism from the Greek word, *baptisma,* means a rite of immersion in water as commanded by Christ, by which one after confessing their sins and professing their faith in Christ, having been born again by the Holy Spirit unto a new life, identifies publicly with the fellowship of Christ and the church. To baptize is *baptizo,* in Greek, which means, "to immerse, to make clean with water, and to wash" is the ritual act with the intent of purification or dedication, with the use of water.

Water is a symbol of purity, cleansing, and separation. The water, which was divided in the Red Sea, served as the separation of the Israelites' demise from Pharaoh's army. Once the Israelites had crossed the Red Sea, another symbol, including baptism, was used to "separate" them as the people of God, was circumcision. Circumcision was a token of their covenant or testament with God.

In the New Testament, the same order and symbolism to indicate the Christian's separation from the world is followed with the Lord's Great Commission, baptism and the Holy Spirit, as an incorporation into the Church. Baptism is not only a bond existing between the person and Christ; to be united to Christ is also to be united with the Church, for the Church is His body. The Church is not an organization, but an organism. As circumcision was incorporation into the spiritual body of Israel, so baptism of water and the Holy Spirit is incorporation into the spiritual body of the Church.

In Jewish teachings, water was the agent as the womb of creation where the earth was birthed out of the deep of the waters. "In the beginning God created the heaven and the earth. And the earth was without form, and void; and darkness was upon the face of the deep. And the Spirit of God moved upon the face of the waters...And God said, Let the waters under the heaven be gathered together unto one place, and let the dry land appear: and it was so. And God called the dry land Earth; and the gathering together of the waters called he Seas: and God saw that it was good" (Genesis 1:1-2, 9-10).

When we are immersed and baptized in water, we are spiritually going back to the agent of creation, being born-again, rebirthed as a *new spiritual creation in the water*. The water baptism reflects the real baptism, the inner sanctification, of the human heart, which comes first. It represents a complete surrender to God, to His will and His Word for our repentance and sanctification, in the name of Jesus and of the Holy Spirit.

According to Scripture, baptism declares that three things happen to believers who are baptized. First, they die with Christ to their old self; second, they rise with Christ to become a new creature; and third, they are incorporated into the family of Christ. Baptism represents the death of the old man and the rebirth of the new man. Romans 6:4–5 makes this clear, "Therefore we are buried with him by baptism into death: that like as Christ was raised up from the dead by the glory of the Father, even so we also should walk in newness of life. For if we have been planted together in the likeness of his death, we shall be also in the likeness of his resurrection." Baptism represents and serves as:

Baptized to Enter the Kingdom of God
- "Jesus answered, Verily, verily, I say unto thee, Except a man be born of water and of the Spirit, he cannot enter into the kingdom of God" (John 3:5).

Baptized to Be Saved
- "He that **believeth and is baptized shall be saved**; but he that believeth not shall be damned" (Mark 16:16, emphasis added).
- "The like figure whereunto even baptism doth also now save us (not the putting away of the filth of the flesh, but the answer of a good conscience toward God,) by the resurrection of Jesus Christ" (I Peter 3:21).

Baptized for the Remission of Sins to Receive the Holy Ghost
- "Arise, and be baptized, and wash away thy sins, calling on the name of the Lord" (Acts 22:16).
- John the Baptist stated, "I indeed baptize you with water unto repentance" (Matthew 3:11).
- "Then Peter said unto them, Repent, and be baptized every one of you in the name of Jesus Christ for the remission of sins, and ye shall receive the gift of the Holy Ghost" (Acts 2:38).
- "Ye shall receive power, after that the Holy Ghost is come upon you" (Acts 1:8).

Christ knew it was necessary that He be baptized to fulfill all righteousness, so shouldn't we? "Then cometh Jesus from Galilee to Jordan unto John, to be baptized of him. But John forbad him, saying, I have need to be baptized of thee, and comest thou to me? And Jesus answering said unto him, Suffer it to be so now: for thus it becometh us to fulfil all righteousness. Then he suffered him. And Jesus, when he was baptized, went up straightway out of the water: and, lo, the heavens were opened unto him, and he saw the Spirit of God descending like a dove, and lighting upon him: And lo a voice from heaven, saying, This is my beloved Son, in whom I am well pleased" (Matthew 3:13–17).

Scripture promises a gift of the Spirit to everyone who has come to Christ and is baptized, but using the gift is conditional. To live the "Spirit-filled" life requires something on our part. Although it is a gift, it is not automatic and needs to be nurtured.

The Holy Spirit also accompanies the reading, meditating, and revelation of God's Word, giving life to the receiver for, "godliness is profitable unto all things, having promise of the life that now is, and of that which is to come" (1 Timothy 4:8).

The Holy Spirit Is Activated and Empowered by the Word of God, which is conveyed by Scripture. Our, loving heavenly, Father provides opportunity for us to know His will, but He has imparted free will that allows us the right of choice, to choose. Consciousness is our God-given knowledge of right and wrong. However, conscience belongs to the natural man and must be taught of God. The natural man's conscience must be, enlightened by the Holy Spirit, which is the Word of God through heavenly spiritual wisdom. 1 Peter 2:2 implores us to, "As newborn babes, desire the sincere milk of the word, that ye may grow thereby."

The Holy Spirit employs the holy Word to work through God's Word to nurture, sustain, and empower our spiritual life. The Word of God is our spiritual food. "It is written, Man shall not live by bread alone, but by every word that proceedeth out of the mouth of God" (Matthew 4:4) and the impartation of the spiritual life is, "Whereby are given unto us exceeding great and precious promises: that by these ye might be partakers of the divine nature" (2 Peter 1:4).

When you read the Bible, you hold a library of sixty-six books; yet, they are of one Spirit that has been inspired by the Holy Spirit. Scripture explains and has written its law on the heart of every person who accepts and welcomes Jesus Christ as their personal Lord and Savior. The Creator's holy nature is revealed to every person through his or her spirit.

God's love revealed in Jeremiah 29:11 says, "For I know the thoughts that I think toward you, saith the LORD, thoughts of peace, and not of evil, to give you an expected end." The Bible reflects God's unconditional love for us through His statues, code of ethics, commandments, and promises. "All scripture is given by inspiration of God, and is profitable for doctrine, for reproof, for correction, for instruction in righteousness" (2 Timothy 3:16).

Remember, the Bible is God-breathed, authoritative, alive, and powerful. Each word and sentence has a purpose and function. "Thy word is a lamp unto my feet, and a light unto my path" (Psalm 119:10). The Holy Spirit is the channel in which we are strengthened, empowered, guided, and evolved to be Christ-like (our higher self).

The Holy Spirit Is the Revelation of the Word. Two aspects of the Holy Spirit's revelation are first, He reveals God's Word, and second, He gives us the ability to understand the revelation. With the written Word comes the Spirit of wisdom and the "spoken Word," or an utterance. This is what is considered as the rhema Word. A rhema is a verse or portion of Scripture that the Holy Spirit brings to our attention with application to a current situation or need for direction. Just as the Spirit of God revealed its Word to holy men of the Bible, the Spirit of God will reveal its contents to the reader. The Holy Bible clearly teaches that the Holy Spirit inspired those who wrote this timeless book. "Knowing this first, that no prophecy of the scripture is of any private interpretation. For the prophecy came not in old time by the will of man: but holy men of God spake as they were moved by the Holy Ghost" (2 Peter 1:20-21).

Knowing Jesus is not the work of human knowledge or intelligence, but the Holy Spirit. Human knowledge and worldly wisdom often hinders the work of the Holy Spirit. To fully understand the Bible, we must discern it through spiritual wisdom as illustrated in 1 Corinthians 2:10–16,

But God hath revealed them unto us by his Spirit: for the Spirit searcheth all things, yea, the deep things of God. For what man knoweth the things of a man, save the spirit of man which is in him? even so the things of God knoweth no man, but the Spirit of God. Now we have received, not the spirit of the world, but the spirit which is of God; that we

71

might know the things that are freely given to us of God. Which things also we speak, not in the words which man's wisdom teacheth, but which the Holy Ghost teacheth; comparing spiritual things with spiritual.

But the natural man receiveth not the things of the Spirit of God: for they are foolishness unto him: neither can he know them, because they are spiritually discerned. But he that is spiritual judgeth all things, yet he himself is judged of no man. For who hath known the mind of the Lord, that he may instruct him? But we have the mind of Christ.

Infilling of the Holy Spirit

When we yield and surrender ourselves to the control and the infusion of the Holy Spirit, an amazing event happens, "Blessed are those who hunger and thirst for righteousness, For they shall be filled" (Matthew 5:6). Scripture commands us to seek the continual filling of the Spirit in Ephesians 5:18–21, "And do not be drunk with wine, in which is dissipation; but be filled with the Spirit, speaking to one another in psalms and hymns and spiritual songs, singing and making melody in your heart to the Lord, giving thanks always for all things to God the Father in the name of our Lord Jesus Christ, submitting to one another in the fear of God."

In 1 Thessalonians 5:19–22, the Apostle Paul warns us not to quench our relationship with the Holy Spirit, because we harm our relationship with God. "Quench not the Spirit. Despise not prophesyings. Prove all things; hold fast that which is good. Abstain from all appearance of evil." The conduct of the *old man grieves* the Holy Spirit and separates us from God. "But your iniquities have separated between you and your God, and your sins have hid his face from you, that he will not hear" (Isaiah 59:2).

These specific actions outlined in Ephesians 4:22–32 will affect our relationship with God:

That ye put off concerning the former conversation the old man, which is corrupt according to the deceitful lusts; And be renewed in the spirit of your mind; And that ye put on the new man, which after God is created in righteousness and true holiness.

Wherefore putting away lying, speak every man truth with his neighbour: for we are members one of another. Be ye angry, and sin not: let not the sun go down upon your wrath: Neither give place to the devil. Let him that stole steal no more: but rather let him labour, working with his hands the thing which is good, that he may have to give to him that needeth. Let no corrupt communication proceed out of your mouth, but that which is good to the use of edifying, that it may minister grace unto the hearers.

And grieve not the holy Spirit of God, whereby ye are sealed unto the day of redemption. Let all bitterness, and wrath, and anger, and clamour, and evil speaking, be put away from you, with all malice: And be ye kind one to another, tender-hearted, forgiving one another, even as God for Christ's sake hath forgiven you.

Since man was made as a free moral agent, God provides opportunity to know His will, but He will never impose upon our will. God has ordained that conscience serve as our moral regulator, but the natural man's conscience must be taught of God and led by the Holy Spirit and enlightened by the Spirit of truth. A conscience divinely enlightened and obedient to the Word of God will guide and serve as a guardian of the soul. As Philippians 2:13 states, "For it is God which worketh in you both to will and to do of his good pleasure."

The infilling of the Spirit depends on our relationship with the Lord and our obedience. Once we accept Christ as our personal Savior, this new nature is called being born-again. *Divine guidance calls for obedience.* In the very process of obeying, the Holy Spirit purifies the soul. "And we are his witnesses of these things; and so is also the Holy Ghost, whom God hath given to them that obey him" (Acts 5:32).

The promptings of the conscience must be regulated by the holy Word. A conscience divinely enlightened and obedient to the Word of God can safely guide and assure one with the fruit of the Spirit. The infilling of the Holy Spirit is an internal relationship between the Holy Spirit and the person. From this internal relationship then flows external evidence, which is exhibited in our lifestyle and in our interactions with one another. When we have yielded to the Spirit, we produce characteristics as indicative in Galatians 5:22, "the fruit of the Spirit is love, joy, peace, longsuffering, gentleness, goodness, faith" and Ephesians 5:9, "for the fruit of the Spirit is in all goodness and righteousness and truth."

Obedience to the holy Word assures one with peace of mind that is absent from worry, doubt, fear, and anxiety. This is what is meant in Isaiah 26:3, "Thou wilt keep him in perfect peace, whose mind is stayed on thee: because he trusteth in thee." "There is no fear in love; but perfect love casteth out fear: because fear hath torment. He that feareth is not made perfect in love. We love him, because he first loved us" (1 John 4:18-19) "by faith which worketh by love" (Galatians 5:6).

When we have been correctly taught, then we know right from wrong. We, however, by our free will, rebuff conscience to comprise, rationalize, and then *justify what we want to do instead of doing what we know is right to do*. This is the first step into the progression of disobedience.

We are in a spiritual battle, the flesh versus the spirit, the natural man versus the spiritual man, and good versus evil. The attack is directed through our mental faculties by what we see, what we hear, and what we think. "Be sober, be vigilant; because your adversary the devil, as a roaring lion, walketh about, seeking whom he may devour" (1 Peter 5:8). This evil is not just a moral force or a vague kind of paganism; it is a cosmic reality, "For we wrestle not against flesh and blood, but against principalities, against powers, against the rulers of the darkness of this world, against spiritual wickedness in high places" (Ephesians 6:12).

The attack is also against the Word of God in an attempt to discredit the validity and the authenticity of truth to separate humanity by appealing to the fallen nature of man. "In whom the god of this world hath blinded the minds of them which believe not, lest the light of the glorious gospel of Christ, who is the image of God, should shine unto them" (2 Corinthians 4:4).

Disobedience to the Word of God impedes and affects the conscience; and constant and unrepented disobedience enables an unholy spirit to work in and through you, as evident in Ephesians 2:2, "According to the prince of the power of the air, the spirit that now worketh in the children of disobedience."

The irresponsive soul grows cold and callous to the promptings of the Spirit. The unlearned, the nonbeliever, the doubter, the undisciplined, the unfaithful, the fearful, and the angry are more susceptible to the *unholy spirit*. "Unto the pure all things are pure: but unto them that are defiled and unbelieving is nothing pure; but even their mind and conscience is defiled" (Titus 1:15).

The Holy Spirit Empowers Us in Spiritual Warfare. The weapons of warfare for the believer are found in Ephesians 6:11–18:

> Put on the whole armour of God, that ye may be able to stand against the wiles of the devil, For we wrestle not against flesh and blood, but against principalities, against powers, against the rulers of the darkness of this world, against spiritual wickedness in high places, and Wherefore take unto you the whole armour of God, that ye may be able to withstand in the evil day, and having done all, to stand. Stand therefore, having your loins girt about with truth, and having on the breastplate of righteousness; And your feet shod with the preparation of the gospel of peace; Above all, taking the shield of faith, wherewith ye shall be able to quench all the fiery darts of the wicked. And take the helmet of salvation, and the sword of the Spirit, which is the word of God: Praying always with all prayer and supplication in the Spirit,

and watching thereunto with all perseverance and supplication for all saints.

2 Corinthians 10:3–5 tells us,

For though we walk in the flesh, we do not war after the flesh: (For the weapons of our warfare are not carnal, but mighty through God to the pulling down of strong holds. Casting down imaginations, and every high thing that exalteth itself against the knowledge of God, and bringing into captivity every thought to the obedience of Christ).

When we are disobedient in the transgression of the law, which is sin, we are then disconnected from the intimacy of fellowship with God as evident in Isaiah 59:2, "But your iniquities have separated between you and your God, and your sins have hid his face from you, that he will not hear."

Secularism, disobedience, and guilt can further lead to condemnation and isolation from God. However, God sends His Holy Spirit to the sinner to bring about reconciliation and restoration of the broken fellowship. The Holy Spirit exposes sin and this conviction is intended to lead us to repentance. When we repent and confess our sins, condemnation goes away. We are reassured in 1 John 1:9, "If we confess our sins, he is faithful and just to forgive us our sins, and to cleanse us from all unrighteousness."

In our walk, there will always be temptations and choices of right and wrong. Even though we have a new nature, we still have an old nature, or sin nature, which remains until redemption is complete. These two natures fight against each other. Christ models this example in Luke 22:31-32, "And the Lord said, Simon, Simon, behold, Satan hath desired to have you, that he may sift you as wheat: But I have prayed for thee, that thy faith fail not: and when thou art converted, strengthen thy brethren."

When the desire of temptation overpowers our new nature, and when we give in to our old nature, we are drawn into sin. This can eventually lead to death, both physically and spiritually, if left unchecked. For example, every sinful temptation is bait, and with the bait is a "hook" with consequences. Using drugs may lead to a drug addiction, and as a result, the person, as well as the family suffers many consequences as a direct or indirect result of their addiction. The consequences can be financial insecurity, job and career loss, health issues, depression, hopelessness, legal ramifications or any other area of destructive consequence in someone's life.

As James 1:14–15 teaches, "But every man is tempted, when he is drawn away of his own lust, and enticed. Then when lust hath conceived, it bringeth forth sin: and sin, when it is finished, bringeth forth death." Romans 8:6 states, "For to be carnally minded is death; but to be spiritually minded is life and peace."

The Apostle Paul also struggled in his process of developing into a spiritual man, for he said, "Now if I do that I would not, it is no more I that do it, but sin that dwelleth in me. I find then a law, that, when I would do good, evil is present with me. For I delight in the law of God after the inward man: But I see another law in my members, warring against the law of my mind, and bringing me into captivity to the law of sin which is in my members. O wretched man that I am! Who shall deliver me from the body of this death? I thank God through Jesus Christ our Lord. So then with the mind I myself serve the law of God; but with the flesh the law of sin" (Romans 7:20–25).

The Presence of the Holy Spirit Will Empower Us to Resist Temptation and make right decisions. "There hath no temptation taken you but such as is common to man: but God is faithful, who will not suffer you to be tempted above that ye are able; but will with the temptation also make a way to escape, that ye may be able to bear it" (1 Corinthians 10:13). 2 Peter 2:9 tells us, "The Lord knoweth how to deliver the godly out of temptations."

God knows that we are frail. Our defense rests in prayer, as instructed in Mark 4:38, "Watch ye and pray, lest ye enter into temptation. The spirit truly is ready, but the flesh is weak." This is one of many reasons that prayer and fasting are the weapons of choice, as the Apostle Paul taught in Romans 12:12, "Rejoicing in hope; patient in tribulation; continuing instant in prayer." Prayerlessness will eventually lead to *spiritual* suicide.

Even though the conflict of moral choices exists and sometimes we may fall short, we are to confess and repent our sins. 1 John 2:1 instructs us, "My little children, these things write I unto you, that ye sin not. And if any man sin, we have an advocate with the Father, Jesus Christ the righteous." Romans 8:3–4 states, "For what the law could not do, in that it was weak through the flesh, God sending his own Son in the likeness of sinful flesh, and for sin, condemned sin in the flesh. That the righteousness of the law might be fulfilled in us, who walk not after the flesh, but after the Spirit." "Looking unto Jesus the author and finisher of our faith" (Hebrews 12:2).

Through the Holy Spirit, We Have Power over Our Flesh. The Spirit through the revealed Word can show our new man how we should interact in the world. Our fallen nature desires to fulfill the lusts of the flesh. The Bible and Jesus, however, are the light in the darkness that will overcome our fallen nature. Jesus declares in John 8:12, "I am the light of the world: he that followeth me shall not walk in darkness, but shall have the light of life."

God is our lawgiver. He has given us a moral code of behavior—a code of ethics, authoritative and comprehensive— the Ten Commandments. "Wherefore the law is holy, and the commandment holy, and just, and good" (Romans 7:12). "And this is his commandment, that we should believe on the name of his Son Jesus Christ, and love one another, as he gave us commandment" (1 John 3:23).

This is the standard of the judgment. There can be no judgment without a law or standard of judgment. Without law, there would be chaos. Sin and disobedience are the result of transgressing the law. "Whosoever committed sin transgresseth also the law: for sin is the transgression of the law" (1 John 3:4).

God has given us spiritual laws, which are a revelation of His character. Jesus, the Christ, was the demonstration of the laws living out the Ten Commandments, and His teachings are made real to us through the Spirit. Christ gives us clear instructions in

John 15:10, "If ye keep my commandments, ye shall abide in my love; even as I have kept my Father's commandments, and abide in his love."

We shall be judged by this law as lived out in the life of Jesus. "For the law of the Spirit of life in Christ Jesus hath made me free from the law of sin and death" (Romans 8:2). When the Holy Spirit directs our thoughts and actions, He fills our purpose to glorify God. "But he that is joined unto the Lord is one spirit. What? know ye not that your body is the temple of the Holy Ghost which is in you, which ye have of God, and ye are not your own? For ye are bought with a price: therefore glorify God in your body, and in your spirit, which are God's" (1 Corinthians 6:17,19–21).

The Power of the Holy Spirit

Lifestyle Principles for Empowerment. Once the person accepts Christ as Lord and Savior, the infilling of the Holy Spirit gives that person power to change and to stop sinning, which they were powerless to do before. This process of transformation is known as sanctification, where we become more like Christ. The sanctified believer behaves as Christ behaved. This is a progressive experience. Sanctification means "purification and holiness" and obedience to the law through the Spirit, which 1 Corinthians 1:30 states, "But of him are ye in Christ Jesus, who of God is made unto us wisdom, and righteousness, and sanctification, and redemption."

The baptism of the Holy Spirit moves us in prayer to complete the sanctification process by praying in and of the Spirit. One who prays with the Spirit, in the Spirit, by the Spirit, and for the Spirit is responding to the promptings of the Spirit. "Likewise the Spirit also helpeth our infirmities: for we know not what we should pray for as we ought: but the Spirit itself maketh intercession for us with groanings which cannot be uttered. And he that searcheth the hearts knoweth what is the mind of the Spirit, because he maketh intercession for the saints according to the will of God" (Romans 8:26–27).

Once you are filled, and *fellowship,* with the Holy Spirit, are *led* and *obedient* to the Holy Spirit you move beyond the *infilling into the power* of the Holy Spirit. Jesus best models this empowerment, as He fasted to begin His public ministry which is illustrated in Luke 4:1–14, where Jesus is led by the Holy Spirit *in obedience, meditation in the Word, speaking the Word*—rebuking Satan, *fasting,* and *prayer,* which are, the weapons of our warfare:

Jesus being full of the Holy Ghost returned from Jordan, and was led by the Spirit into the wilderness, Being forty days tempted of the devil. And in those days he did eat nothing: and when they were ended, he afterward hungered. And the devil said unto him, If thou be the Son of God, command this stone that it be made bread.

And Jesus answered him, saying, It is written, That man shall not live by bread alone, but by every word of God. And the devil, taking him up into an high mountain, shewed unto him all the kingdoms of the world in a moment of time. And the devil said unto him, All this power will I give thee, and the glory of them: for that is delivered unto me; and to whomsoever I will I give it. If thou therefore wilt worship me, all shall be thine.

And Jesus answered and said unto him, Get thee behind me, Satan: for it is written, Thou shalt worship the Lord thy God, and him only shalt thou serve. And he brought him to Jerusalem, and set him on a pinnacle of the temple, and said unto him, If thou be the Son of God, cast thyself down from hence: For it is written, He shall give his angels charge over thee, to keep thee: And in their hands they shall bear thee up, lest at any time thou dash thy foot against a stone.

And Jesus answering said unto him, It is said, Thou shalt not tempt the Lord thy God. And when the devil had ended all the temptation, he departed from him for a season. And Jesus returned in the power of the Spirit into Galilee: and there went out a fame of him through all the region round about.

As illustrated, Jesus was filled with the Holy Ghost and was ready for spiritual combat, and when confronted and tested in the battle by Satan, Jesus deployed His arsenal and weapons of warfare which were the Word of God, Scripture, combined with the power of fasting. After His victory in battle, He excelled in "the power of the Spirit."

Understanding Fasting: Fasting is intentional abstinence from physical pleasures, such as eating and sexual relations. It is a determined discipline to abstain for a time from these pleasures, accompanied with prayer, in order to gain essential spiritual benefits. Fasting and prayer does not change God, it changes us. Fasting should be a natural part of the life of the believer. It is a time set apart to seek the presence of the Holy Spirit and intensifies our worship with God. It brings divine revelation and divine rewards. It empowers us for spiritual warfare. It appeals to God for protection, for victory, for forgiveness, and for pardon.

It is through fasting and prayer that enables our spirit to be more receptive to the presence and promptings of the Holy Spirit. Fasting produces spiritual examination and introspection, spiritual confession, humility and repentance, spiritual intercession, and developing discipline.

Spiritual confession: Fasting puts us in harmony with an All-Powerful God who demands humility from those who wish to be close to Him. Fasting humbles the flesh. Spiritual elevation is a prerequisite for true repentance. One way to achieve spiritual elevation is to abstain from the physical.

Spiritual intercession: Fasting allows us to hear and receive guidance, wisdom, instruction, and knowledge from God through the Holy Spirit. It is the greatest spiritual discipline for seeking the power of the Holy Spirit. Only through prayer and fasting can some hindrances, yokes of oppression, and spiritual warfare be conquered. As Jesus said in Mark 9:29, "This kind can come forth by nothing, but by prayer and fasting."

Developing discipline: Fasting and praying, when combined, is a powerful method that empowers us to discipline our physical body so that we become more in tune with our spiritual body. Fasting exerts discipline over our physical appetites to bring the body under subjection to what the Holy Spirit desires.

Examples of the Power of Prayer and Fasting: Throughout the Bible, fasting with prayer was the discipline practiced where prayers, spiritual power, and revelation was manifested in a person's circumstance.

Daniel, the Prophet, fasted for the fulfillment of God's promises and he received mighty revelations from God. "And I set my face unto the Lord God, to seek by prayer and supplications, with fasting, and sackcloth, and ashes...Yea, whiles I was speaking in prayer, even the man Gabriel, whom I had seen in the vision at the beginning, being caused to fly swiftly, touched me about the time of the evening oblation. And he informed me, and talked with me, and said, O Daniel, I am now come forth to give thee skill and understanding. At the beginning of thy supplications the commandment came forth, and I am come to shew thee; for thou art greatly beloved: therefore understand the matter, and consider the vision" (Daniel 9:3, 21-23).

- "Defraud ye not one the other, except it be with consent for a time, that ye may give yourselves to fasting and prayer; and come together again, that Satan tempt you not for your incontinency" (1 Corinthians 7:5).
- "Is not this the fast that I have chosen? to loose the bands of wickedness, to undo the heavy burdens, and to let the oppressed go free, and that ye break every yoke" (Isaiah 58:6)?
- "But thou, when thou fastest, anoint thine head, and wash thy face; That thou appear not unto men to fast, but unto thy Father which is in secret: and thy Father, which seeth in secret, shall reward thee openly" (Matthew 6:17–18).
- "Therefore also now, saith the LORD, turn ye even to me with all your heart, and with fasting, and with weeping, and with mourning: And rend your heart, and not your

garments, and turn unto the LORD your God: for he is gracious and merciful, slow to anger, and of great kindness, and repenteth him of the evil" (Joel 2:12–13).

- "Then I proclaimed a fast there, at the river of Ahava, that we might afflict ourselves before our God, to seek of him a right way for us, and for our little ones, and for all our substance. So we fasted and besought our God for this: and he was intreated of us" (Ezra 8:21, 23).

Through each victorious experience, we have defeating the deceptions of the devil, resisting temptation, and walking in the Spirit, we are empowered and further developed spiritually in the process of sanctification to be Christ-like.

Spirituality is frequently defined as our path to enlightenment to evolve to our higher consciousness and purpose. We are all called in purpose and responsibility to minister and edify the gospel. This responsibility is not only delegated to the pastor, the preacher, the teacher, but it is also delegated to each person individually, irrespective of his or her title, role, or function. The church is not only built of brick and mortar, but it is also made up of believers, as well. "Know ye not that ye are the temple of God, and that the Spirit of God dwelleth in you" (1 Corinthians 3:16)?

The Holy Spirit's work in convicting of righteousness encompasses more than convicting the sinner that Christ is righteous; it also includes convincing us that we have the same righteousness and power through the Holy Spirit. As a result, you receive "power" from God's Holy Spirit to complete the task given you to accomplish through the Spirit. Along with the power, the Spirit has a "gift" for the believer as he or she completes the task.

The Gifts of the Holy Spirit is designed to accomplish the work of the Spirit, equipping the believer. "Now ye are the body of Christ, and members in particular. And God hath set some in the church, first apostles, secondarily prophets, thirdly teachers, after that miracles, then gifts of healings, helps, governments, diversities of tongues" (1 Corinthians 12:28).

I Corinthians 12:31 encourages us to, "earnestly desire the best gifts":

> Now there are diversities of gifts, but the same Spirit. And there are differences of administrations, but the same Lord. And there are diversities of operations, but it is the same God which worketh all in all. But the manifestation of the Spirit is given to every man to profit withal.

> For to one is given by the Spirit the word of wisdom; to another the word of knowledge by the same Spirit;

> To another faith by the same Spirit; to another the gifts of healing by the same Spirit;

> To another the working of miracles; to another prophecy; to another discerning of spirits; to another divers kinds of tongues; to another the interpretation of tongues:

> But all these worketh that one and the selfsame Spirit, dividing to every man severally as he will. (1 Corinthians 12:4–11)

Jesus Our Gift: Jesus came so we could have a relationship with God. "Whosoever denieth the Son, the same hath not the Father: he that acknowledgeth the Son hath the Father also" (1 John 2:23). Jesus stated in John 10:10, "The thief cometh not, but for to steal, and to kill, and to destroy: I am come that they might have life, and that they might have it more abundantly."

He also came to restore fallen humanity and to establish His Church. Jesus gave the Church its purpose in Matthew 28:18–24 where we are told, "All power is given unto me in heaven and in earth. Go ye therefore, and teach all nations, baptizing them in the name of the Father, and of the Son, and of the Holy Ghost: Teaching them to observe all things whatsoever I have commanded you: and, lo, I am with you always, even unto the end of the world."

Before Christ departed, He specifically told His disciples to remain in Jerusalem until they received *power from Heaven*. This power comes from the Holy Spirit, giving us the ability to accomplish the impossible. "But you shall receive power when the Holy Spirit has come upon you; and you shall be witnesses to Me in Jerusalem, and in all Judea and Samaria, and to the end of the earth" (Acts 1:8).

The union of the divine with our human conscience brings power—invincible power. When we are under the power and influence of the Holy Spirit, we have access to the authority of Christ. We go forward with His authority and power. We represent the authority of Heaven on this Earth. We have the Holy Spirit as our guarantee, validating and proving our divine authority to effect earthly manifestations. As believers, we have the spiritual authority (influence) and the right of (privilege) to act in the authority of Christ's name. "But as many as received him, to them gave he power to become the sons of God, even to them that believe on his name" (John 1:12).

A Spirit-filled prayer life is not only for our personal desires, but prayer also empowers us to overcome temptation and sin, and prayer is the vehicle that fulfills the purposes of God on Earth, so God can work on the Earth through us. This is what Christ meant when He said, "And he that sent me is with me: the Father hath not left me alone; for I do always those things that please him" (John 8:29). As we develop our faith and our spirituality by living in the Spirit, Scripture states in Galatians 5:25, "If we live in the Spirit, let us also walk in the Spirit."

The mind, the body, and the spirit are connected to the extent that now even science is researching and redefining how thinking and spiritual aspects profoundly affect our body. It just validates what people of faith have known all along—there is power, restoration, and healing in the Word.

Therefore, is it actually miraculous, or is mankind finally coming in tune with our innate ability by entering into a relationship with our Creator? Are we finally surrendering to His will and purpose for our lives? Are we finally connecting to our purpose and fulfillment in our relationship with God? Are we finally evolving to be more CHRIST-like?

The Body of Christ is called to preach the gospel (the good news); however, not only for our eternal salvation, but also for earthly manifestation. What a glorious day it will be when "followers of Christ" come into their true power and revelation of their true manifestation as sons and daughters of God.

It is in our process of spiritual development, maturity, and *obedience* that we become sensitive to and aware of the voice of the Holy Spirit. The same Holy Spirit that spoke to the holy men of the Bible can speak to us today. The same Holy Spirit that led Christ Jesus can lead us today, if we follow the example of Christ. Jesus said in John 14:6, "I am the way, the truth, and the life: no man cometh unto the Father, but by me."

The following Scriptures are biblical truths in biblical meditations on how to acquire the Holy Spirit, how the Holy Spirit is manifested, and how the Holy Spirit works.

How Do You Acquire the Holy Spirit?
Accepting Christ as Lord and Savior
- "Whosoever shall confess that Jesus is the Son of God, God dwelleth in him, and he in God" (1 John 4:15).
- "That if thou shalt confess with thy mouth the Lord Jesus, and shalt believe in thine heart that God hath raised him from the dead, thou shalt be saved. For with the heart man believeth unto righteousness; and with the mouth confession is made unto salvation" (Romans 10:9–10).

Obedience to God
- "And we are his witnesses of these things; and so is also the Holy Ghost, whom God hath given to them that obey him" (Acts 5:32).

Baptism
- "Then Peter said unto them, Repent, and be baptized every one of you in the name of Jesus Christ for the remission of

sins, and ye shall receive the gift of the Holy Ghost" (Acts 2:38).

Asking God

- "If ye then, being evil, know how to give good gifts unto your children: how much more shall your heavenly Father give the Holy Spirit to them that ask him" (Luke 11:13)?

Trusting God

- "Trust in the LORD with all thine heart; and lean not unto thine own understanding. In all thy ways acknowledge him, and he shall direct thy paths" (Proverbs 3:5–6).

How Is the Holy Spirit Manifested?

Gifts from God

- "Now there are diversities of gifts, but the same Spirit. And there are differences of administrations, but the same Lord. And there are diversities of operations, but it is the same God which worketh all in all. But the manifestation of the Spirit is given to every man to profit withal. For to one is given by the Spirit the word of wisdom; to another the word of knowledge by the same Spirit; To another faith by the same Spirit; to another the gifts of healing by the same Spirit; To another the working of miracles; to another prophecy; to another discerning of spirits; to another divers kinds of tongues; to another the interpretation of tongues: But all these worketh that one and the selfsame Spirit, dividing to every man severally as he will" (1 Corinthians 12:4–11).
- "Not by might, nor by power, but by my spirit, saith the LORD of hosts" (Zechariah 4:6).

Wisdom and the Knowledge of the Holy Word

- "Give instruction to a wise man, and he will be yet wiser: teach a just man, and he will increase in learning. The fear of the LORD is the beginning of wisdom: and the knowledge of the holy is understanding" (Proverbs 9:9–10).

Relationship with God and Jesus
- "Whosoever denieth the Son, the same hath not the Father: he that acknowledgeth the Son hath the Father also" (1 John 2:23).
- "Wherefore I give you to understand, that no man speaking by the Spirit of God calleth Jesus accursed: and that no man can say that Jesus is the Lord, but by the Holy Ghost" (1 Corinthians 12:3).
- "If any man will come after me, let him deny himself, and take up his cross daily, and follow me" (Luke 9:23).
- "If we walk in the light, as he is in the light, we have fellowship one with another, and the blood of Jesus Christ his Son cleanseth us from all sin" (1 John 1:7).
- "Know ye not that ye are the temple of God, and that the Spirit of God dwelleth in you?" (1 Corinthians 3:16)

Sanctification
- "The very God of peace sanctify you wholly; and *I pray God* your whole spirit and soul and body be preserved blameless unto the coming of our Lord Jesus Christ" (1 Thessalonians 5:23).
- "Put on the new man, which after God is created in righteousness and true holiness" (Ephesians 4:24).
- "Because it is written, Be ye holy; for I am holy" (1 Peter 1:16).

Obedience
- "He that hath my commandments, and keepeth them, he it is that loveth me: and he that loveth me shall be loved of my Father, and I will love him, and will manifest myself to him" (John 14:21).
- "Jesus answered and said unto him, If a man love me, he will keep my words: and my Father will love him, and we will come unto him, and make our abode with him. He that

loveth me not keepeth not my sayings: and the word which ye hear is not mine, but the Father's which sent me. These things have I spoken unto you, being yet present with you. But the Comforter, which is the Holy Ghost, whom the Father will send in my name, he shall teach you all things, and bring all things to your remembrance, whatsoever I have said unto you" (John 14:23–26).

- "And whatsoever we ask, we receive of him, because we keep his commandments, and do those things that are pleasing in his sight. And this is his commandment, That we should believe on the name of his Son Jesus Christ, and love one another, as he gave us commandment. And he that keepeth his commandments dwelleth in him, and he in him. And hereby we know that he abideth in us, by the Spirit which he hath given us" (1 John 3:22–24).
- "Turn you at my reproof: behold, I will pour out my spirit unto you, I will make known my words unto you" (Proverbs 1:23).

Worship

- "True worshippers shall worship the Father in spirit and in truth: for the Father seeketh such to worship him" (John 4:23).
- "Glory and honour are in his presence; strength and gladness are in his place" (1 Chronicles 16:27).
- "He that dwelleth in the secret place of the most High shall abide under the shadow of the Almighty" (Psalm 91:1).

Righteous Living

- "And grieve not the holy Spirit of God, whereby ye are sealed unto the day of redemption. Let all bitterness, and wrath, and anger, and clamour, and evil speaking, be put away from you, with all malice: And be ye kind one to another, tenderhearted, forgiving one another, even as God for Christ's sake hath forgiven you" (Ephesians 4:30-32).
- "(For the fruit of the Spirit is in all goodness and righteousness and truth)" (Ephesians 5:9).

- "The fruit of the Spirit is love, joy, peace, longsuffering, gentleness, goodness, faith, meekness, temperance: against such there is no law" (Galatians 5:22-23).

How the Holy Spirit Works
Why the Spirit?

- "Except a man be born of water and of the Spirit, he cannot enter into the kingdom of God" (John 3:5).

To Worship God

- "God is a Spirit: and they that worship him must worship him in spirit and in truth" (John 4:24).
- "For through him we both have access by one Spirit unto the Father" (Ephesians 2:18).

To Glorify God

- "But he that is joined unto the Lord is one spirit. What? know ye not that your body is the temple of the Holy Ghost which is in you, which ye have of God, and ye are not your own? For ye are bought with a price: therefore glorify God in your body, and in your spirit, which are God's" (1 Corinthians 6:17, 19–20).

To Discern Wisdom

- "But God hath revealed them unto us by his Spirit: for the Spirit searcheth all things, yea, the deep things of God. For what man knoweth the things of a man, save the spirit of man which is in him? even so the things of God knoweth no man, but the Spirit of God. Now we have received, not the spirit of the world, but the spirit which is of God; that we might know the things that are freely given to us of God. Which things also we speak, not in the words which man's wisdom teacheth, but which the Holy Ghost teacheth; comparing spiritual things with spiritual. But the natural man receiveth not the things of the Spirit of God: for they are foolishness unto him: neither can he know them, because they are spiritually discerned. But he that is spiritual judgeth all things, yet he himself is judged of no man. For who hath known the mind of the Lord, that he may instruct him? But we have the mind of Christ" (1 Corinthians 2:10–15).

- "But the Comforter, which is the Holy Ghost, whom the Father will send in my name, he shall teach you all things, and bring all things to your remembrance, whatsoever I have said unto you" (John 14:26).
- "Howbeit when he, the Spirit of truth, is come, he will guide you into all truth: for he shall not speak of himself; but whatsoever he shall hear, that shall he speak: and he will shew you things to come. He shall glorify me: for he shall receive of mine, and shall shew it unto you" (John 16:13–14).
- "But ye have an unction from the Holy One, and ye know all things" (1 John 2:20).

Intercession (Connects You to God)
- "The LORD is nigh unto them that are of a broken heart; and saveth such as be of a contrite spirit" (Psalm 34:18).
- "For thus saith the high and lofty One that inhabiteth eternity, whose name is Holy; I dwell in the high and holy place, with him also that is of a contrite and humble spirit, to revive the spirit of the humble, and to revive the heart of the contrite ones" (Isaiah 57:15).
- "It is the spirit that quickeneth; the flesh profiteth nothing: the words that I speak unto you, they are spirit, and they are life" (John 6:63).

Strengthens You to Overcome Sin
- "This I say then, Walk in the Spirit, and ye shall not fulfill the lust of the flesh" (Galatians 5:16).
- "For the law of the Spirit of life in Christ Jesus hath made me free from the law of sin and death" (Romans 8:2).

Empowers and Strengthens You to Be Holy

- "That the righteousness of the law might be fulfilled in us, who walk not after the flesh, but after the Spirit. For they that are after the flesh do mind the things of the flesh; but they that are after the Spirit the things of the Spirit. For to be carnally minded is death; but to be spiritually minded is life and peace. Because the carnal mind is enmity against God: for it is not subject to the law of God, neither indeed can be. So then they that are in the flesh cannot please God. But ye are not in the flesh, but in the Spirit, if so be that the Spirit of God dwell in you. Now if any man have not the Spirit of Christ, he is none of his.

  And if Christ be in you, the body is dead because of sin; but the Spirit is life because of righteousness. But if the Spirit of him that raised up Jesus from the dead dwell in you, he that raised up Christ from the dead shall also quicken your mortal bodies by his Spirit that dwelleth in you" (Romans 8:4–11).
- "For if ye live after the flesh, ye shall die: but if ye through the Spirit do mortify the deeds of the body, ye shall live. For as many as are led by the Spirit of God, they are the sons of God" (Romans 8:13–14).
- "For we through the Spirit wait for the hope of righteousness by faith" (Galatians 5:5).

Defense in Spiritual Warfare

- "Be strong in the Lord, and in the power of his might. Put on the whole armour of God, that ye may be able to stand against the wiles of the devil. For we wrestle not against flesh and blood, but against principalities, against powers, against the rulers of the darkness of this world, against spiritual wickedness in high places" (Ephesians 6:10–12).
- "Wherefore take unto you the whole armour of God, that ye may be able to withstand in the evil day, and having done all, to stand. Stand therefore, having your loins girt about with truth, and having on the breastplate of righ-

teousness; And your feet shod with the preparation of the gospel of peace; Above all, taking the shield of faith, wherewith ye shall be able to quench all the fiery darts of the wicked" (Ephesians 6:13–16).

- "And take the helmet of salvation, and the sword of the Spirit, which is the word of God: Praying always with all prayer and supplication in the Spirit, and watching thereunto with all perseverance and supplication for all saints; And for me, that utterance may be given unto me, that I may open my mouth boldly, to make known the mystery of the gospel" (Ephesians 6:17–19).
- "When the enemy shall come in like a flood, the Spirit of the LORD shall lift up a standard against him" (Isaiah 59:19).
- "Submit yourselves therefore to God. Resist the devil, and he will flee from you" (James 4:7).

Increases Your Faith

- "Now the God of hope fill you with all joy and peace in believing, that ye may abound in hope, through the power of the Holy Ghost" (Romans 15:13).
- "But ye, beloved, building up yourselves on your most holy faith, praying in the Holy Ghost" (Jude 1:20).

Intercessor to Help You Pray

- "Likewise the Spirit also helpeth our infirmities: for we know not what we should pray for as we ought: but the Spirit itself maketh intercession for us with groanings which cannot be uttered. And he that searcheth the hearts knoweth what is the mind of the Spirit, because he maketh intercession for the saints according to the will of God" (Romans 8:26–27).
- "For the Holy Ghost shall teach you in the same hour what ye ought to say" (Luke 12:12).
- "For he that speaketh in an unknown tongue speaketh not unto men, but unto God: for no man understandeth him; howbeit in the spirit he speaketh mysteries" (1 Corinthians 14:2).

Power and Authority through Prayer

- "But ye shall receive power, after that the Holy Ghost is come upon you" (Acts 1:8).
- "And if Christ be in you, the body is dead because of sin; but the Spirit is life because of righteousness. But if the Spirit of him that raised up Jesus from the dead dwell in you, he that raised up Christ from the dead shall also quicken your mortal bodies by his Spirit that dwelleth in you" (Romans 8:10–11).
- "By stretching forth thine hand to heal; and that signs and wonders may be done by the name of thy holy child Jesus. And when they had prayed, the place was shaken where they were assembled together; and they were all filled with the Holy Ghost, and they spake the word of God with boldness" (Acts 4:30–31).

We pray...

"The grace of the Lord Jesus Christ, and the love of God, and the communion of the Holy Ghost, be with you all. Amen" (2 Corinthians 13:14).

CHAPTER 4

Honoring God

―――――

"Furthermore we have had fathers of our flesh which corrected us, and we gave them reverence: shall we not much
rather be in subjection unto the Father of spirits, and live?"
(Hebrews 12:9)

*H*onor is the reverent respect, humility, sincerity, and love
with which we acknowledge, magnify, and celebrate God
in worship and live a submitted life in obedience according to
His Word. Worship and honor connects us to the presence of
the most holy for, "Thou art worthy, O Lord, to receive glory and
honour and power: for thou hast created all things, and for thy
pleasure they are and were created" (Revelation 4:11).

Jesus declared, "Ye worship ye know not what: we know
what we worship: for salvation is of the Jews" (John 4:22).
Christ was Jewish as were His disciples and they both honored and kept God's Holy Days, "the Feasts of the LORD," and
The Commandments. Christ said, "Think not that I am come to
destroy the law, or the prophets: I am not come to destroy, but
to fulfil. Whosoever therefore shall break one of these least commandments, and shall teach men so, he shall be called the least

in the kingdom of heaven: but whosoever shall do and teach them, the same shall be called great in the kingdom of heaven" (Matthew 5:17-19).

> **Our Hebraic-Judaeo-Christian Roots:** "For he is not a Jew, which is one outwardly; neither is that circumcision, which is outward in the flesh: But he is a Jew, which is one inwardly; and circumcision is that of the heart, in the spirit, and not in the letter; whose praise is not of men, but of God" (Romans 2:28).

> "There is neither Jew nor Greek, there is neither bond nor free, there is neither male nor female: for ye are all one in Christ Jesus" (Galatians 3:28).

The word *Jew* comes from the Hebrew name of the ancestor of *"Judah."* The word *Judah* means, "praised" which is derived from the Shoresh, meaning *yadah*, to "give thanks and praise." Later, the term meant anyone who descended from Israel. In modern usage, one is a Jew if he or she has Jewish parents or has undergone Jewish conversion in accordance to Jewish law. The Greek word for "Christian" is *Christianos*, which means "follower of Christ."

As Christians, we should honor the birth, death, burial, Resurrection and Ascension of our Lord and Savior. Christians generally do not celebrate the Holy Days and the observance of The Commandments has been debatable and, often, misunderstood. However, if Jesus, the Master, honored and kept the Holy Days, Sabbath, and The Commandments shouldn't we? As followers of Christ, it would be apparent that we should, as well. The Bible in its entirety is the Word of God. "For precept must be upon precept, precept upon precept; line upon line, line upon line" (Isaiah 28:10), "rightly dividing the word of truth" (2 Timothy 2:15).

"What advantage then hath the Jew? or what profit is there of circumcision? Much every way: chiefly, because that unto them were committed the oracles of God" (Romans 3:1-2). "Seeing it is one God, which shall justify the circumcision by faith, and uncircumcision through faith. Do we then make void the law through faith? God forbid: yea, we establish the law" (Romans 3:30-31).

The Mosaic Law, Law of Moses, was intended to be perpetual. On the other hand, as a legal code, it would be abolished. So Jesus, the Messiah, came not to abolish the perfect Law of God, but to perfect the imperfect legal code of Moses. The Messianic prophecy in Isaiah 42:21tells us that Christ, "...will magnify the law, and make it honorable."

We are told in Galatians 3:24–26, "Wherefore the law was our schoolmaster to bring us unto Christ, that we might be justified by faith. But after that faith is come, we are no longer under a schoolmaster. For ye are all the children of God by faith in Christ Jesus."

This does not mean that Christians should discard The Commandments as if they have no relevance today. *Christ's example is the written code lived out,* an internal spiritual principle and lifestyle, of godly living, not just a written code of one that is only defined by rules and regulations. This perspective is clearly seen in Romans 7:6, "But now we are delivered from the law, that being dead wherein we were held; that we should serve in newness of spirit, and not in the oldness of the letter."

Jesus redefined the law, based on the principles of the law, and showed its full spiritual intent as love, the principled and qualifying factor of spirituality and Christianity. "Thou shalt love the Lord thy God with all thy heart, and with all thy soul, and with all thy mind. This is the first and great commandment. And the second is like unto it, Thou shalt love thy neighbour as thyself. On these two commandments hang all the law and the prophet" (Matthew 22:37-40).

When the Holy Spirit directs our life He fills the letter (the written Word) by the Spirit, and obedience to the written Word, that the righteousness of the law is fulfilled in us. As reflected in 2 Corinthians 3:3, 6, "Who also hath made us able ministers of the new testament; not of the letter, but of the spirit: for the letter killeth, but the spirit giveth life...ye are manifestly declared to be the epistle of Christ ministered by us, written not with ink, but with the Spirit of the living God; not in tables of stone, but in fleshy tables of the heart."

"The fruit of the Spirit is love, joy, peace, longsuffering, gentleness, goodness, faith, meekness, temperance: against such there is no law" (Galatians 5:22).

God is our lawgiver; He has given us a moral code of behavior, authoritative and comprehensive—the Ten Commandments. The Ten Commandments are the Laws of God and the foundational groundwork for right behavior. "Wherefore the law is holy, and the commandment holy, and just, and good" (Romans 7:12).

Recall, the law is the standard of the judgment. There can be no judgment without a law or standard of judgment. "Whosoever committed sin transgresseth also the law: for sin is the transgression of the law" (1 John 3:4). The transgression of law is not walking in the full measure of the promises of God in this life; and the judgment, of the transgression of the law, is not partaking in the eternal, promised, after-life in heaven or the consequences of: "death and hell were cast into the lake of fire. This is the second death. And whosoever was not found written in the book of life was cast into the lake of fire" (Revelations 20:14-15).

"This I say then, Walk in the Spirit, and ye shall not fulfill the lust of the flesh" (Galatians 5:16). "For the law of the Spirit of life in Christ Jesus hath made me free from the law of sin and death" (Romans 8:2).

The Apostle Paul's conclusion concerning the law is found in Romans 13:8-10, "Owe no man any thing, but to love one another: for he that loveth another hath fulfilled the law. For this, Thou shalt not commit adultery, Thou shalt not kill, Thou shalt not steal, Thou shalt not bear false witness, Thou shalt not covet; and if there be any other commandment, it is briefly comprehended in this saying, namely, Thou shalt love thy neighbour as thyself. Love worketh no ill to his neighbour: therefore love is the fulfilling of the law." "Therefore cast off the works of darkness, and let us put on the armour of light...put ye on the Lord

Jesus Christ, and make not provision for the flesh, to fulfil the lusts thereof" (Roman 13:12-14).

God has given us spiritual laws, a revelation of His character. Jesus Christ was the demonstration of the laws living by the Ten Commandments and honoring the Holy Days. "If ye keep my commandments, ye shall abide in my love; even as I have kept my Father's commandments, and abide in his love" (John 15:10). Love and honor is the qualifying factor in God's purpose and spiritual intent for our divine original nature to prevail.

God's Holy Days and Appointed Times

The divine order of God is based in His principles, power, and law. The fulfillment for us to receive the promises of God is based on our honor of, reverence for, and obedience to those principles, order, and law.

The Holy Days set by God were to be remembered among the Israelites for all generations, and testified that God had been their deliverer, provider, and source. God commanded ancient Israel to actively keep three festivals each year.

Those aware of these festivals generally believe they were meant only for ancient Israel and ceased after Jesus' crucifixion and Resurrection. However, Scripture explains that Jesus fulfills in Himself everything to which the Old Testament Scriptures point and illustrates how the Law of God, and observance of the Holy Days, given to Israel is transformed through its fulfillment in Him.

Jesus fulfilled, and continues to fulfill, in Himself all the types, shadows, and prophecies of the Old Testament that pointed to Him and of the New Testament prophecies to come. These festivals reveal the unfolding of God's plan for humanity and how He will establish His Kingdom on earth. "For the law having a shadow of good things to come, and not the very image of the things, can never with those sacrifices which they offered year by year continually make the comers thereunto perfect" (Hebrews 10:1).

The Scripture most often quoted by Christians stating that the Old Testament law and ordinances are not relevant is Colossians 2:14, "Blotting out the handwriting of ordinances that was against us, which was contrary to us, and took it out of the way, nailing it to his cross."

Jesus by His death, on the Cross, made a new class of man (one new man) the church, "and hath broken down the middle wall of partition between us; Having abolished in his flesh the enmity, even the law of commandments contained in ordinances; for to make in himself of [two] twain one new man, so making peace; And that he might reconcile both unto God in one body by the cross, having slain the enmity thereby: And came and preached peace to you [Gentiles] which were afar off, and to them that were nigh [Jews]" (Ephesians 2:14-17).

The Gentiles, "being aliens from the commonwealth of Israel, and strangers from the covenants of promise, having no hope, and without God in the world" (Ephesians 2:12) *are* "now in Christ Jesus ye who sometimes were far off are made nigh by the blood of Christ... For through him we both have access by one Spirit unto the Father. Now therefore ye are no more strangers and foreigners, but fellowcitizens with the saints, and of the household of God; And are built upon the foundation of the apostles and prophets, Jesus Christ himself being the chief corner stone" (Ephesians 2:13,18-20). Christ also *annulled the penalty of the law*, figuratively, by "nailing it to the cross," so mankind could have a new start in life again before God as a new creation, purged from sin, to be reconciled to God.

Legalism is obeying the law to try and earn entrance into the kingdom by works and if this is the only motive, then it is in vain. When legalities become the practice, then worship becomes a ritualistic religion, as opposed to us living in the Spirit and experiencing a fellowship and relationship with God; then our faith is based on "works, lest any man should boast" (Ephesians 2:9). Earthly principles and customs are contrary to the gospel, in that they do not change the inner man, as evident in Colossians 2:20–23, "Wherefore if ye be dead with Christ from the rudiments of the world, why, as though living in the world, are ye subject to ordinances, (Touch not; taste not; handle not; Which all are to perish with the using;) after the commandments and doctrines of men? Which things have indeed a shew of wisdom in will worship, and humility, and neglecting of the body: not in any honour to the satisfying of the flesh."

Jesus did not nail the principles of the Ten Commandments or the "feasts of the LORD" to the cross; he nailed the practice of legalities and ritualistic religion based on rules, ceremonial rites, traditions, man-made laws and the sin offerings; because He was the fulfillment of such practices. These practices included the temporary sacrificial sanctuary system, which involved animal sacrificial ceremonies for the atonement of sin, which of course are no longer necessary since Jesus became the true Lamb of God. The ceremonial law with its sacrificial system pointed the people to the coming of Christ. When Christ died on the Cross of Calvary the veil of the temple curtain was torn from top to bottom, to signify that the entire ceremonial system was forever finished, and by His blood we now have access to the Throne of God.

The New Testament shows both Jesus observing God's Holy Days, and the disciples following His example after His death, burial, and Resurrection. Jews, Christian Jews, Messianic Jews (Jew and Gentile), and some Christians commonly observe the festivals. Traditionally, however, non-Jewish Bible believers understand the festivals to be exclusively Jewish feasts. Leviticus 23:1-2, 4 tells us very clearly, "Concerning the feasts of the LORD, which ye shall proclaim to be holy convocations, even these are my feasts.... These are the feasts of the LORD, even holy convocations, which ye shall proclaim in their seasons."

In Hebrew feast means *mow'ed*; the word *mow'ed* has several meanings: "an appointment, a fixed time or season, a cycle or year, an assembly, an appointed time, and a set time or exact time." By understanding the Hebrew meaning of the English word "feast," we can see that God is telling us that He is ordaining a "set time or exact time or an appointed time" when He has an appointment with humanity to fulfill certain events in the redemption.

The festivals are God's feasts, "these are the feasts of the LORD," not only Jewish feasts, they are His appointed times that we are to observe. In Exodus 23:20–33, we also see that God promised seven blessings to those who observe His feasts as follows: God will be an enemy to your enemies (verse 22). God will assign an angel to you (verse 23). God will give you prosperity (verse 25). God will take sickness away from you (verse 25). God will give you long life (verse 26). God will bring increase and inheritance (verse 30).

While the seven Torah festivals were, indeed, given to the Jewish people, Gentiles (Christians) who have been engrafted into God's family tree of salvation, and covenant relationship, by faith in Jesus Christ have also been attached to this part of the root system that provides richness and blessings to God's people.

Scholars attest that Christians once practiced the feasts, however, "in AD 325, the Roman emperor, Constantine stopped the Passover as a church practice. Since that time, the holy convocations (the feasts) have not been observed by most Christians." These appointed times, weekly and annual Sabbaths, were determined by God Himself, and God calls upon us to set aside set times and seasons for sacred appointments with Him. There is far more meaning and significance to these "feasts of the LORD" than is noted here. In summation, they are powerful spiritual lessons in honoring God and they are summarized as the feasts of faith, feasts of joy and thanksgiving, feasts of promise, feasts of rehersals, and the feasts of love.

Honoring the Holy Convocations

Ancient Israel, under the First Covenant, is recorded in the following Scriptures honoring the Holy Days. As New Covenant believers, however, we need not be concerned with ancient ritualism from which followers of Christ are liberated in Christ according to Hebrews 9:10, "Which stood only in meats and drinks, and divers washings, and carnal ordinances, imposed on them until the time of reformation." But, however, under the New

Covenant, we should remember, and celebrate, the Holy Days as His appointed times for their prophetic, spiritual, divine, memorial, sacred, and eternal seasons; not as, a matter of legalistic law, but one of intimacy, worship, and honor with the "LORD".

> Three times thou shalt keep a feast unto me in the year. Thou shalt keep the feast of unleavened bread: (thou shalt eat unleavened bread seven days, as I commanded thee, in the time appointed of the month Abib; for in it thou camest out from Egypt: and none shall appear before me empty:) And the feast of harvest, the firstfruits of thy labours, which thou hast sown in the field: and the feast of ingathering, which is in the end of the year, when thou hast gathered in thy labours out of the field. (Exodus 23:14–16)

> Leviticus 23: Concerning the feasts of the LORD, which ye shall proclaim to be holy convocations, even these are my feasts. Six days shall work be done: but the seventh day is the sabbath of rest, an holy convocation; ye shall do no work therein: it is the sabbath of the LORD in all your dwellings. These are the feasts of the LORD, even holy convocations, which ye shall proclaim in their seasons. In the fourteenth day of the first month at even is the LORD's passover. And on the fifteenth day of the same month is the feast of unleavened bread unto the LORD: seven days ye must eat unleavened bread. In the first day ye shall have an holy convocation: ye shall do no servile work therein ... Even unto the morrow after the seventh sabbath shall ye number fifty days; and ye shall offer a new meat offering unto the LORD.

> Ye shall bring out of your habitations two wave loaves of two tenth deals; they shall be of fine flour; they shall be baken with leaven; they are the firstfruits unto the LORD ... And ye shall proclaim on the selfsame day, that it may be an holy convocation unto you: ye shall do no servile work therein: it shall be a statute for ever in all your dwellings throughout your generations. And when ye reap the harvest of your land,

thou shalt not make clean riddance of the corners of thy field when thou reapest, neither shalt thou gather any gleaning of thy harvest: thou shalt leave them unto the poor, and to the stranger: I am the LORD your God ... In the seventh month, in the first day of the month, shall ye have a Sabbath, a memorial of blowing of trumpets, an holy convocation. Ye shall do no servile work therein: but ye shall offer an offering made by fire unto the LORD.

And the LORD spake unto Moses, saying, Also on the tenth day of this seventh month there shall be a day of atonement: it shall be an holy convocation unto you; and ye shall afflict your souls, and offer an offering made by fire unto the LORD. And ye shall do no work in that same day: for it is a day of atonement, to make an atonement for you before the LORD your God. For whatsoever soul it be that shall not be afflicted in that same day, he shall be cut off from among his people. And whatsoever soul it be that doeth any work in that same day, the same soul will I destroy from among his people. Ye shall do no manner of work: it shall be a statute for ever throughout your generations in all your dwellings. It shall be unto you a sabbath of rest, and ye shall afflict your souls: in the ninth day of the month at even, from even unto even, shall ye celebrate your sabbath. These are the feasts of the LORD, which ye shall proclaim to be holy convocations.

Following are the seven feasts instituted by God for His believers, which will be further discussed below:

Passover
Feast of Unleavened Bread
Feast of Firstfruits
Feast of Weeks (also known as Harvest, the Day of Firstfruits, Pentecost)
Feast of Trumpets
The Day of Atonement
Feast of Tabernacles

Passover is the first of the seven annual festivals celebrated and is considered being Israel's foundational feast upon which the other six feasts follow. The *Feast of Unleavened Bread* follows Passover, because only unleavened bread was eaten during the seven days immediately following Passover. The third feast occurs on the second day of the *Feast of Unleavened Bread*; it is called the *Feast of Firstfruit.* The *Feast of Weeks* also known as *Harvest* (Exodus 23:16), the *Day of Firstfruits* (Numbers 28:26) or *Pentecost in the New Testament.*

The *Feast of Trumpets* is the first of the fall feasts. It begins the "ten days of awe" before the *Day of Atonement.* The Jewish people call this feast *Rosh Hashanah*, which literally means "Head of the Year" and it is observed as the start of the civil year (in contrast with the religious year which starts with Passover) on the Jewish calendar.

The Day of Atonement (Yom Kippur) occurred ten days after the Feast of Trumpets. The ten days from Trumpets to the Day of Atonement are known as "the days of awe," which include penitence, prayer, and fasting in preparation for the most solemn day of the Jewish religious calendar, the Feast of Tabernacles. The seventh and final "Feast of the Lord" is the *Feast of Tabernacles.* It occurs five days after the Day of Atonement.

The Significance of Passover: Exodus 12:24, "And ye shall observe this thing for an ordinance to thee and to thy sons for ever." The Passover celebrated God's deliverance of Israel out of four hundred years bondage in Egypt. In Exodus, Chapters 7–12, God sent plagues on the Egyptians. The last plague was the death of the firstborn in every family in Egypt (Exodus 12:29–30). God told the people of Israel to kill a spotless lamb and put its blood on the doorposts and the crosspiece of their homes. When the angel of death came to kill all the firstborn in Egypt, he would see the blood and pass over that house (Exodus 12:3–13). After the firstborn had been killed, Pharaoh sent Israel out of Egypt, which was God's deliverance of them. So the celebration of the Passover commemorated the sacrificial lamb whose blood enabled Israel to escape the judgment of God.

Jesus Honoring the Passover: Jesus Christ was crucified during the Passover event. He and His disciples ate a Passover meal together on the eve of His death. Matthew 26:18–19, "The Master saith, My time is at hand; I will keep the passover at thy house with my disciples. And the disciples did as Jesus had appointed them; and they made ready the passover."

The Passover as the Lord's Last Supper: During the celebration of Passover this meal became known as the Lord's Supper in Luke 22:15–20 Jesus, "said unto them, With desire I have desired to eat this Passover with you before I suffer: For I say unto you, I will not any more eat thereof, until it be fulfilled in the kingdom of God. And he took the cup, and gave thanks, and said, Take this, and divide it among yourselves: For I say unto you, I will not drink of the fruit of the vine, until the kingdom of God shall come. And he took bread, and gave thanks, and brake it, and gave unto them, saying, This is my body which is given for you: this do in remembrance of me. Likewise also the cup after supper, saying, This cup is the new testament in my blood, which is shed for you."

- *New Testament Meaning*: This holy day forms the primary background for understanding the events of the symbolism of the Lord's Table (Communion) and the meaning of the Messiah's (Jesus) death. It became a symbol of Jesus, God's Passover Lamb, whose blood enables one to escape the eternal judgment of God.

All of the lambs sacrificed in Egypt, one per household, pointed to the one true Lamb of God who takes away the sin of the world, as stated in John 1:29, "The next day John seeth Jesus coming unto him, and saith, Behold the Lamb of God, which taketh away the sin of the world." Writing to the Corinthians, the Apostle, Paul noted that Christ was the ultimate Passover Lamb reconciling all Christians to God the Father.

- "For even Christ our passover is sacrificed for us: Therefore let us keep the feast" (I Corinthians 5:7-8).

Christ was our Passover Lamb, and this is all the more reason Christians should celebrate Passover.

The Feast of Unleavened Bread follows Passover, because only unleavened bread was eaten during the seven days immediately following Passover. The Israelites were instructed in Deuteronomy 16:3, "Thou shalt eat no leavened bread with it; seven days shalt thou eat unleavened bread therewith, even the bread of affliction; for thou camest forth out of the land of Egypt in haste: that thou mayest remember the day when thou camest forth out of the land of Egypt all the days of thy life."

- *New Testament Meaning:* The Apostle Paul records, "Therefore let us keep the feast, not with old leaven, neither with the leaven of malice and wickedness; but with the unleavened bread of sincerity and truth" (1 Corinthians 5:8).

Unleavened bread pictures the Christian's duty to "put out sin" from a life yielded to Jesus Christ and to grow in grace and in knowledge.

The Significance of the Feast of Firstfruit: The third feast occurs on the second day of the Feast of Unleavened Bread; it is called the *Feast of Firstfruit*, where ancient Israel would present their first grain harvest to the priest in thanksgiving and recognition of God's continued provision and blessing. (Leviticus 23:9-14)

- *New Testament Meaning:* **The Son of God arose from the grave on Firstfruits**. Paul specifically calls Jesus' Resurrection the *first fruits* of those who will rise from the dead in 1 Corinthians 15: 20–24: "But now Christ is risen from the dead, and has become the first fruits of those who have fallen asleep. For since by man came death, by Man also came the resurrection of the dead. For as in Adam all die, even so in Christ all shall be made alive. But each one in his own order: Christ the first fruits, afterward those who are Christ's at His coming. Then comes the end, when He delivers the kingdom to God the Father, when He puts an end to all rule and all authority and power."

The Significance of the Feast of Weeks, also known as *Feast of Harvest* (Exodus 23:16), and the *Day of Firstfruits* (Numbers 28:26). This holy day is celebrated fifty days after Passover as a festival of joy and thanksgiving celebrating the completion of the harvest season and as a time to honor the Lord for blessing the firstfruits of their labors.

This feast day was referred to as "Feast of Weeks" because it was celebrated seven weeks after the offering of the barley sheaf (Exodus 34:22; Deuteronomy 16:9–10). Also known as the "Feast of the Harvest" (Exodus 23:16) because it came at the end of the barley harvest, and it was also known as the "Day of First Fruits" (Exodus 34:22; Numbers 28:26) because it marked the beginning of the first fruits of the wheat harvest being offered at the temple. It is referred to in the New Testament as *"Pentecost"* a term derived from the Greek word *pentekoste* (meaning "fiftieth").

- *New Testament* Meaning: The Feast of Harvest—The Feast of Weeks—*Day of Pentecost* is a symbolic festival which pointed to Christians receiving God's Holy Spirit and the birthday of the Christian Church.

The Christian Church came into being on the holy *Day of Pentecost* as worshipers, including the disciples, were celebrating Pentecost with fasting and praying; and the baptism of the Holy Spirit descended upon them. "And when the day of Pentecost was fully come, they were all with one accord in one place. And suddenly there came a sound from heaven as of a rushing mighty wind, and it filled all the house where they were sitting. And there appeared unto them cloven tongues like as of fire, and it sat upon each of them. And they were all filled with the Holy Ghost, and began to speak with other tongues, as the Spirit gave them utterance" (Acts 2:1–4).

- *New Testament Meaning:* The Day of Firstfruits also points to the prophetic 144,000 saints who follow the Lamb. Revelation 14:4 states, "These are they which were not defiled with women; for they are virgins. These are they which follow the Lamb whithersoever he goeth. These were redeemed from among men, being the firstfruits unto God and to the Lamb."

The Significance of the Feast of Trumpets: This celebration marks the beginning of the Holy Days on the Jewish calendar. The Bible refers to Rosh Hashanah as the Feast of Trumpets, and it begins the Ten Days of Awe that conclude with Yom Kippur—the Day of Atonement. It is celebrated as a reminder of the event in Exodus 19:18-19 as the sound of the cosmic trumpets announced the manifestation of God's presence to the Israelites on Mt. Sinai. "And mount Sinai was altogether on a smoke, because the LORD descended upon it in fire: and the smoke thereof ascended as the smoke of a furnace, and the whole mount quaked greatly. And when the voice of the trumpet sounded long, and waxed louder and louder, Moses spake, and God answered him by a voice."

- *New Testament* Meaning: Portrays Christ's Second Coming to be announced "with the trump of God" in 1 Thessalonians 4:16-17, "For the Lord himself shall descend from heaven with a shout, with the voice of the archangel, and with the trump of God: and the dead in Christ shall rise first: Then we which are alive and remain shall be caught up together with them in the clouds, to meet the Lord in the air: and so shall we ever be with the Lord."

The Significance of the Day of Atonement (Yom Kippur): In Hebrew, *Yom* means "day" (marked from sunset to sunset, as instructed by God), and *Kippur* means to "pardon," or "condone." The word *atonement* means to *make amends* or *to reconcile*—to become "at one." The Lord commanded the Day of Atonement as a solemn annual observance for the Israelites. It's unique in that it is the only of the annual God-commanded biblical Holy Days in which fasting was required. The fast was such a strict requirement that anyone who failed to do so would be cut off from the community.

This day is the holiest day of the Jewish year. Atonement may also be termed the Day of Purgation (cleansing). Leviticus 16:30–31 describes it as "a sabbath of sabbaths." It is an opportunity, year by year, to obtain divine forgiveness of sin, repentance, and to cleanse oneself before the LORD, restoring oneself to a state of wholeness and holiness. "And ye shall be holy unto me: for I the LORD am holy, and have severed you from other people, that ye should be mine" (Leviticus 20:26).

Each year the high priest, repeated his sin offerings for his own sin, as well as for the sins of the people. This ritual was an annual reminder that perfect and permanent atonement had not yet been made; but Jesus, through His very own blood, accomplished eternal redemption for us.

- *New Testament* Meaning: The focal point of this feast involved the high priest entering the Holy of Holies performing specific rituals as outlined in detail in Leviticus 16. As the high priest of the Old Testament entered the Holy of Holies with the blood of sacrificial animals, Jesus entered Heaven itself to appear on our behalf in front of the Father. This ritual is a symbol of the atoning work of Jesus Christ, our Great High Priest, who did not need to make any sacrifice for Himself but rather shed His own blood for our sins. The sacrifice of Jesus did what all the lambs, goats, and bulls could never do-take away sin forever.

According to Hebrews 9:11–12,

"But Christ being come an high priest of good things to come, by a greater and more perfect tabernacle, not made with hands, that is to say, not of this building; Neither by the

110

blood of goats and calves, but by his own blood he entered in once into the holy place, having obtained eternal redemption for us."

"For it is not possible that the blood of bulls and of goats should take away sins" (Hebrews 10:4).

The Significance of the Feast of Tabernacles (Feast of Ingathering): At its most basic level, it is a fall festival, celebrating the abundance of God's blessings in connection with the ingathering of the fall harvest (similar to the holiday festivities of Thanksgiving). It is also a memorial of the Exodus, when the Israelites wandered in the wilderness, living in tabernacles, or tents, en route to the Promised Land. It is, therefore, a representation of faith in God's protection and promises. They were to keep this holiday in thankfulness to God for all the increase of the year.

"And ye shall keep it a feast unto the LORD seven days in the year. It shall be a statute for ever in your generations: ye shall celebrate it in the seventh month ... That your generations may know that I made the children of Israel to dwell in booths, when I brought them out of the land of Egypt: I am the LORD your God" (Leviticus 23:41–43).

Jesus Honoring the Feast of Tabernacles: "Now the Jew's feast of tabernacles was at hand. His brethren therefore said unto him, Depart hence, and go into Judaea, that thy disciples also may see the works that thou doest ... Then Jesus said unto them, My time is not yet come: but your time is alway ready. The world cannot hate you; but me it hateth, because I testify of it, that the works thereof are evil. Go ye up unto this feast: I go not up yet unto this feast: for my time is not yet full come. When he had said these words unto them, he abode still in Galilee. But when his brethren were gone up, then went he also up unto the feast, not openly, but as it were in secret" (John 7:2–10).

- *New Testament* Meaning: The Feast of Tabernacles looks forward to the time God will "tabernacle" on earth again with all humanity. To "tabernacle" means to dwell or live with. This feast looks forward to Jesus and His resurrected and transformed saints that will reign on the earth during the 1,000 year Millennium as, the Apostle, John prophesied in Revelation 20:4-6,

  And I saw thrones, and they sat upon them, and judgment was given unto them: and I saw the souls of them that were beheaded for the witness of Jesus, and for the word of God, and which had not worshipped the beast, neither his image, neither had received his mark upon their foreheads, or in their hands; and they lived and reigned with Christ a thousand years. But the rest of the dead lived not again until the thousand years were finished. This is the first resurrection. Blessed and holy is he that hath part in the first resurrection: on such the second death hath no power, but they shall be priests of God and of Christ, and shall reign with him a thousand years.

  Zechariah 14:16 prophesied that all nations and all people will tabernacle with the Lord in Jerusalem: "And it shall come to pass, that every one that is left of all the nations which came against Jerusalem shall even go up from year to year to worship the King, the LORD of hosts, and to keep the feast of tabernacles."

  Revelation 21:3 prophesies "a new Heaven and a new Earth." "And I heard a great voice out of heaven saying, Behold, the tabernacle of God is with men, and he will dwell with them, and they shall be his people, and God himself shall be with them, and be their God."

- The New Testament interpretations illustrated have been derived from scholars and theologians based on biblical Scriptures. The feasts are prophetic symbols and examples foreshadowing the ministry of Jesus the Messiah; that brings into sharper focus the plan of God and the purpose for Christ's first and the Second Coming of Christ.

The Weekly Sabbath: "God blessed the seventh day, and sanctified it: because that in it he had rested from all his work which God created and made" (Genesis 2:3). Jesus said, "The Sabbath was made for man, and not man for the Sabbath" (Mark 2:27). In God's infinite wisdom, He knew we needed a day of rest to refresh, recharge, and purposely REST in Him. "There remaineth therefore a rest to the people of God. For he that is entered into his rest, he also hath ceased from his own works, as God did from his" (Hebrews 4:9-10).

The purpose of the Sabbath is a time to study the Word, and attend church to fellowship in corporate prayer with praise and worship. "Not forsaking the assembling of ourselves together, as the manner of some is; but exhorting one another: and so much the more ..." (Hebrews 10:25). It is a permanent commandment in that we give honor to God, Elohim, our Creator of the universe. In the following Scriptures, we see God will honor us when we honor Him.

Blessed is the man that doeth this, and the son of man that layeth hold on it; that keepeth the sabbath from polluting it, and keepeth his hand from doing any evil. Also the sons of the stranger, that join themselves to the LORD, to serve him, and to love the name of the LORD, to be his servants, every one that keepeth the sabbath from polluting it, and taketh hold of my covenant; Even them will I bring to my holy mountain, and make them joyful in my house of prayer: ...for mine house shall be called an house of prayer for all people. (Isaiah 56:1, 6-7)

If thou turn away thy foot from the Sabbath, from doing thy pleasure on my holy day; and call the sabbath a delight, the holy of the LORD, honourable; and shalt honour him, not doing thine own ways, nor finding thine own pleasure, nor speaking thine own words: Then shalt thou delight thyself in the LORD; and I will cause thee to ride upon the high places of the earth, and feed thee with the heritage of Jacob thy father: for the mouth of the LORD hath spoken it. (Isaiah 58:13–14)

Remember the Sabbath day, to keep it holy. Six days shalt thou labour, and do all thy work: But the seventh day is the Sabbath of the LORD thy God: in it thou shalt not do any work, thou, nor thy son, nor thy daughter, thy manservant, nor thy maidservant, nor thy cattle, nor thy stranger that is within thy gates. (Exodus 20:8–10)

Jesus and the Disciples Honoring the Sabbath: As recorded in the gospels, Jesus kept the Sabbath, "And he came to Nazareth, where he had been brought up: and, as his custom was, he went into the synagogue on the Sabbath day, and stood up for to read" (Luke 4:16).

"And he [Paul] reasoned in the synagogue every sabbath, and persuaded the Jews and the Greeks" (Acts 18:4).

Communion—Observance of the Lord's Supper

In observing Holy Communion we are remembering the life of Christ, His sacrifice, His death, His burial, and The Resurrection. Jesus instructed the disciples during the last Passover meal to, "Do this in remembrance of me" (1 Corinthians 11:24). It is one of the two holy ordinances instituted by Christ in the New Testament recorded in Luke 22:15–20, the other being baptism.

The term communion refers to the inner unity and fellowship of believers, one with another, through their union in Christ. The Lord's Table symbolizes this fellowship and even brings about that unity, "For we being many are one bread, and one body: for we are all partakers of that one bread" (1 Corinthians 10:17). Stated simply, to have communion with God means to have a share in His divine purpose; He lives in us and we in Him.

Worship at the Lord's Table embraces a variety of terms in the New Testament known as breaking bread, communion, and the Lord's Supper.

Partaking in the Lord's Table is to, "proclaim the Lord's death until he comes" (1 Corinthians 11:26). The wine we bless is symbolic of Christ's blood and the bread we break is symbolic of His body.

The first element is "unleavened bread." Christ tells us "... Take, eat; this is my body" (Matthew 26:26). The second element is "the cup." Christ provides us with the interpretation, "This cup is the new testament in my blood, which is shed for you" (Luke 22:20). The cup, which contains the fruit of the vine, represents the covenant through which we have our reconciliation to God. The third element is the "fruit of the vine" that is contained in the cup. Again, Christ provides us with the meaning, "For this is my blood of the new testament, which is shed for many for the remission of sins" (Matthew 26:28).

When we partake of the Lord's Supper we should bring to remembrance the following:

- Like the Passover, the Lord's Supper was also instituted to help us remember the blood of the Lamb, Christ our Passover Lamb, and by the blood our deliverance to salvation.
- The crucifixion and the Resurrection has a continuing significance to all who take up their cross daily to follow Jesus. Jesus tells us in Luke 9:23, "If any man will come after me, let him deny himself, and take up his cross daily, and follow me."
- The Lord's Supper helps us look inward in self-examination and to look up in rededication. "He must increase, but I must decrease" (John 3:30).

Wherefore whosoever shall eat this bread, and drink this cup of the Lord, unworthily, shall be guilty of the body and blood of the Lord. But let a man examine himself, and so let him eat of that bread, and drink of that cup. For he that eateth and drinketh unworthily, eateth and drinketh damnation to himself, not discerning the Lord's body. For this cause many are weak and sickly among you, and many sleep.

For if we would judge ourselves, we should not be judged. But when we are judged, we are chastened of the Lord, that we should not be condemned with the world. Wherefore, my brethren, when ye come together to eat, tarry one for another. (I Corinthians 11:27–33)

When we partake of Holy Communion not only do we remember the life of Christ; but also, we honor Him in memory by paying due diligence to the Word and Laws of God. Remember, "and the Word was made flesh and dwelt among us." Therefore, if figuratively we eat "the body," we eat the Word and when "we drink His blood," we are covered and redeemed "by the blood." Jesus as recorded in John 6:48-51,

I am that bread of life. Your fathers did eat manna in the wilderness, and are dead. This is the bread which cometh down from heaven, that a man may eat thereof, and not die. I am the living bread which came down from heaven: if any man eat of this bread, he shall live for ever: and the bread that I will give is my flesh, which I will give for the life of the world.

Jesus as recorded in John 6:53-54,

Verily, verily, I say unto you, Except ye eat the flesh of the Son of man, and drink his blood [refers to the seat of life], ye have no life in you. Whoso eateth my flesh, and drinketh my blood, hath eternal life; and I will raise him up at the last day.

First Fruits and Tithes

First Fruits: The principle of first fruits has many applications. The basic principle means the first in place, order, and rank, the beginning, or principle things. It is a principle of placing and honoring God, first, in everything that we do. When we place God first we seek His wisdom, purpose, and direction.

When we offer the first part of our day unto the Lord in worship and prayer, it sets the course for the remainder of the day. We honor Him as a priority and as an expression of our gratitude we devote and give those things that are most meaningful to us, to Him.

We see the practice of the Israelites honoring God with the "firstfruit" of their substance, children, and worship as an outward expression that God was their only, and main, Source of the manifestation of everything that they had. Although, this practice was based under the law, we as followers of Christ apply the principles out of love, and not the law.

In God's pattern, whatever is first establishes the rest. The first is the root, from which the rest is determined. The Apostle Paul explains in Romans 11:16, "For if the firstfruit be holy, the lump is also holy: and if the root be holy, so are the branches." It furthermore aligns us with His covenant blessings. When we apply the principle of firstfruits in our lives, we begin to see that all "firsts" should be given to the Lord.

Christ is also called the "firstfruit." Firstfruit is not only referring to the Messiah resurrecting from the grave, but it also represents those souls that are resurrected spiritually, persons consecrated to God for all time, a spiritual rebirth to a divine nature. "Of his own will begat he us with the word of truth, that we should be a kind of firstfruits of his creatures. Wherefore lay apart all filthiness and superfluity of naughtiness, and receive with meekness the engrafted word, which is able to save your souls" (James 1:18, 21).

"But seek ye first the kingdom of God, and his righteousness; and all these things shall be added unto you" (Matthew 6:33).

"Honour the LORD with thy substance, and with the first-fruits of all thine increase: So shall thy barns be filled with plenty, and thy presses shall burst out with new wine" (Proverbs 3:9–10).

Tithing: Tithing is a biblical ordinance and principle of giving to God a tenth of all of your first increase to support God's work and the ministry on Earth. We give out of an acknowledgment of God's ownership and source of everything as an act of love, gratefulness, and thanksgiving that we can give, and that it is by Him that we are able to give. It is also an act of obedience that connects you to the protection and the blessings of God. Believers should realize that God is their source and is the owner of everything that we possess. Psalm 24:1 acknowledges that, "The earth is the LORD's, and the fulness thereof; the world, and they that dwell therein."

> "But thou shalt remember the LORD thy God: for it is he that giveth thee power to get wealth that he may establish his covenant which he sware unto thy fathers, as it is this day" (Deuteronomy 8:18).

> Even from the days of your fathers ye are gone away from mine ordinances, and have not kept them. Return unto me, and I will return unto you, saith the LORD of hosts. But ye said, Wherein shall we return? Will a man rob God? Yet ye have robbed me. But ye say, Wherein have we robbed thee? In tithes and offerings. Ye are cursed with a curse: for ye have robbed me, even this whole nation. Bring ye all the tithes into the storehouse, that there may be meat in mine house, and prove me now herewith, saith the LORD of hosts, if I will not open you the windows of heaven, and pour you out a blessing, that there shall not be room enough to receive it.

> And I will rebuke the devourer for your sakes, and he shall not destroy the fruits of your ground; neither shall your vine cast her fruit before the time in the field, saith the LORD of hosts. And all nations shall call you blessed: for ye shall be a delightsome land, saith the LORD of hosts. (Malachi 3:7–12)

> "Thou shalt truly tithe all the increase of thy seed, that the field bringeth forth year by year" (Deuteronomy 14:22).

Our Love Walk

"God is love" (1 John 4:8) and "God so loved the world, that he gave his only begotten Son, that whosoever believeth in him should not perish, but have everlasting life" (John 3:16). God's grace is, "to make all men see what is the fellowship of the mystery..." (Ephesians 3:9).

The love of God is not just the gift of the Anointed One, Christ, but it is also the example of God's power to us, and in us, which is manifested by and through the Holy Spirit in prayer in the revelation of the, "righteousness of Christ in us." The grace of God is that you, "be strengthened with might by his Spirit in the inner man; That Christ may dwell in your hearts by faith; that ye, being rooted and grounded in love" (Ephesians 3:16-17) which is the soil we must grow in and, the foundation, on which we must build.

We must further come to the revelation that we, "May be able to comprehend with all saints what is the breadth, and length, and depth, and height; And to know the love of Christ, which passeth knowledge, that ye might be filled with all the fullness of God (Ephesians 3:18-19). Simply stated, love is a divine exchange. We must grow in the love of God, and the love for God, with the enfoldment of realization that God loves us.

To walk in and receive the full measure of God's grace and promises is the development of faith that, "the love of God is shed abroad in our hearts by the Holy Ghost which is given unto us" (Romans 5:5). The more you grow in unconditional love the more you grow in His divine presence and His power, "for faith worketh by love" (Galatians 5:6). When you are operating and functioning in the love of God, and the power and anointing of the Holy Spirit, it empowers your love walk with the right of privilege of your redeemed authority and power in prayer. You rise above the snares, deceptions, traps, and pettiness of the "evil one," which results in offences, strongholds, unforgiveness, and walking out of love that become hindrances to answered prayer.

"Who is a wise man and endued with knowledge among you? let him shew out of a good conversation his works with meekness of wisdom. But if ye have bitter envying and strife in your hearts, glory not, and lie not against the truth. This wisdom descendeth not from above, but is earthly, sensual, devilish. For where envying and strife is, there is confusion and every evil work" (James 3:13-16).

Obedience to God's Word is the key to receiving and walking in the blessings and anointing of God. As we are obedient to walk in His Word, we will walk in His favor, might, promises, blessings, and power in prayer. "And whatsoever we ask, we receive of him, because we keep his commandments, and do those things that are pleasing in his sight" (1 John 3:22).

We honor God by serving Him; and we serve Him by serving others. We are all connected to one another. Recall, Jesus briefly summed up the Ten Commandment law, as it was first recorded in the Old Testament, by saying, "And thou shalt love the Lord thy God with all thy heart, and with all thy soul, and with all thy mind, and with all thy strength: this is the first commandment. And the second is like, namely this, Thou shalt love thy neighbour as thyself. There is none other commandment greater than these" (Mark 12:30–31).

The first four of the Ten Commandments, found in Deuteronomy 5:6–21, specifically call for man to give honor and respect to God, and the remaining six commandments call for man to honor and respect each other.

1. You shall have no other gods before me.
2. You shall not make for yourself any carved image, or any likeness of anything that is in heaven above, or that is in the earth beneath, or that is in the water under the earth; you shall not bow down to them nor serve them. For I, the Lord your God, am a jealous God, visiting the iniquity of the fathers on the children to the third and fourth generations of those who hate me, but showing mercy to thousands, to those who love Me and keep My commandments.
3. You shall not take the name of the Lord your God in vain, for the Lord will not hold him guiltless who takes His name in vain.

4. Remember the Sabbath day, to keep it holy. Six days you shall labor and do all your work, but the seventh day is the Sabbath of the Lord your God. In it you shall do no work: you, nor your son, nor your daughter, nor your manservant, nor your maidservant, nor your cattle, nor your stranger who is within your gates. For in six days the Lord made the heavens and the earth, the sea, and all that is in them, and rested the seventh day. Therefore the Lord blessed the Sabbath day and hallowed it.
5. Honor your father and your mother, that your days may be long upon the land which the Lord your God is giving you.
6. You shall not murder.
7. You shall not commit adultery.
8. You shall not steal.
9. You shall not bear false witness against your neighbor.
10. You shall not covet your neighbor's house; you shall not covet your neighbor's wife, nor his manservant, nor his maidservant, nor his ox, nor his donkey, nor anything that is your neighbor's.

- "Blessed are they that do his commandments, that they may have right to the tree of life, and may enter in through the gates into the city" (Revelation 22:14).
- "If ye keep my commandments, ye shall abide in my love; even as I have kept my Father's commandments, and abide in his love" (John 15:10).
- Good Master, what good thing shall I do, that I may have eternal life? And he said unto him, Why callest thou me good? there is none good but one, that is, God: but if thou wilt enter into life, keep the commandments. He saith unto him, Which? Jesus said, Thou shalt do no murder, Thou shalt not commit adultery, Thou shalt not steal, Thou shalt not bear false witness, Honour thy father and thy mother: and, Thou shalt love thy neighbour as thyself. (Matthew 19:16–19)

The Spirit of Love: Our lifestyle should be a reflection of the characteristics and attributes of Christ, a divine *agape* love. "A new commandment I give unto you, That ye love one another; as I have loved you, that ye also love one another. By this shall all men know that ye are my disciples, if ye have love one to another" (John 13:34–35).

- "Let brotherly love continue. Be not forgetful to entertain strangers: for thereby some have entertained angels unawares" (Hebrews 13:1–2).
- Though I speak with the tongues of men and of angels, and have not charity [brotherly love], I am become as sounding brass, or a tinkling cymbal. And though I have the gift of prophecy, and understand all mysteries, and all knowledge; and though I have all faith, so that I could remove mountains, and have not charity [brotherly love], I am nothing. And though I bestow all my goods to feed the poor, and though I give my body to be burned, and have not charity [brotherly love], it profiteth me nothing.

Charity never faileth: but whether there be prophecies, they shall fail; whether there be tongues, they shall cease; whether there be knowledge, it shall vanish away. And now abideth faith, hope, charity, these three; but the greatest of these is charity [brotherly love]" (1 Corinthians 13: 1-3, 8, 13).

The Spirit of Giving: Whatever you are standing in need of, give to someone. As long as you are giving, you will be receiving. Love gives. "Remember the words of the Lord Jesus, how he said, It is more blessed to give than to receive" (Acts 20:35).

- For I was an hungred, and ye gave me no meat: I was thirsty, and ye gave me no drink: I was a stranger, and ye took me not in: naked, and ye clothed me not: sick, and in prison, and ye visited me not. Then shall they also answer him, saying, Lord, when saw we thee an hungred, or athirst, or

a stranger, or naked, or sick, or in prison, and did not minister unto thee? Then shall he answer them, saying, Verily I say unto you, Inasmuch as ye did it not to one of the least of these, ye did it not to me. And these shall go away into everlasting punishment: but the righteous into life eternal. (Mathew 25:41-46)
- "Give, and it shall be given unto you; good measure, pressed down, and shaken together, and running over, shall men give into your bosom. For with the same measure that ye mete withal it shall be measured to you again" (Luke 6:38).
- "He that giveth unto the poor shall not lack: but he that hideth his eyes shall have many a curse" (Proverbs 28:27).
- "Therefore all things whatsoever ye would that men should do to you, do ye even so to them: for this is the law and the prophets" (Matthew 7:12).
- "But this I say, He which soweth sparingly shall reap also sparingly; and he which soweth bountifully shall reap also bountifully. Every man according as he purposeth in his heart, so let him give; not grudgingly, or of necessity: for God loveth a cheerful giver" (2 Corinthians 9:6-7).
- "Be not deceived; God is not mocked: for whatsoever a man soweth, that shall he also reap" (Galatians 6:7).

The Spirit of Charity: "Pure religion and undefiled before God and the Father is this, To visit the fatherless and widows in their affliction, and to keep himself unspotted from the world" (James 1:27).

- Is it not to deal thy bread to the hungry, and that thou bring the poor that are cast out to thy house? when thou seest the naked, that thou cover him; and that thou hide not thyself from thine own flesh?

Then shall thy light break forth as the morning, and thine health shall spring forth speedily: and thy righteousness shall go before thee; the glory of the LORD shall be thy reward. Then shalt thou call, and the LORD shall answer;

thou shalt cry, and he shall say, Here I am. If thou take away from the midst of thee the yoke, the putting forth of the finger, and speaking vanity; And if thou draw out thy soul to the hungry, and satisfy the afflicted soul; then shall thy light rise in obscurity, and thy darkness be as the noon day: And the LORD shall guide thee continually, and satisfy thy soul in drought, and make fat thy bones: and thou shalt be like a watered garden, and like a spring of water, whose waters fail not.

And they that shall be of thee shall build the old waste places: thou shalt raise up the foundations of many generations; and thou shalt be called, The repairer of the breach, The restorer of paths to dwell in. (Isaiah 58:7–12)

- "And above all things have fervent charity among yourselves: for charity shall cover the multitude of sins" (1 Peter 4:8).
- "He that hath pity upon the poor lendeth unto the LORD; and that which he hath given will he pay him again" (Proverbs 19:17).

When we honor God, He will honor us:
- When the Son of man shall come in his glory, and all the holy angels with him, then shall he sit upon the throne of his glory: And before him shall be gathered all nations: and he shall separate them one from another, as a shepherd divideth his sheep from the goats: And he shall set the sheep on his right hand, but the goats on the left. Then shall the King say unto them on his right hand, Come, ye blessed of my Father, inherit the kingdom prepared for you from the foundation of the world. (Matthew 25:31-34)
- "That all men should honour the Son, even as they honour the Father. He that honoureth not the Son honoureth not the Father which hath sent him" (John 5:23).
- "The LORD saith, Be it far from me; for them that honour me I will honour" (1 Samuel 2:30).

- Jesus states, "If any man serve me, let him follow me; and where I am, there shall also my servant be: if any man serve me, him will my Father honour" (John 12:26).
- Ye have said, It is vain to serve God: and what profit is it that we have kept his ordinance, and that we have walked mournfully before the LORD of hosts? And now we call the proud happy; yea, they that work wickedness are set up; yea, they that tempt God are even delivered. Then they that feared the LORD spake often one to another: and the LORD hearkened, and heard it, and a book of remembrance was written before him for them that feared the LORD, and that thought upon his name.

And they shall be mine, saith the LORD of hosts, in that day when I make up my jewels; and I will spare them, as a man spareth his own son that serveth him. Then shall ye return, and discern between the righteous and the wicked, between him that serveth God and him that serveth him not. (Malachi 3:14-18)

Our Prayer Life

"Let your light so shine before men, that they may see your good works, and glorify your Father which is in heaven" (Matthew 5:16). The purpose of the Christian's power of attorney, in Christ's name, is to glorify God. It glorifies God to answer all prayers, heal, save, and bless humanity. However, He cannot do so unless we ask in faith, "nothing wavering."

There is a balance between grace and faith. If your prayers are riddled with unbelief, and a lack of trust, you are not honoring God and God cannot honor you. "But without faith it is impossible to please him: for he that cometh to God must believe that he is, and that he is a rewarder of them that diligently seek him" (Hebrews 11:6).

CHAPTER 5

Understanding the Power of Prayer

"And all things, whatsoever ye shall ask in prayer, believing, ye shall receive" (Matthew 21:22).

Random House Dictionary's definition for prayer: A devout petition to, or any form of spiritual communion with God... Webster's Dictionary: an expression... of devout petition addressed to God or a deity ...

The Hebraic meaning for pray is the word *palal,* which literally means to "fall down to the ground in the presence of one in authority pleading a cause." Pray has several meanings in Greek, one is *erotao,* meaning "request, beseech, entreat, ask, or desire."

There is power in prayer. The power of prayer is principled upon the faithfulness of God to perform that which He has promised in His Word, and our faith and trust to believe His Word. "God is not a man, that he should lie; neither the son of man, that he should repent: hath he said, and shall he not do it? or hath he spoken, and shall he not make it good?" (Numbers 23:19)

The power of prayer should never be underestimated because it draws on the glory and might of the divine omnipotent, omnipresent, omniscient, and omnificent powers of the God of the Universe!

The study of Jesus and the lives of great men and women in Scripture reveal how the lifestyle of prayer was woven into the pattern of their lives. This lifestyle and pattern of prayer played out in miraculous powers, triumphs in battles, overcoming insurmountable odds, healing of the sick, deliverance, salvation, and countless victories. This power flows through prayer. So then the question arises, why is it we are not seeing and experiencing results and manifestations in a profound manner of biblical proportions to our prayers? Why are we depressed, sick, poor, mean spirited, ineffective, and powerless when as, "followers of Christ" "we have this treasure in earthen vessels, that the excellency of the power may be of God, and not of us" (2 Corinthians 4:7)?

What has changed? God has not changed. "For I am the LORD, I change not" (Malachi 3:6). Perhaps humanity has changed in how we perceive, interact with, relate to, fellowship with, worship, honor and respond to God. Throughout time, the power of prayer has been questioned by science. Although, most of us who possess the practice and the belief that prayer can and does work do not require scientific, quantitative proof of the power of prayer. The analytical mind of some scientists even calls for proof of the existence of a higher being, disregarding that God is the science, and the evidence of God's hand in the creation of mankind and the universe as a whole.

Religion does not give you power, but having a personal and intimate relationship with the Godhead (God, Jesus Christ, and the Holy Spirit) does! It's the power that comes when we honor, obey, believe, have faith in, walk in, and live in God's precepts. To have a right relationship with God, we must also pursue right relationships with people. "And whatsoever we ask, we receive of him, because we keep his commandments, and do those things that are pleasing in his sight" (1 John 3:22).

Why Pray?

First, and foremost, God commands us to pray, "that men ought always to pray, and not to faint" (Luke 18:1). We pray because God is our Source and our Sustainer, our lifeline, and we depend on Him. We were created to fellowship with Him, and through prayer, we receive the guidance, wisdom, comfort, strength, power and all the other resources that we need for life-both naturally and spiritually.

We are to deploy prayer as our arsenal in spiritual warfare, "watch ye and pray, lest ye enter into temptation. The spirit truly is ready, but the flesh is weak" (Mark 4:38). It will combat worry, fear, anxiety, doubt, lust, jealousy, envy, and pride, to name only a few of the contradictions to the Word of God. Prayer is used to enable us to reform and realign our thinking in the process of renewing our minds. Prayer is used to resist temptation when confronted with sin, to encourage when hopeless, to heal when sick, to strengthen, to petition God for our personal needs and desires, to seek wisdom, to pray for the salvation of others, and to stand in the gap and intercede for someone or something (a ministry, a community, a nation) that is in need of prayer.

Prayer also increases your awareness of God in your life and the role that God plays in your life, acknowledging and giving thanks to Him in everything. The most vital part of any prayer, whether it is a prayer of a petition, of thanksgiving, of praise of God, or of confession, is the introspection it provides, seeing our role on earth and our relationship with the Father, God.

Prayer is humanity executing the privilege of authority, as agents of God, on Earth to invoke Heaven's influence on Earth. Hebrews 2:6–8 states, "But one in a certain place testified, saying, What is man, that thou art mindful of him? or the son of man that thou visitest him? Thou madest him a little lower than the angels; thou crownedst him with glory and honour, and didst set him over the works of thy hands: Thou hast put all things in subjection under his feet. For in that he put all in subjection under him, he left nothing that is not put under him."

Prayer is the medium through which your spirit is purposed to affect, and be affected, by God. In prayer, it is our privilege to know the fellowship and the communion of the Holy Spirit. It is discovering and seeking the will of God through the Holy Spirit by heavenly spiritual wisdom of the what, the how, and the when of God. Prayer should take the form of a conversation, both talking and listening.

Prayer not only establishes a relationship with God, it is vital to maintaining our relationship with God. A meaningful relationship is dependent on intimacy and quality two-way communication; and therefore, your relationship with the Lord, or anyone, will never grow and develop without communication. Once we make our petitions, we should then listen to what the Holy Spirit has to say to us.

How Does God Work through Prayer?

While we can never fully understand this, fundamentally, it is no different than the way God works through any of our actions. On our own, under our own power, we can accomplish nothing of eternal significance. But God chooses to work through us, so that when we pray His will is accomplished through us. God chooses to use us as His vessels, as representatives of Christ, in accomplishing His purposes and allows us to participate in the execution of His power through our prayers.

God calls us to obey, *believe* and *trust* Him—to know beyond all doubt, with complete conviction, confidence, and expectation in Him that we are an integral, divine aspect and channel of expression of Him, to co-effect by and through Him by faith; prayer executes this manifestation.

When we pray, we are reminded of who God is, of what He has done, of what He will do, and what He has promised. We are reminded that, "God is faithful." As we develop confidence in truth, knowledge, understanding and wisdom of Him, we will walk in greater courage, peace, trust, victory and authority. The authority you exercise is the result of divine exchange in operation, in your life.

The following Scriptures are biblical truths in biblical meditations on why prayer works:

Why Does Prayer Work?

God's Promises of Prayer

- According as his divine power hath given unto us all things that pertain unto life and godliness, through the knowledge of him that hath called us to glory and virtue: Whereby are given unto us exceeding great and precious promises: that by these ye might be partakers of the divine nature, having escaped the corruption that is in the world through lust.

  And beside this, giving all diligence, add to your faith virtue; and to virtue knowledge; And to knowledge temperance; and to temperance patience; and to patience godliness; And to godliness brotherly kindness; and to brotherly kindness charity. For if these things be in you, and abound, they make you that ye shall neither be barren nor unfruitful in the knowledge of our Lord Jesus Christ.

  But he that lacketh these things is blind, and cannot see afar off, and hath forgotten that he was purged from his old sins. Wherefore the rather, brethren, give diligence to make your calling and election sure: for if ye do these things, ye shall never fall. (2 Peter 1:3–10)

- "For all the promises of God in him are yea, and in him Amen, unto the glory of God by us" (2 Corinthians 1:20).
- "God is not a man, that he should lie; neither the son of man, that he should repent: hath he said, and shall he not do it? or hath he spoken, and shall he not make it good?" (Numbers 23:19)
- "Godliness is profitable unto all things, having promise of the life that now is, and of that which is to come" (1 Timothy 4:8).
- "And all things, whatsoever ye shall ask in prayer, believing, ye shall receive" (Matthew 21:22).
- "He that believeth on me, the works that I do shall he do also; and greater works than these shall he do; because I go unto my Father. And whatsoever ye shall ask in my

name, that will I do, that the Father may be glorified in the Son. If ye shall ask any thing in my name, I will do it" (John 14:12–14).

- "And this is the confidence that we have in him, that if we ask any thing according to his will, he heareth us: And if we know that he hear us whatsoever we ask, we know that we have the petitions that we desired of him" (1 John 5:14–15).
- "The Lord is not slack concerning his promise, as some men count slackness; but is longsuffering to us-ward, not willing that any should perish, but that all should come to repentance" (2 Peter 3:9).
- "For the eyes of the Lord are over the righteous, and his ears are open unto their prayers: but the face of the Lord is against them that do evil" (1 Peter 3:12).
- "Be not deceived; God is not mocked: for whatsoever a man soweth, that shall he also reap" (Galatians 6:7).
- "God shall supply all your need according to his riches in glory by Christ Jesus" (Philippians 4:19).
- "And whatsoever we ask, we receive of him, because we keep his commandments, and do those things that are pleasing in his sight" (1 John 3:22).
- "Let us hold fast the profession of our faith without wavering (for he is faithful that promised)" (Hebrews 10:23).

God's Love for Us

- "If ye then, being evil, know how to give good gifts unto your children, how much more shall your Father which is in heaven give good things to them that ask him?" (Matthew 7:11)
- "Ye have not chosen me, but I have chosen you, and ordained you, that ye should go and bring forth fruit, and that your fruit should remain: that whatsoever ye shall ask of the Father in my name, he may give it you" (John 15:16).
- "We love him, because he first loved us" (1 John 4:19).

- "He that spared not his own Son, but delivered him up for us all, how shall he not with him also freely give us all things?" (Romans 8:32)
- "For God so loved the world, that he gave his only begotten Son, that whosoever believeth in him should not perish, but have everlasting life" (John 3:16).
- "But God commendeth his love toward us, in that, while we were yet sinners, Christ died for us" (Romans 5:8).

Man's Authority on Earth

- "But one in a certain place testified, saying, What is man, that thou art mindful of him? or the son of man that thou visitest him? Thou madest him a little lower than the angels; thou crownedst him with glory and honour, and didst set him over the works of thy hands: Thou hast put all things in subjection under his feet. For in that he put all in subjection under him, he left nothing that is not put under him" (Hebrews 2:6–8).
- "For whatsoever is born of God overcometh the world: and this is the victory that overcometh the world, even our faith" (1 John 5:4).

Belief

- "And all things, whatsoever ye shall ask in prayer, believing, ye shall receive" (Matthew 21:22).
- "What things soever ye desire, when ye pray, believe that ye receive them, and ye shall have them" (Mark 11:24).

Faith

- "If ye have faith as a grain of mustard seed, ye shall say unto this mountain, Remove hence to yonder place; and it shall remove; and nothing shall be impossible unto you" (Matthew 17:20).

Power in Speaking God's Word

- "Being born again, not of corruptible seed, but of incorruptible, by the word of God, which liveth and abideth for ever. For all flesh is as grass, and all the glory of man as the flower of grass. The grass withereth, and the flower thereof falleth away: But the word of the Lord endureth forever. And this is the word which by the gospel is preached unto you" (1 Peter 1:23–25).

- "Death and life are in the power of the tongue: and they that love it shall eat the fruit thereof" (Proverbs 18:21).
- "For by thy words thou shalt be justified, and by thy words thou shalt be condemned" (Matthew 12:37).
- "As for God, his way is perfect: the word of the LORD is tried: he is a buckler to all those that trust in him" (Psalm 18:30).
- "For the word of God is quick, and powerful, and sharper than any two edged sword, piercing even to the dividing asunder of soul and spirit, and of the joints and marrow, and is a discerner of the thoughts and intents of the heart" (Hebrews 4:12).
- "Every word of God is pure: he is a shield unto them that put their trust in him" (Proverbs 30:5).

God's Saving Grace

- "For the LORD God is a sun and shield: the LORD will give grace and glory: no good thing will he withhold from them that walk uprightly" (Psalm 84:11).
- "And God is able to make all grace abound toward you; that ye, always having all sufficiency in all things, may abound to every good work" (2 Corinthians 9:8).
- "Let us therefore come boldly unto the throne of grace, that we may obtain mercy, and find grace to help in time of need" (Hebrews 4:16).
- "For by grace are ye saved through faith; and that not of yourselves: it is the gift of God" (Ephesians 2:8).
- "My grace is sufficient for thee: for my strength is made perfect in weakness. Most gladly therefore will I rather glory in my infirmities, that the power of Christ may rest upon me" (2 Corinthians 12:9).

Relationship with Jesus

- "I am the true vine, and my Father is the husbandman. Every branch in me that beareth not fruit he taketh away: and every branch that beareth fruit, he purgeth it, that it may bring forth more fruit. Now ye are clean through the word which I have spoken unto you. Abide in me, and I in you. As the branch cannot bear fruit of itself, except it abide in the vine; no more can ye, except ye abide in me. I am the vine, ye are the branches: He that abideth in me, and I in him, the same bringeth forth much fruit: for without me ye can do nothing" (John 15:1–5).

- "If a man abide not in me, he is cast forth as a branch, and is withered; and men gather them, and cast them into the fire, and they are burned. If ye abide in me, and my words abide in you, ye shall ask what ye will, and it shall be done unto you. Herein is my Father glorified, that ye bear much fruit; so shall ye be my disciples. As the Father hath loved me, so have I loved you: continue ye in my love. If ye keep my commandments, ye shall abide in my love; even as I have kept my Father's commandments, and abide in his love" (John 15:6–10).

- "And whatsoever we ask, we receive of him, because we keep his commandments, and do those things that are pleasing in his sight. And this is his commandment, That we should believe on the name of his Son Jesus Christ, and love one another, as he gave us commandment. And he that keepeth his commandments dwelleth in him, and he in him. And hereby we know that he abideth in us, by the Spirit which he hath given us" (1 John 3:22–24).

Authority and Power in the Name of Jesus

- "Wherefore God also hath highly exalted him, and given him a name which is above every name: That at the name of Jesus every knee should bow, of things in heaven, and things in earth, and things under the earth" (Philippians 2:9–10).

- "I say unto you, Whatsoever ye shall ask the Father in my name, he will give it you" (John 16:23).
- "He that believeth on me, the works that I do shall he do also; and greater works than these shall he do; because I go unto my Father. And whatsoever ye shall ask in my name, that will I do, that the Father may be glorified in the Son" (John 4:12–13).
- "Beware lest any man spoil you through philosophy and vain deceit, after the tradition of men, after the rudiments of the world, and not after Christ. For in him dwelleth all the fulness of the Godhead bodily. And ye are complete in him, which is the head of all principality and power" (Colossians 2:8–10).

The Principles of Kingdom Authority
- "The sower soweth the word" (Mark 4:14).
- "Every kingdom divided against itself is brought to desolation; and a house divided against a house falleth" (Luke 11:17).
- "Jesus Christ the same yesterday, and to day, and for ever" (Hebrews 13:8).
- "The things which are impossible with men are possible with God" (Luke 18:27).

The Holy Spirit
- "But the Comforter, which is the Holy Ghost, whom the Father will send in my name, he shall teach you all things, and bring all things to your remembrance, whatsoever I have said unto you. Peace I leave with you, my peace I give unto you: not as the world giveth, give I unto you. Let not your heart be troubled, neither let it be afraid" (John 14:26–27).
- "But ye shall receive power, after that the Holy Ghost is come upon you" (Acts 1:8).
- "He that hath my commandments, and keepeth them, he it is that loveth me: and he that loveth me shall be loved of my Father, and will love him, and will manifest myself to him" (John 14:21).

CHAPTER 6

How to Pray Effectively

"And this is the confidence that we have in him, that if we ask any thing according to his will, he heareth us: And if we know that he hear us whatsoever we ask, we know that we have the petitions that we desired of him" (1 John 5:14–15).

I t is not vain repetition of prayers that Heaven respects, nor the eloquence of our speech, nor the length of the prayer. Rather, it is our personal relationship with the Godhead, our sincerity, humility, passion, supplication, love-walk, faith, obedience, conviction, belief, trust, confidence, and patience that our prayers will be answered that Heaven recognizes.

We pray as a lifestyle, not to be performed only in times of the crisis or in times of the need, but every day. Prayer should be as normal to the believer as eating and sleeping. The Psalmist David wrote, "Evening, and morning, and at noon, will I pray, and cry aloud: and he shall hear my voice" (Psalm 55:17). Prayer requires practice, and the more we practice, the more proficient we will become in it. Jesus stated in Luke 18:1, "that men ought always to pray, and not to faint." The Apostle Paul stated in Colossians 4:2, "Continue in prayer, and watch in the same with thanksgiving." The Apostle Paul then raised the standard and instructed us to, "pray without ceasing" (1 Thessalonians 5:17). In other words, we should maintain a mindset of prayer. God wants us to keep a constant internal dialogue with Him, asking and expecting Him to be made manifest in our daily lives and the lives of our brethren.

Prayer may take on different degrees of passion. Prayer can be a casual acknowledgment to God, thanking Him for waking you this morning, as the first fruit of your praise. We may pray in our car on our way to work; but we know when we are in a serious crisis, we will really seek the face and presence of God. This is when we will fall to our knees with uplifted holy hands, "and look unto the hills, from whence cometh my [our] help" (Psalm 121:1).

However, in order for prayer to become effective and powerful it needs to be a consistent discipline in seeking and spending time alone with the Lord. We should, however, be mindful that our prayer time should be viewed as a growing intimate relationship with the Lord, not a rigid requirement, ritual or exercise. In that very act, there should be a dialogue, with a release of our faith in confidence and expectation with thanksgiving of a manifestation of the very thing that we ask for.

Developing a balanced prayer life means incorporating all of the principles that build intimacy with the Lord and expanding our prayers to reflect kingdom principles and priorities by praying in the will of God.

Scripture illustrates the practice, the method, frequency, order, the when, where, and how, of the science of prayer. Numerous Scriptures refer to the application of prayer as instantaneous, fervent, without ceasing, private, corporate, meditative, authoritative, vigilant, sincere, appreciative, unified, repentant, worship, praise and thanksgiving, humble and faithful.

There are different kinds, or functions, of prayers each with its particular purpose and intended result. Many times, the prayers will blend together as you are praying more than one kind of prayer at the same time.

In application, you can use different types of prayer methods during your prayer times, such as praise, thanksgiving, worship, confession, supplication (asking), consecration, intercessory, and agreement. In all styles of prayer, whether they are formal, conversational, meditative, devotional, corporate, or spontaneous, there is an underlying eternal principle that they all share, and that is we commune with, and in faith trust, God. The types of prayer include:

- Prayer of confession (repentance or forgiveness)
- Prayer of supplication (petition, need, want, request or ask)
- Prayer of thanksgiving
- Prayer of praise and worship (honoring and loving God)
- Prayer of consecration (to make or declare sacred and holy)
- Prayer of agreement (one accord-one mind)
- Intercessory prayer (praying for others)
- Prayer of binding and loosening (spiritual warfare)
- Prayer of faith

Prayer is learned. Jesus' disciples witnessed the power of prayer firsthand and asked Jesus to teach them to pray. The Lord's Prayer can be seen both, as a model and a guideline on how to pray, and can also be repeated as part of your daily prayer. The Lord's Prayer represents four of the five types of prayer: praise, thanksgiving, confession, and supplication or petition.

The Model Prayer, Which Jesus Taught His Disciples
But thou, when thou prayest, enter into thy closet, and when thou hast shut thy door, pray to thy Father which is in secret; and thy Father which seeth in secret shall reward thee openly. But when ye pray, use not vain repetitions, as the heathen do: for they think that they shall be heard for their much speaking. Be not ye therefore like unto them: for your Father knoweth what things ye have need of, before ye ask him.

After this manner therefore pray ye: Our Father which art in heaven, Hallowed be thy name. Thy kingdom come, Thy will be done in earth, as it is in heaven. Give us this day our daily bread. And forgive us our debts, as we forgive our debtors. And lead us not into temptation, but deliver us from evil: For thine is the kingdom, and the power, and the glory, for ever. Amen. For if ye forgive men their trespasses, your heavenly Father will also forgive you: But if ye forgive not men their trespasses, neither will your Father forgive your trespasses. (Matthew 6:6–15)

Jesus Teaches Us How to Pray

- Verse 6: "When thou prayest, enter into thy closet, and when thou hast shut thy door, pray to thy Father which is in secret; and thy Father which seeth in secret shall reward thee openly."

According to Jewish tradition, Jewish men wear a garment called a *tallit* or prayer shawl during prayer. The *tallit* serves as their prayer closet or private sanctuary. It is their practice that they place and wrap their *tallit* over their head and hands, to aid in attaining a proper mood of reverence for God's presence and a prayerful spirit during worship.

The sole significance of the *tallit* is in the *tzitzit* (fringes). The four corners of the *tallit* are often called "wings" or "fringes" that serve as a visual reminder to follow the divine Commandments as recorded in Deuteronomy 22:12, "Thou shalt make thee fringes upon the four quarters of thy vesture, wherewith thou coverest thyself." "And it shall be unto you for a fringe, that ye may look upon it, and remember all the commandments of the LORD, and do them" (Numbers 15:39). There is far more meaning and significance to the symbolism of the *tallit* than noted here.

- Verse 7: Christ instructs us to "use not vain repetitions." What is "vain repetition?" Vain is defined as "without real significance, value, or importance." The Greek word for vain is *battalogeo* meaning, "to repeat the same things over and over, to use many idle words." We could probably agree, then, that it includes all prayers that are repeated over and over again, going through the motions or formalities without any heartfelt emotion. More often than not, the more times a prayer is repeated, the less thought will enter into it. At that point, it has truly become a prayer in vain.

When a prayer becomes routine, our words may well become routine. God wants sincerity, humility, conviction, and faith in the spirit of prayer. God wants us to not just say our prayers, but also feel them. The Apostle Paul makes this clear in Colossians 4:2 when he writes, "Continue earnestly in prayer, being vigilant in it with thanksgiving." The distinction to be noted here is *earnestly*. *Earnestly* is defined as "fervent, serious in intention of purpose, and sincerely zealous."

A prayer should be a deep-felt sincere desire of the soul, calling out to God in faith and belief. We must also take into consideration that if we truly feel that God has heard our prayer, we can have confidence that He will answer our petition. Then we will concur with the Apostle, John, in 1 John 5:14–15, "And this is the confidence that we have in him, that, if we ask any thing according to his will, he heareth us: And if we know that he hear us, whatsoever we ask, we know that we have the petitions that we desired of him."

Therefore, with this being said, there is no need to constantly repeat and become redundant in the prayer that we are praying. This does not mean, however, we are not to persevere and be instant in prayer as Romans 12:12 instructs, "Rejoicing in hope; patient in tribulation; continuing instant in prayer."

- Verse 9: Establishes our relationship with God; we declare His authority in giving honor, respect, and reverence in His holy name, for He is our Source and our Sustainer; He is worthy of praise and worship. When you approach the Throne of God, recognize God as your loving Father, the Holy Spirit as your Comforter and guide, and Jesus as your best friend as He is recorded in John 15:14 as saying, "Ye are my friends, if ye do whatsoever I command you."

- Verse 10: "Thy kingdom come": His authority, principles, and His purpose. "Thy will be done in earth, as it is in heaven," we are praying for the fulfillment of God working through us to fulfill His purpose of heavenly manifestation in earthly matters. Thy will be done is frequently interpreted as a sense of deference to what has already happened; however, its full significance is that it is a creative and faith-filled operative to the manifestation of an act that we also participate in. We are to pray according to the authority of His Word, based on the promise of His Word and His purpose for us, through the instrument of faith, in expectation and with thanksgiving.
- Verse 11: We are to pray for daily provision, whatever our needs are and the needs of others.
- Verse 12: We are to pray and ask for forgiveness for our sins and for others who have wronged us.
- Verse 13: We are to pray and ask God to keep us from being tempted; to empower us to be in right standing with Him; to deliver and empower us from the schemes of Satan (to protect us), and that we have through Him all power over the enemy.
- Verse 14: We need to forgive in order to be forgiven. To receive God's forgiveness when we pray, we must have the same attitude toward others that we expect Him to have toward us.

The following Scriptures are biblical truths in biblical meditations:

Seek God First
- "And ye shall seek me, and find me, when ye shall search for me with all your heart" (Jeremiah 29:13).
- "But seek ye first the kingdom of God, and his righteousness; and all these things shall be added unto you" (Matthew 6:33).

Be in Right Standing with God

- "Ye ask, and receive not, because ye ask amiss, that ye may consume it upon your lusts" (James 4:3).
- "Submit yourselves therefore to God. Resist the devil, and he will flee from you" (James 4:7).
- "For the eyes of the Lord are over the righteous, and his ears are open unto their prayers: but the face of the Lord is against them that do evil" (1 Peter 3:12).

Be Thankful

- "Be careful for nothing, but in everything by prayer and supplication with thanksgiving make your request known unto God: and the peace of God, which passeth all understanding, shall keep your hearts and minds through Christ Jesus" (Philippians 4:6–7).
- "In every thing give thanks: for this is the will of God in Christ Jesus concerning you" (1 Thessalonians 5:18).

Be Vigilant with Thanksgiving

- "Continue earnestly in prayer, being vigilant in it with thanksgiving" (Colossians 4:2).
- "Men ought always to pray, and not to faint" (Luke 18:1).

Trust God

- "The LORD is good, a strong hold in the day of trouble; and he knoweth them that trust in him" (Nahum 1:7).

You Must Believe—Faith

- "Jesus said unto him, If thou canst believe, all things are possible to him that believeth" (Mark 9:23).
- "And all things, whatsoever ye shall ask in prayer, believing, ye shall receive" (Matthew 21:22).
- "I will therefore that men pray every where, lifting up holy hands, without wrath and doubting" (1 Timothy 2:8).

Why Does Prayer Appear Unanswered?

Knowledge, understanding of knowledge, and the application of knowledge are power. No knowledge, and misunderstanding of knowledge, produces wrong thinking; wrong thinking produces wrong believing; and wrong believing produces wrong actions. Your belief system is fundamental and it governs your life, therefore, it is important to know why you believe what you believe and why you believe it. So how does that affect our prayers? If what you believe when you pray or what you believe about prayer is untrue, or principles you should know, but don't know about prayer, then your prayers will be ineffective or not as effective as they could be.

"Jesus answered and said unto them, Ye do err, not knowing the scriptures, nor the power of God" (Matthew 22:29).

"Full well ye reject the commandment of God, that ye may keep your own tradition. Making the word of God of none effect through your tradition, which ye have delivered: and many such like things do ye" (Mark 7:9, 13).

If you are not experiencing the results that the Bible promises, then it is apparent there is either something wrong with what you are doing, or not doing, or the way you understand what you believe.

Understanding Scripture (spiritual knowledge) is not only achieved through study, but it is also a matter of the heart in relationship with Christ, accepting it in faith. To increase in faith, you have to honor, obey, and trust God by, "Casting all your care [worry, anxiety] upon him; for he careth for you" (1 Peter 5:7). Your conscience and heart are very important in your relationship with God. Christ prayed for the disciples and the believer, "Sanctify them through thy truth: thy word is truth." Sanctify in Greek is *hagiazō* meaning, "to be holy, to purify internally by renewing of the soul, to purify by expiation: free from the guilt of sin, and to separate from profane things and dedicate to God."

The living Word is *truth.* If you are walking in the truth, and if the truth abides in you, then you can, "ask whatsoever you will, and it shall be done unto you." The putting to death of our sin nature of body and mind is a perquisite. When we walk in "truth" we have the Spirit of wisdom, the mind of Christ, and the power of the Holy Spirit, and in this power, we have all things.

Christ is recorded in Luke 6:46-49 as saying,

And why call ye me, Lord, Lord, and do not the things which I say? Whosoever cometh to me, and heareth my sayings, and doeth them, I will shew you to whom he is like: He is like a man which built an house, and digged deep, and laid the foundation on a rock: and when the flood arose, the stream beat vehemently upon that house, and could not shake it: for it was founded upon a rock.

But he that heareth, and doeth not, is like a man that without a foundation built an house upon the earth; against which the stream did beat vehemently, and immediately it fell; and the ruin of that house was great.

It has been stated the responses to prayer are yes, not yet, and no. Most often, our prayer requests are not answered because of our own lifestyle choices and sabotaging behavior as follows:

No Understanding
- When any one heareth the word of the kingdom, and understandeth it not, then cometh the wicked one, and catcheth away that which was sown in his heart. This is he which received seed by the way side. But he that received the seed into stony places, the same is he that heareth the word, and anon with joy receiveth it; Yet hath he not root in himself, but dureth for a while: for when tribulation or persecution ariseth because of the word, by and by he is offended. He also that received seed among the thorns is he that heareth the word; and the care of this world, and

the deceitfulness of riches, choke the word, and he becometh unfruitful.

- But he that received seed into the good ground is he
that heareth the word, and understandeth it; which also
beareth fruit, and bringeth forth, some an hundredfold,
some sixty, some thirty. (Matthew 13:19–23)

Unbelief and Doubt

- "If any of you lack wisdom, let him ask of God, that giveth to
all men liberally, and upbraideth not; and it shall be given
him. But let him ask in faith, nothing wavering. For he that
wavereth is like a wave of the sea driven with the wind and
tossed. For let not that man think that he shall receive any
thing of the Lord. A double minded man is unstable in all
his ways" (James 1:5–8).
- "And these are they by the way side, where the word is
sown; but when they have heard, Satan cometh immediately, and taketh away the word that was sown in their
hearts" (Mark 4:15).
- "He [Jesus] could there do no mighty work, save that he
laid his hands upon a few sick folk, and healed them. And
he marvelled because of their unbelief" (Mark 6:5-6).
- "So we see that they could not enter in because of unbelief" (Hebrews 3:19).
- "And he [Jesus] did not many mighty works there because
of their unbelief" (Matthew 13:58).

No Faith

- "Then came the disciples to Jesus apart, and said, Why
could not we cast him out? And Jesus said unto them,
Because of your unbelief: for verily I say unto you, If ye
have faith as a grain of mustard seed, ye shall say unto
this mountain, Remove hence to yonder place; and it
shall remove; and nothing shall be impossible unto you"
(Matthew 17:19–20).
- "But without faith it is impossible to please him; for he
that cometh to God must believe that he is, and that he

is a rewarder of them that diligently seek him" (Hebrews 11:6).

- "Let us therefore fear, lest, a promise being left us of entering into his rest, any of you should seem to come short of it. For unto us was the gospel preached, as well as unto them: but the word preached did not profit them, not being mixed with faith in them that heard it" (Hebrews 4:1–2).

No Patience

- "That ye be not slothful, but followers of them who through faith and patience inherit the promises" (Hebrews 6:12).

Fear

- "And seek not ye what ye shall eat, or what ye shall drink, neither be ye of doubtful mind. For all these things do the nations of the world seek after: and your Father knoweth that ye have need of these things. But rather seek ye the kingdom of God; and all these things shall be added unto you. Fear not, little flock; for it is your Father's good pleasure to give you the kingdom" (Luke 12:29-32).
- "The fear of man bringeth a snare: but whoso putteth his trust in the LORD shall be safe" (Proverbs 29:25).

Worry

- "Which of you by taking thought can add one cubit unto his stature? Wherefore, if God so clothe the grass of the field, which to day is, and to morrow is cast into the oven, shall he not much more clothe you, O ye of little faith? Therefore take no thought, saying, What shall we eat? or, What shall we drink? or, Wherewithal shall we be clothed? (For after all these things do the Gentiles seek:) for your heavenly Father knoweth that ye have need of all these things.

  But seek ye first the kingdom of God, and his righteousness; and all these things shall be added unto you. Take therefore no thought for the morrow: for the morrow shall take thought for the things of itself. Sufficient unto the day is the evil thereof" (Matthew 6:27–34).

- "Now the just shall live by faith: but if any man draw back, my soul shall have no pleasure in him" (Hebrews 10:38).

Faith without Works

- But wilt thou know, O vain man, that faith without works is dead? Was not Abraham our father justified by works, when he had offered Isaac his son upon the altar? Seest thou how faith wrought with his works, and by works was faith made perfect? And the scripture was fulfilled which saith, Abraham believed God, and it was imputed unto him for righteousness: and he was called the Friend of God.

  Ye see then how that by works a man is justified, and not by faith only. Likewise also was not Rahab the harlot justified by works, when she had received the messengers, and had sent them out another way? For as the body without the spirit is dead, so faith without works is dead also. (James 2:20–26)

- "But be ye doers of the word, and not hearers only, deceiving your own selves" (James 1:22).
- "For not the hearers of the law are just before God, but the doers of the law shall be justified" (Romans 2:13).

Unforgiveness

- "And when ye stand praying, forgive, if ye have ought against any: that your Father also which is in heaven may forgive you your trespasses" (Mark 11:25).

Required Fasting

- "Jesus ... rebuked the foul spirit, saying unto him, Thou dumb and deaf spirit, I charge thee, come out of him, and enter no more into him. And the spirit cried, and rent him sore, and came out of him: and he was as one dead; insomuch that many said, He is dead. But Jesus took him by the hand, and lifted him up; and he arose. And when he was come into the house, his disciples asked him privately, Why could not we cast him out? And he said unto them, This kind can come forth by nothing, but by prayer and fasting" (Mark 9:25–29).

- "But thou, when thou fastest, anoint thine head, and wash thy face; That thou appear not unto men to fast, but unto thy Father which is in secret: and thy Father, which seeth in secret, shall reward thee openly" (Matthew 6:17–18).
- "Then came to him the disciples of John, saying, Why do we and the Pharisees fast oft, but thy disciples fast not? And Jesus said unto them, Can the children of the bride-chamber mourn, as long as the bridegroom is with them? but the days will come, when the bridegroom shall be taken from them, and then shall they fast" (Matthew 9:14–15).

Vain Repetitions (Prayer without Value)
- "But when ye pray, use not vain repetitions, as the heathen do: for they think that they shall be heard for their much speaking. Be not ye therefore like unto them: for your Father knoweth what things ye have need of, before ye ask him" (Matthew 6:7–8).

No Relationship with Christ
- "Abide in me, and I in you. As the branch cannot bear fruit of itself, except it abide in the vine; no more can ye, except ye abide in me. I am the vine, ye are the branches: He that abideth in me, and I in him, the same bringeth forth much fruit: for without me ye can do nothing. If a man abide not in me, he is cast forth as a branch, and is withered; and men gather them, and cast them into the fire, and they are burned. If ye abide in me, and my words abide in you, ye shall ask what ye will, and it shall be done unto you" (John 15:4–7).

Blatantly Living in Sin (Grieving the Holy Spirit)

- "Submit yourselves therefore to God. Resist the devil, and he will flee from you. Draw nigh to God, and he will draw nigh to you. Cleanse your hands, ye sinners; and purify your hearts, ye double minded. Humble yourselves in the sight of the Lord, and he shall lift you up" (James 4:7–10).
- "The LORD is far from the wicked, But He hears the prayer of the righteous" (Proverbs 15:29).
- "But your iniquities have separated between you and your God, and your sins have hid his face from you, that he will not hear" (Isaiah 59:2).
- "Ye ask, and receive not, because ye ask amiss, that ye may consume it upon your lusts" (James 4:3).
- "For the eyes of the Lord are over the righteous, and his ears are open unto their prayers: but the face of the Lord is against them that do evil" (1 Peter 3:12).
- "He that turneth away his ear from hearing the law, even his prayer shall be abomination" (Proverbs 28:9).

Consider Your Ways (Your Lifestyle)

- "Now the works of the flesh are manifest, which are these; Adultery, fornication, uncleanness, lasciviousness, Idolatry, witchcraft, hatred, variance, emulations, wrath, strife, seditions, heresies, Envyings, murders, drunkenness, revellings, and such like: of the which I tell you before, as I have also told you in time past, that they which do such things shall not inherit the kingdom of God" (Galatians 5:19–21).
- "Now therefore thus saith the LORD of hosts; Consider your ways. Ye have sown much, and bring in little; ye eat, but ye have not enough; ye drink, but ye are not filled with drink; ye clothe you, but there is none warm; and he that earneth wages earneth wages to put it into a bag with holes. Thus saith the LORD of hosts; Consider your ways" (Haggai 1:5–7).
- "Whoso stoppeth his ears at the cry of the poor, he also shall cry himself, but shall not be heard" (Proverbs 21:13).

- "Likewise, ye husbands, dwell with them according to knowledge, giving honour unto the wife, as unto the weaker vessel, and as being heirs together of the grace of life; that your prayers be not hindered" (1 Peter 3:7).

Not Praying in God's Will – Wrong Motives
- "Ye ask, and receive not, because ye ask amiss, that ye may consume it upon your lusts" (James 4:3).

Unholy Practices
- When thou art come into the land which the LORD thy God giveth thee, thou shalt not learn to do after the abominations of those nations. There shall not be found among you any one that maketh his son or his daughter to pass through the fire, or that useth divination, or an observer of times, or an enchanter, or a witch. Or a charmer, or a consulter with familiar spirits, or a wizard, or a necromancer [the practice of communicating with the spirits of the dead in order to predict the future.] For all that do these things are an abomination unto the LORD: and because of these abominations the LORD thy God doth drive them out from before thee. Thou shalt be perfect with the LORD thy God. For these nations, which thou shalt possess, hearkened unto observers of times, and unto diviners: but as for thee, the LORD thy God hath not suffered thee so to do. (Deuteronomy 18:9–14)

To Everything There Is a Season
- To every thing there is a season, and a time to every purpose under the heaven: A time to be born, and a time to die; a time to plant, and a time to pluck up that which is planted; A time to kill, and a time to heal; a time to break down, and a time to build up; A time to weep, and a time to laugh; a time to mourn, and a time to dance; A time to cast away stones, and a time to gather stones together; a time to embrace, and a time to refrain from embracing; A time to get, and a time to lose; a time to keep, and a time

to cast away; A time to rend, and a time to sew; a time to keep silence, and a time to speak; A time to love, and a time to hate; a time of war, and a time of peace. (Ecclesiastes 3:1– 8)

What Makes Prayer Work?

Why are all of these factors important for the empowerment of prayer? The Bible is a book of covenant. A covenant deals with the conditional promises made to man by God as revealed in Scripture. God is faithful in His promises when we are faithful to operate within His order, laws, and principles. "... Blessed are those who hear the word of God, and keep it" (Luke 11:28).

It has been a common practice for people when they pray to say, "if it be Thy will be done?" This statement, of (if), raises a question of doubt and unbelief. What is not realized, is that this prayer request has been negated before and after it was spoken. To have faith that your prayers are going to be answered, you need a foundation (substance) of truth to your requests. Ephesians 5:17 advises, "Wherefore be ye not unwise, but understanding what the will of the Lord is." The appropriate prayer request should be as Jesus taught, "Thy will be done, as in heaven, so in earth" (Luke 11:2).

The Word and Spirit of God reveal His will. The Holy Bible is the representation of His will, principles, order, promises, and commands. These privileges are declared the will of God for His children! We do not have to guess if it is God's will for us - or even to ask if it is His will - if He said it, in His Word, then it is ours, if we are faithful and obedient to His Word!

Therefore, prayers must have honorable motives, "Ye ask, and receive not, because ye ask amiss [wrongly], that ye may consume it upon your lusts" (James 4:3). "For the LORD seeth not as man seeth; for man looketh on the outward appearance, but the LORD looketh on the heart" (1 Samuel 16:7).

God's desire is that we would unite with Him. We are to dwell in Him and He in us. In 1 Corinthians 1:9 we read, "God, who has called you into fellowship with his Son, Jesus Christ our Lord, is faithful." "...truly our fellowship is with the Father and with His Son Jesus Christ" (1 John 1:3). Fellowship is the Greek word *koinonia*, which literally means "partnership and communion."

In this fellowship is humility. Humility is the reverence and honor in which we know all things are governed and made possible by God through His grace, mercy and sovereign authority. "Not that we are sufficient of ourselves to think any thing as of ourselves; but our sufficiency is of God" (2 Corinthians 3:5).

Our prayers must be offered in humility. Our proper posture in prayer is to admit our own unworthiness apart from Christ for in Him only, "we might be made the righteousness of God in him" (2 Corinthians 5:21). "It is of the LORD's mercies that we are not consumed, because his compassions fail not. They are new every morning: great is thy faithfulness" (Lamentations 3:22–23). Mercy is the kindness and compassion in excess that goes beyond what is deserved and grace is the recompense of the favor, and the benefits, extended from mercy.

Pride and arrogance sees all the ways we would commend ourselves to God. Humility understands all the ways in which we are dependent upon His mercy. It is God's grace given to us freely through Jesus Christ and the gift of the Holy Spirit that changes and empowers us, and God's omnificent provisions that sustains us; and the only proper response to grace is humility, gratefulness, and thanksgiving.

It is in this relationship and partnership of communion predicated in our divine ability to meet humility with His grace and operate within these principles with our love, confidence, belief, and faith in God's promises that makes prayer powerful and effective.

"The prayer of faith shall save the sick, and the Lord shall raise him up; and if he have committed sins, they shall be forgiven him" (James 5:15). The "prayer of faith" secures the manifestation. The word sick in Greek is *astheneō* defined as, "to be weak in means, needy, poor" and "to be weak, feeble, to be without strength, powerless." The "prayer of faith" will not only heal the physically sick, but also manifest changes in circumstances to affect conditions of impoverishment.

Every prayer should be prayed in *faith* with an expected manifestation; and if there is no manifestation, Scripture instructs us to, "Examine yourselves, whether ye be in the faith; prove your own selves. Know ye not your own selves, how that Jesus Christ is in you, except ye be reprobates" (2 Corinthians 13:5)?

According to Scripture, if we are faithful, there will be proof of the evidence; in other words, RESULTS! You build strength in *faith* the same way you build strength in muscle, by exercise, consistency, practice, commitment, discipline, and in the knowledge, understanding, and trust of these applications, and in God, that you will achieve the results that are desired. The following Scriptures are biblical truths in biblical meditations on *what makes prayer work*:

Relationship with God
- "But seek ye first the kingdom of God, and his righteousness; and all these things shall be added unto you" (Matthew 6:33).
- "And ye shall seek me, and find me, when ye shall search for me with all your heart" (Jeremiah 29:13).

Relationship with Jesus
- "And whatsoever we ask, we receive of him, because we keep his commandments, and do those things that are pleasing in his sight. And this is his commandment, That we should believe on the name of his Son Jesus Christ, and love one another, as he gave us commandment. And he that keepeth his commandments dwelleth in him, and he in him. And hereby we know that he abideth in us, by the Spirit which he hath given us" (1 John 3:22–24).
- "Abide in me, and I in you. As the branch cannot bear fruit of itself, except it abide in the vine; no more can ye, except ye abide in me. I am the vine, ye are the branches: He that abideth in me, and I in him, the same bringeth forth much fruit: for without me ye can do nothing. If a man abide not in me, he is cast forth as a branch, and is withered; and men gather them, and cast them into the fire, and they are

burned. If ye abide in me, and my words abide in you, ye shall ask what ye will, and it shall be done unto you" (John 15:4–7).

- "Beware lest any man spoil you through philosophy and vain deceit, after the tradition of men, after the rudiments of the world, and not after Christ. For in him dwelleth all the fulness of the Godhead bodily. And ye are complete in him, which is the head of all principality and power" (Colossians 2:8–10).
- "For through him we both have access by one Spirit unto the Father" (Ephesians 2:18).

Relationship with the Holy Spirit

- "God is a Spirit: and they that worship him must worship him in spirit and in truth" (John 4:24).
- "Likewise the Spirit also helpeth our infirmities: for we know not what we should pray for as we ought: but the Spirit itself maketh intercession for us with groanings which cannot be uttered. And he that searcheth the hearts knoweth what is the mind of the Spirit, because he maketh intercession for the saints according to the will of God" (Romans 8:26–27).

The Love of God

- "But as it is written, Eye hath not seen, nor ear heard, neither have entered into the heart of man, the things which God hath prepared for them that love him" (1 Corinthians 2:9).
- "And we have known and believed the love that God hath to us. God is love; and he that dwelleth in love dwelleth in God, and God in him" (1 John 4:16).
- "For whatsoever is born of God overcometh the world: and this is the victory that overcometh the world, even our faith" (1 John 5:4).
- "But God commendeth his love toward us, in that, while we were yet sinners, Christ died for us" (Romans 5:8).

Repentance and Humility to God

- "If my people, which are called by my name, shall humble themselves, and pray, and seek my face, and turn from their wicked ways; then will I hear from heaven, and will forgive their sin, and will heal their land" (2 Chronicles 7:14).
- "The LORD is nigh unto them that are of a broken heart; and saveth such as be of a contrite spirit" (Psalm 34:18).
- "If we confess our sins, he is faithful and just to forgive us our sins, and to cleanse us from all unrighteousness" (1 John 1:9).
- "But he giveth more grace. Wherefore he saith, God resisteth the proud, but giveth grace unto the humble" (James 4:6).
- "For thus saith the high and lofty One that inhabiteth eternity, whose name is Holy; I dwell in the high and holy place, with him also that is of a contrite and humble spirit, to revive the spirit of the humble, and to revive the heart of the contrite ones" (Isaiah 57:15).

Believing and Receiving the Promises of God

- "God is not a man, that he should lie; neither the son of man, that he should repent: hath he said, and shall he not do it? or hath he spoken, and shall he not make it good?" (Numbers 23:19)
- "Let us hold fast the profession of our faith without wavering; (for he is faithful that promised)" (Hebrews 10:23).
- "For all the promises of God in him are yea, and in him Amen" (2 Corinthians 1:20).

Praying in God's Will

- "And this is the confidence that we have in him, that, if we ask any thing according to his will, he heareth us: And if we know that he hear us, whatsoever we ask, we know that we have the petitions that we desired of him" (1 John 5:14–15).

Praise and Worship
- "The garment of praise for the spirit of heaviness" (Isaiah 61:3).

The Grace of God
- "For by grace are ye saved through faith; and that not of yourselves: it is the gift of God" (Ephesians 2:8).
- "And God is able to make all grace abound toward you; that ye, always having all sufficiency in all things, may abound to every good work" (2 Corinthians 9:8).

The Power of God's Word
- "As for God, his way is perfect: the word of the LORD is tried: he is a buckler to all those that trust in him" (Psalm 18:30).
- "For the word of God is quick, and powerful, and sharper than any two edged sword, piercing even to the dividing asunder of soul and spirit, and of the joints and marrow, and is a discerner of the thoughts and intents of the heart" (Hebrews 4:12).
- "Being born again, not of corruptible seed, but of incorruptible, by the word of God, which liveth and abideth for ever. For all flesh is as grass, and all the glory of man as the flower of grass. The grass withereth, and the flower thereof falleth away: The word of the Lord endureth for ever. And this is the word which by the gospel is preached unto you" (1 Peter 1:23-25).
- "Thy word is a lamp unto my feet, and a light unto my path" (Psalm 119:10).

The Power of Your Words (What You Say)
- "Even so the tongue is a little member, and boasteth great things. Behold, how great a matter a little fire kindleth! And the tongue is a fire, a world of iniquity: so is the tongue among our members, that it defileth the whole body, and setteth on fire the course of nature; and it is set on fire of hell" (James 3:5–6).

- "Death and life are in the power of the tongue: and they that love it shall eat the fruit thereof" (Proverbs 18:21).
- "For by thy words thou shalt be justified, and by thy words thou shalt be condemned" (Matthew 12:37).
- "We having the same spirit of faith, according as it is written, I believed, and therefore have I spoken; we also believe, and therefore speak" (2 Corinthians 4:13).
- "For a good tree bringeth not forth corrupt fruit; neither doth a corrupt tree bring forth good fruit. For every tree is known by his own fruit ... A good man out of the good treasure of his heart bringeth forth that which is good; and an evil man out of the evil treasure of his heart bringeth forth that which is evil: for of the abundance of the heart his mouth speaketh" (Luke 6:43–45).

Asking
- "Ask, and it shall be given you; seek, and ye shall find; knock, and it shall be opened unto you" (Matthew 7:7).
- "I say unto you, Whatsoever ye shall ask the Father in my name, he will give it you" (John 16:23).

Being Forgiving—Being Committed
- "See that none render evil for evil unto any man; but ever follow that which is good, both among yourselves, and to all men. Rejoice evermore. Pray without ceasing" (1 Thessalonians 5:15–17).

Being Thankful
- "In every thing give thanks: for this is the will of God in Christ Jesus concerning you. Quench not the Spirit" (1 Thessalonians 5:18–19).
- "Make a joyful noise unto the LORD, all ye lands. Serve the LORD with gladness: come before his presence with singing. Know ye that the LORD he is God: it is he that hath made us, and not we ourselves; we are his people, and the sheep of his pasture. Enter into his gates with thanks-

giving, and into his courts with praise: be thankful unto him, and bless his name" (Psalm 100:1–4).

- "By him therefore let us offer the sacrifice of praise to God continually, that is, the fruit of our lips giving thanks to his name" (Hebrews 13:15).

Fervent Prayer
- "Confess your faults one to another, and pray one for another, that ye may be healed. The effectual fervent prayer of a righteous man availeth much" (James 5:16).

Baptized to Enter the Kingdom of God
- "Except a man be born of water and of the Spirit, he cannot enter into the kingdom of God" (John 3:5).

Baptized for the Remission of Sins to Receive the Holy Ghost
- "Then Peter said unto them, Repent, and be baptized every one of you in the name of Jesus Christ for the remission of sins, and ye shall receive the gift of the Holy Ghost" (Acts 2:38).
- "Ye shall receive power, after that the Holy Ghost is come upon you" (Acts 1:8).

Fasting
- "Is not this the fast that I have chosen? to loose the bands of wickedness, to undo the heavy burdens, and to let the oppressed go free, and that ye break every yoke?" (Isaiah 58:6)
- "But thou, when thou fastest, anoint thine head, and wash thy face; That thou appear not unto men to fast, but unto thy Father which is in secret: and thy Father, which seeth in secret, shall reward thee openly" (Matthew 6:17–18).
- "Then I proclaimed a fast there, at the river of Ahava, that we might afflict ourselves before our God, to seek of him a right way for us, and for our little ones, and for all our substance. So we fasted and besought our God for this: and he was intreated of us" (Ezra 8:21, 23).

The Power of Agreement

- "That if two of you shall agree on earth as touching any thing that they shall ask, it shall be done for them of my Father which is in heaven. For where two or three are gathered together in my name, there am I in the midst of them" (Matthew 18:19–20).
- "How should one chase a thousand, and two put ten thousand to flight" (Deuteronomy 32:30).

You Must Believe

- "Jesus said unto him, If thou canst believe, all things are possible to him that believeth" (Mark 9:23).
- "And Jesus answering saith unto them, Have faith in God. For verily I say unto you, That whosoever shall say unto this mountain, Be thou removed, and be thou cast into the sea; and shall not doubt in his heart, but shall believe that those things which he saith shall come to pass; he shall have whatsoever he saith. Therefore I say unto you, What things soever ye desire, when ye pray, believe that ye receive them, and ye shall have them" (Mark 11:22–24).
- "And all things, whatsoever ye shall ask in prayer, believing, ye shall receive" (Matthew 21:22).

Hope

- "For we are saved by hope: but hope that is seen is not hope: for what a man seeth, why doth he yet hope for? But if we hope for that we see not, then do we with patience wait for it" (Romans 8:24–25).
- "Rejoicing in hope; patient in tribulation; continuing instant in prayer" (Romans 12:12).
- "Be of good courage, and he shall strengthen your heart, all ye that hope in the LORD" (Psalm 31:24).
- "The LORD is my portion, saith my soul; therefore will I hope in him. The LORD is good unto them that wait for him, to the soul that seeketh him" (Lamentations 3:24–25).

Trusting in God
- "Trust in the LORD with all thine heart; and lean not unto thine own understanding. In all thy ways acknowledge him, and he shall direct thy paths" (Proverbs 3:5–6).
- "And this is the confidence that we have in him, that, if we ask any thing according to his will, he heareth us: And if we know that he hear us, whatsoever we ask, we know that we have the petitions that we desired of him" (1 John 5:14–15).
- "The LORD is good, a strong hold in the day of trouble; and he knoweth them that trust in him" (Nahum 1:7).

Patience
- "But that on the good ground are they, which in an honest and good heart, having heard the word, keep it, and bring forth fruit with patience" (Luke 8:15).
- "But let patience have her perfect work, that ye may be perfect and entire, wanting nothing" (James 1:4).

Our Love Walk
- "Master, which is the great commandment in the law? Jesus said unto him, Thou shalt love the Lord thy God with all thy heart, and with all thy soul, and with all thy mind. This is the first and great commandment. And the second is like unto it, Thou shalt love thy neighbour as thyself. On these two commandments hang all the law and the prophets" (Matthew 22:36–40).

Your Discipline and Commitment
- And these are they by the way side, where the word is sown; but when they have heard, Satan cometh immediately, and taketh away the word that was sown in their hearts. And these are they likewise which are sown on stony ground; who, when they have heard the word, immediately receive it with gladness; And have no root in themselves, and so endure but for a time: afterward, when affliction or per-

secution ariseth for the word's sake, immediately they are offended.

- And these are they which are sown among thorns; such as hear the word, And the cares of this world, and the deceitfulness of riches, and the lusts of other things entering in, choke the word, and it becometh unfruitful.
- "And these are they which are sown on good ground; such as hear the word, and receive it, and bring forth fruit, some thirtyfold, some sixty, and some an hundred" (Mark 4:15–20).

Faith

- "The prayer of faith shall save the sick, and the Lord shall raise him up; and if he have committed sins, they shall be forgiven him" (James 5:15).
- "And Jesus answered and said unto him, What wilt thou that I should do unto thee? The blind man said unto him, Lord, that I might receive my sight. And Jesus said unto him, Go thy way; thy faith hath made thee whole. And immediately he received his sight, and followed Jesus in the way" (Mark 10:51–52).
- "And Jesus said unto them, Because of your unbelief: for verily I say unto you, If ye have faith as a grain of mustard seed, ye shall say unto this mountain, Remove hence to yonder place; and it shall remove; and nothing shall be impossible unto you" (Matthew 17:20).
- "The Hall of Faith"—outlines miracles that were accomplished by and through faith. (Hebrews 11:3–35)
- "But without faith it is impossible to please him; for he that cometh to God must believe that he is, and that he is a rewarder of them that diligently seek him" (Hebrews 11:6).

Principles for Prayer

Love and relationships are at the core of humanity, and to know, and to love someone is to learn about them. Knowing of God does not equate to knowing God. To believe in God is not simply affirming a fact, but to engage in a trust relationship; and an intimate relationship is cultivated by love, trust, quality time, and two-way communication. Therefore, a one-sided conversation does not promote intimacy. Relationship in communion with God is through prayer, by talking, meditating and listening. We are receiving communications from God both through His Word and the Holy Spirit. Believers are to embrace the same intimacy with the Father that Jesus lived out.

Walk in accordance to God's Word. "Grieve not the holy Spirit of God, whereby ye are sealed unto the day of redemption" (Ephesians 4:30). You cannot live any way that you want to and expect God to answer your prayer. The Bible is a book of covenant based on a code of honor in order, principle, law, love, truth, relationship, and obedience to the holy Word. Once we walk in these precepts then, "whatsoever we ask, we receive of him, because we keep his commandments, and do those things that are pleasing in his sight" (1 John 3:22).

> "The LORD is far from the wicked: but He heareth the prayer of the righteous" (Proverbs 15:29) and "the eyes of the Lord are over the righteous, and his ears are open unto their prayers: but the face of the Lord is against them that do evil" (1 Peter 3:12).

> "The effectual fervent prayer of a righteous man availeth much" (James 5:16).

The Word of God is what cleanses us from sin. When you engage the Word of God, you meditate in it, you do it, you confess it (speak it), you BELIEVE it—this is sowing the Word of God. "The sower soweth the word" (Mark 4:14). Regarding the Word of God, "they are spirit, and they are life" (John 6:63).

Avoid prayer hindrances. The barriers to answered prayer are: ignorance to the Word of God, unbelief, worry, fear, doubt, self condemnation (guilt), unconfessed sin, unforgiveness, wrong motives, involvement in the occult, undeveloped faith, and rejection of spiritual authority and spiritual principles. You cannot violate the principles of God without consequence. These violations include both natural, and spiritual, as well as eternal consequences.

> Who is a wise man and endued with knowledge among you? let him shew out of a good conversation his works with meekness of wisdom. But if ye have bitter envying and strife in your hearts, glory not, and lie not against the truth. This wisdom descendeth not from above, but is earthly, sensual, devilish. For where envying and strife is, there is confusion and every evil work. But the wisdom that is from above is first pure, then peaceable, gentle, and easy to be intreated, full of mercy and good fruits, without partiality, and without hypocrisy. (James 3:13-17)

Avoid involvement in the occult. Certain practices, such as ouija boards, palm readers, tarot cards, séances, witchcraft, and black magic are entrances to demonic gateways, and unknowingly, we give permission to hindrances and strongholds to influence our lives by entertaining such practices.

Our Father in Heaven to whom we address our prayers is, "a jealous God" (Exodus 20:5). He considers these practices as idol worship and any attempt to find guidance from other sources is futile and with negative consequences. He alone is truth and only from Him can we learn to live correctly on earth.

It is written in Deuteronomy 18:9–14,

> When thou art come into the land which the LORD thy God giveth thee, thou shalt not learn to do after the abominations of those nations. There shall not be found among you any one that maketh his son or his daughter to pass through the fire, or that useth divination, or an observer of times, or an enchanter, or a witch. Or a charmer, or a consulter with familiar spirits, or a wizard, or a necromancer [the practice of communicating with the spirits of the dead in order to predict the future.] For all that do these things are an

abomination unto the LORD: and because of these abominations the LORD thy God doth drive them out from before
thee. Thou shalt be perfect with the LORD thy God. For these
nations, which thou shalt possess, hearkened unto observers
of times, and unto diviners: but as for thee, the LORD thy God
hath not suffered thee so to do.

The fact is, what we believe about God determines how we
live our life, whom we are living it for, and where we go for help
and guidance when we need assistance. It determines whether
we are worshipping and seeking the living God of the Bible or
seeking the spirits of the dead and methods of the occult.

Avoid unholy practices. "Mortify therefore your members which are upon the earth; fornication, uncleanness, inor-
dinate affection, evil concupiscence, and covetousness, which
is idolatry: For which things' sake the wrath of God cometh on
the children of disobedience: But now ye also put off all these;
anger, wrath, malice, blasphemy, filthy communication out of
your mouth. And have put on the new man, which is renewed in
knowledge after the image of him that created him" (Colossians
3:5-6, 8, 10).

"Let us lay aside every weight, and the sin which doth so
easily beset us, and let us run with patience the race that is set
before us, Looking unto Jesus the author and finisher of our
faith" (Hebrews 12:1-2).

Walk in love. To honor God is to love Him and others, and to
love Him is to obey Him. "Put on therefore, as the elect of God,
holy and beloved, bowels of mercies, kindness, humbleness of
mind, meekness, longsuffering; Forbearing one another, and forgiving one another, if any man have a quarrel against any: even
as Christ forgave you, so also do ye. And above all these things
put on charity [brotherly love], which is the bond of perfectness"
(Colossians 3:12-14). As we see in John 14:21, "He that hath my
commandments, and keepeth them, he it is that loveth me: and
he that loveth me shall be loved of my Father, and I will love him,
and will manifest myself to him."

Repent of your sins and forgive others and yourself. Effective prayer calls for us to be in right standing with God. Sin grieves the Holy Spirit and thereby separates us from God. Consistent confession and repentance is essential to maintain a Spirit-filled life. The depth and power of your prayer life will never be greater than the depth of your daily confession, cleansing, and sanctification. We are told in 2 Chronicles 7:14, "If my people, which are called by my name, shall humble themselves, and pray, and seek my face, and turn from their wicked ways; then will I hear from heaven, and will forgive their sin, and will heal their land."

Unforgiveness toward yourself leads to guilt and condemnation, thereby making you feel unworthy to fellowship with God; but Scripture reassures us that, "If we confess our sins, he is faithful and just to forgive us our sins, and to cleanse us from all unrighteousness" (1 John 1:9). Unforgiveness toward others results in resentment, bitterness, and anger; both forms of unforgiveness are toxic emotions and will hinder your prayers.

Not only do we need to ask God for His forgiveness, but also Matthew 18:15 instructs us to, "Moreover if thy brother shall trespass against thee, go and tell him his fault between thee and him alone: if he shall hear thee, thou hast gained thy brother." "Take heed to yourselves: If thy brother trespass against thee, rebuke him; and if he repent, forgive him" (Luke 17:3).

Forgiveness is one of the deepest parts of love because it is probably one of the most difficult to give. In some instances it is only by the presiding power of the Holy Spirit that we are able to forgive and love with the heart of God. It was by the sovereignty of the Holy Spirit that Jesus while on the cross was able to say, "Father, forgive them; for they know not what they do" (Luke 23:34).

To receive God's forgiveness when we pray, we must have the same attitude toward others that we expect God to have toward us; and "when ye stand praying, forgive, if ye have ought against any: that your Father also which is in heaven may forgive you your trespasses" (Mark 11:25).

Prioritize and make God and prayer first. This emphasizes that your prayer time is a priority that you plan, schedule, and maintain. Without question, the development of a powerful effective prayer life requires consistent quality time alone with God. In order to do this, Scripture states, "Seek ye first the kingdom of God, and his righteousness; and all these things shall be added unto you" (Matthew 6:33). Seeking God in prayer should be your first resource, not your last resort.

Worship the Father in Spirit and in truth. "True worshippers shall worship the Father in spirit and in truth: for the Father seeketh such to worship him. God is a Spirit: and they that worship him must worship him in spirit and in truth" (John 4:23-24). "But he that **doeth truth cometh to the light, that his deeds may be made manifest,** that they are wrought in God" (John 3:21, emphasis added).

The Greek word for truth is *aletheia* defined as "a personal excellence" and "what is true in things appertaining to God and the duties of man, moral and religious truth." The word light in the Greek is defined as *metaph* "the **power of understanding especially moral and spiritual truth; of truth and its knowledge, together with the spiritual purity associated with it."**

Developing a powerful effective prayer life requires discipline to grow in spiritual knowledge and understanding, along with sanctification. The more you are sanctified with the truth, the more you will manifests in "deeds" prayers.

Christ prayed to the Father, "Sanctify them through thy truth: thy word is truth. And the glory which thou gavest me I have given them; that they may be one, even as we are one: I in them, and thou in me, that they may be made perfect in one..." (John 17:17, 22-23)

We must not only worship God in Spirit, but also in truth, which is the spiritual intellect of the mind by the process of, "be not conformed to this world: but be ye transformed by the renewing of your mind" (Romans 12:2). Renewing the mind means to exchange and align your thoughts, ideas, and belief systems for God's Word which is spiritual wisdom.

Worship by definition, according to Random House dictionary means, "reverent honor and homage paid to God or a sacred personage or to any object regarded as sacred." It is also defined as "to idolize." An idol by definition is "any person or thing devotedly or excessively admired or valued." Therefore, worship starts when we devote our attention, focus, respect, time, and aspire to be like someone or want more and more of something. "Therefore let no man glory in men" (1 Corinthians 3:21).

Because our human nature is influenced and thereby conformed to what we admire, value and respect, is so persuasive, we need to worship God. When we consciously choose to be influenced by His ethics and values, and prioritize, focus, respect, honor and love the Father, we aspire and gradually conform to His image to, "put on the new man, which is renewed in knowledge after the image of him that created him" (Colossians 3:10).

Create an atmosphere for worship and praise. The underlying concept of worship in Scripture is that of love, reverence and service to the most Holy, God. This understanding expands the application of worship far beyond the walls of a church building of the sanctuary. Worship is not only during the corporate assembly of church service or a congregational setting; but it enlarges the practice and lifestyle of worship beyond, and in addition to, the formal setting. In other words, worship expands into the home, into "your prayer closet," or where the Spirit arises.

Listen to spiritual and gospel music. "Speaking to yourselves in psalms and hymns and spiritual songs, singing and making melody in your heart to the Lord" (Ephesians 5:19).

How to Enter God's Presence for Prayer:
"Thou wilt shew me the path of life: in thy presence is fulness of joy; at thy right hand there are pleasures for evermore" (Psalm 16:11). The heart of prayer is love; the posture of prayer is humility; the focus of prayer is worship; the power of prayer is the Holy Spirit; the authority of prayer is Christ; the principle of

prayer is faith; the manifestation of prayer is change by the glory of God.

"He that dwelleth in the secret place of the most High shall abide under the shadow of the Almighty. I will say of the LORD, He is my refuge and my fortress: my God; in him will I trust... Because thou hast made the LORD, which is my refuge, even the most High, thy habitation; There shall no evil befall thee, neither shall any plague come nigh thy dwelling. For he shall give his angels charge over thee, to keep thee in all thy ways." (Psalm 91:1-2, 9-11).

Prayer should begin with silence where you will not be interrupted or distracted. Become silent and gather yourself. Scriptures calls for us to, "Be still, and know that I am God" (Psalm 46:10).

"Humble yourselves in the sight of the Lord, and he shall lift [exalt] you up" (James 4:10, emphasis added). "Whosoever shall exalt himself shall be abased; and he that shall humble himself shall be exalted" (Matthew 23:12).

As you enter prayer, prepare your heart to fellowship with God by meditating on biblical Scriptures. Biblical meditation is the art of reflection in the Word, because meditating on the Word of God incorporates the presence and working of the Holy Spirit. The key and most important element in biblical meditation is not just reading or even committing to memory what has been read, which is important, but more importantly, it is *believing* what you have read. Anyone may repeat a Scripture, but the source of power is in your belief and your faith of what is being said.

Reflect and meditate on key points of Scriptures that apply to your circumstance. The process of meditating on God's Word and promises will bring hope and illumination to build and sustain your faith.

The goal of biblical meditation is to *internalize and personalize the Scriptures so that their truth can affect how we think*. As we renew our mind in the Word we prepare ourselves to pray in faith.

"Enter into his gates with thanksgiving, and into his courts with praise" (Psalm 100:4, emphasis added). He is worthy to be exalted! Blessed are you God, King of the universe; blessed is your Holy name. Thank God for the results of prayer, both before, and after you see the results. Thanking God will increase your faith for what you don't yet see because you believe it is already done. Praising God will also increase your faith since you will begin to focus your thoughts on God, His faithfulness, promises, and power and not your circumstance.

Every blessing received should prompt us to praise God in prayer. How can God give us greater blessings if we do not appreciate those already given? Being thankful opens a gateway for additional blessings to flow to you and expands your capacity to receive more. It also validates your appreciation for what you do have, and it acknowledges your belief, faith, and confidence in God to manifest what you are praying for.

"Let every thing that hath breath praise the LORD. Praise ye the LORD" (Psalm 150:6, emphasis added). Our primary purpose is to glorify the Father, "For ye are bought with a price: therefore glorify God in your body, and in your spirit, which are God's" (1 Corinthians 6:20). When we reflect on who God is and all He has done for us, even the little things we may take for granted, praise becomes natural and spontaneous. Praise comes out of worship from a rooted personal and intimate relationship with God and a deep, heartfelt release of your testimony of who God is and what He has done for you.

Praise creates the atmosphere and the anointing of God's presence, for "God's presence inhabits the praises of His people." Your praise invites God's presence to invade your circumstance and is, "the garment of praise for the spirit of heaviness" (Isaiah 61:3). Your praise mixed with faith produces an atmosphere to process the promises of God.

Allow the Holy Spirit to lead you into prayer. In Ephesians 6:18–20, Paul stresses that we cannot pray effectively in our own power; and that we should pray, "always with all prayer and supplication in the Spirit, and watching thereunto with all perseverance and supplication for all saints; ... that utterance may be given unto [you] me, that I [you] may open my [your] mouth boldly, to make known the mystery of the gospel, For which I am [you are] an ambassador in bonds: that therein I [you] may speak boldly, as I [you] ought to speak."

Always ask for God's anointing as you pray. Powerful prayer is enabled through the Holy Spirit. "Ye shall receive power, after that the Holy Ghost is come upon you" (Acts 1:8).

Romans 8:26-27 says,

Likewise the Spirit also helpeth our infirmities: for we know not what we should pray for as we ought: but the Spirit itself maketh intercession for us with groanings which cannot be uttered. And he that searcheth the hearts knoweth what is the mind of the Spirit, because he maketh intercession for the saints according to the will of God.

The baptism of the Holy Spirit, known as the speaking of "tongues" is supernatural, spiritual gifts. This is a gift of the Holy Spirit as 1 Corinthians 12:7, 10 explains, "The manifestation of the Spirit is given to every man to profit withal… to another divers kinds of tongues; to another the interpretation of tongues."

There is a supernatural exchange that takes place as we pray in unknown or other tongues and, therefore, can be of immense help to us. "He that speaketh in an unknown tongue edifieth himself" (1 Corinthians 14:4). We generally do not understand the words but our prayer is spiritual. It is our spirit that is in direct communication with the Holy Spirit, God. "For he that speaketh in an unknown tongue speaketh not unto men, but unto God: for no man understandeth him; howbeit in the spirit he speaketh mysteries" (1 Corinthians 14:2).

Your prayer life will enable you to become more sensitive and aware of the promptings of the Holy Spirit, and with this awareness, "ye have an unction from the Holy One, and ye know all things" (1 John 2:20). "For the Holy Ghost shall teach you in the same hour what ye ought to say" (Luke 12:12). Some may call this intuition, a prompting, a nudge, a hunch, or a knowing in your inner spirit.

Effective prayer follows putting on the armor of God. The passage Ephesians 6:10 begins by telling us to "be strong in the Lord, and in the power of his might." Ephesians 6:11 calls for us to "Put on the whole armour of God, that ye may be able to stand against the wiles of the devil." Remember, the word stand in Greek is *histemi*, and it means, "to abide in established covenant." This word is important because when we stand, we abide in the covenant promises of God. The whole armor of God helps us to ward off the attacks of the enemy.

"Wherefore take unto you the whole armour of God, that ye may be able to withstand in the evil day, and having done all, to stand. Stand therefore, having your loins girt about with truth, and having on the breastplate of righteousness; And your feet shod with the preparation of the gospel of peace; Above all, taking the shield of faith, wherewith ye shall be able to quench all the fiery darts of the wicked. And take the helmet of salvation, and the sword of the Spirit, which is the word of God" (Ephesians 6:13–17).

If we do not, first, put on the armor (which is the Word of God), we will pray out of misconceptions concerning the truth of who we are in Christ, and our authority in praying in His name, and our understanding of who God is. When you pray, understand who you are in Christ, "that we might be made the righteousness of God in him" (2 Corinthians 5:21). As a member of the royal family, we do not plead or beg, but ask, expect, receive, and thank our heavenly Father for granting the results in response to our prayer.

Pray with an attitude of authority in the name of Jesus. A correct form of prayer is through the Holy Spirit by the name of Jesus unto the Father. "For through him we both have access by one Spirit unto the Father" (Ephesians 2:18). It is Christ... that is risen again, who is even at the right hand of God, who also maketh intercession for us" (Romans 8:34). Christ intercedes for us in Heaven and the Holy Spirit intercedes through us on earth.

The authority we have in Jesus' name through prayer is based on a covenantal authority by the blood covenant relationship with God through Christ. Praying in the name and authority and power of Jesus is giving Him authority to intercede on our behalf when you make requests of the Father God. All Christians have a blood bought, promised, redemptive, covenant, legal and family right to use the name of Jesus.

Praying in the name of Jesus isn't telling us to just use His name; rather, He is *also* calling on us to believe, to understand His nature, His attributes, His power, *and to develop in it to conform to His image*, and appropriate it in faith. "But we all, with unveiled face, beholding as in a mirror the glory of the Lord, are being transformed into the same image from glory to glory, just as by the Spirit of the Lord" (2 Corinthians 3:18).

Jesus taught, "He that believeth on me, the works that I do shall he do also; and greater works than these shall he do; because I go unto my Father. And whatsoever ye shall ask in my name, that will I do, that the Father may be glorified in the Son. If ye shall ask any thing in my name, I will do it" (John 14:12–14).

Pray in the name of Jesus. Praying in the specific name of Jesus personalizes the characteristic and the divinity of nature specified for the designated petition. It can be understood, therefore, how the divine name is often spoken of as equivalent to the divine presence or power. If we want God to meet our need when we pray "in the name of Jesus," we must pray based on the divine name that meets our particular need at the time. It is important to understand that the name of Jesus is given to us to use in relation to our needs.

Recorded in Exodus 3:13-14, "Moses said unto God, Behold, when I come unto the children of Israel, and shall say unto them, The God of your fathers hath sent me unto you; and they shall say to me, What is his name? what shall I say unto them? And God said unto Moses, I AM THAT I AM: and he said, Thus shalt thou say unto the children of Israel, I AM hath sent me unto you." God is what you need Him to be in whatever your need is.

If you are sick you call on Jehovah-Rapha, the God who heals (Exodus 15:26), or if you need peace call on Jehovah-Shalom, the

Lord is peace. "Whatsoever ye shall ask the Father in my name, he will give it you" (John 16:23).

"Heavenly Father, El Elyon (The Most High God), I come before you in the authority and in the name of Jesus Christ, Jehovah Raah (The Lord My Shepherd), (your petition)... thank you Father..." If you forget or do not know the names of God, just call on Jesus!

"Come boldly unto the throne of grace that we [you] may obtain mercy, and find grace to help in time of need" (Hebrews 4:16, emphasis added). When we expect little from prayer, we will not have much power and authority in prayer. When we question the power of prayer, we lose the power of it. "Ye are of God, little children, and have overcome them: because greater is he that is in you, than he that is in the world" (1 John 4:4).

Pray the solution, not the problem. God knows what we have need of before we ask; however, it is in the act of praying that we need to ask. We speak the words of Scripture (His promises) in our prayers and appropriate our faith. "Ye have not, because ye ask not" (James 4:2). We speak to the "mountain" not about the "mountain." We speak specifically to the problem with specific requests that are Scripture-based. Jesus tells us in Mark 11:23, "That whosoever shall say unto this mountain, Be thou removed, and be thou cast into the sea; and shall not doubt in his heart, but shall believe that those things which he saith shall come to pass; he shall have whatsoever he saith."

As we know "faith comes by hearing and hearing by the Word of God." Speaking your prayers out loud also has the effect of increasing your faith. In the same way, when reading your Bible, read it out loud and turn what you're reading into prayer. Agreeing with God and His Word is a powerful act of intercession. As we declare the Word, we are *prophesying* into our circumstance according to God's Word.

Angels hear, obey, and act on your behalf when you speak God's Word. God's Word releases God's Spirit into action. "Bless the LORD, ye his angels, that excel in strength, that do his commandments, hearkening unto the voice of his word" (Psalm 103:20).

Pray for spiritual wisdom so God may direct your steps, "for the steps of a good man are ordered by the LORD: and he delighteth in his way" (Psalm 37:23). "If any of you lack wisdom, let him ask of God, that giveth to all men liberally, and upbraideth not; and it shall be given him. But let him ask in faith, nothing wavering. For he that wavereth is like a wave of the sea driven with the wind and tossed. For let not that man think that he shall receive any thing of the Lord" (James 1:5–7).

Fast and pray. Prayer, to be effective, often requires fasting. Fasting exerts discipline over our physical appetites to bring the body under subjection to what the Spirit desires. Fasting combined with prayer, they, together, make up the most critical weapons of spiritual warfare and deliverance in our lives. Only through prayer and fasting can some hindrances, yokes of oppression, and spiritual warfare be conquered. As Jesus said in Mark 9:29, "This kind can come forth by nothing, but by prayer and fasting." "That thou appear not unto men to fast, but unto thy Father which is in secret: and thy Father, which seeth in secret, shall reward thee openly" (Matthew 6:18).

Destroy and cancel assignments of darkness. The assignment of the devil falls into three categories, "steal, kill, and destroy." Some are principalities and powers, rulers of darkness, and others are spiritual wickedness in high places. Their assignments are against the purposes of God and are directed toward believers. Assignments can only take affect with your permission. Your permission may be unknowingly due to unholy practices, unconfessed sin, unforgiveness, fear, and other entrances that create hindrances to answered prayers.

In this form of spiritual warfare we are to pray to rebuke the works of the devil. We are to repent and cease from sin, and command these assignments to be bound and to leave their positions of influence or authority *in the name of Jesus* and release the power of the written Word. We cannot come against Satan and be in agreement with him at the same time. Remember, Jesus stated in Mark 3:23-27, "How can Satan cast out Satan? And if a kingdom be divided against itself, that kingdom cannot stand. And if a house be divided against itself, that house cannot stand. And if Satan rise up against himself, and be divided, he cannot stand, but hath an end."

Christ has given Christians, "the keys of the kingdom of heaven: and whatsoever thou shalt bind on earth shall be bound in heaven: and whatsoever thou shalt loose on earth shall be loosed in heaven" (Matthew 16:19). "As it is written, For thy sake we are killed all the day long; we are accounted as sheep for the slaughter. Nay, in all these things we are more than conquerors through him that loved us" (Romans 8:36–37).

Allow God to lead you to pray for others. We have a joint responsibility for every member of the Body of Christ. "...there should be no schism [dissension] in the body; but that the members should have the same care one for another. And whether one member suffer, all the members suffer with it; or one member be honoured, all the members rejoice with it. Now ye are the body of Christ, and members in particular" (1 Corinthians 12:25–27).

We are guarding and praying for each other. We should conduct ourselves as prayer warriors in a battle. We are on the alert. When we hear of an enemy attack, we assist the weak point in the defense; we send reinforcements to fortify its strength.

Intercede for others. Intercession is primarily focused on the needs of others. To intercede for someone is to spiritually stand in the gap and pray for the advancement of God's interest in the world, a person, a ministry, or a community. It is seen in 1 Timothy 2:1-2, "that, first of all, supplications, prayers, intercessions, and giving of thanks, be made for all men; For kings, and for all that are in authority; that we may lead a quiet and peaceable life in all godliness and honesty."

Our heavenly Father looks for those to stand in the gap as 2 Chronicles 16:9 affirms, "For the eyes of the LORD run to and fro throughout the whole earth, to shew himself strong in the behalf of them whose heart is perfect toward him."

Agree with the Word of God. Christ has commissioned and released into the life of every Christian according to John 17:15-23 the ability to affect divine activity by cooperating and agreeing with the Word of God.

There is *power in agreement* and *power in numbers* in united prayer. The principal governing the prayer of agreement illustrates the power of unity, praying "in one accord [one mind]." Engaging the faith of at least two *believers* brings power to prayer. "How should one chase a thousand, and two put ten thousand to flight" (Deuteronomy 32:30).

Jesus declared in Matthew 18:19–20, "I say unto you, That if two of you shall agree on earth as touching any thing that they shall ask, it shall be done for them of my Father which is in heaven. For where two or three are gathered together in my name, there am I in the midst of them."

When selecting a prayer partner be extremely selective. Pray with someone that has the same basic viewpoints and doctrines as yours. It is important that each person sincerely pray in agreement, focused as one mind, believing, so that you can both stand together.

Pray blessings for your enemies and pray for their salvation. Christ instructs in Matthew 5:44, 48, "Love your enemies, bless them that curse you, do good to them that hate you, and pray for them which despitefully use you, and persecute you ... Be ye therefore perfect, even as your Father which is in heaven is perfect."

"Recompense to no man evil for evil. Provide things honest in the sight of all men. Dearly beloved, avenge not yourselves, but rather give place unto wrath: for it is written, Vengeance [justice] is mine; I will repay, saith the Lord" (Romans 12:17, 19).

"If thine enemy be hungry, give him bread to eat; and if he be thirsty, give him water to drink: For thou shalt heap coals of fire upon his head, and the LORD shall reward thee" (Proverbs 25:21–22).

Principles following prayer:
Maintain a mindset of belief, faith and expectancy for, "Surely goodness and mercy shall follow me [you] all the days of my [your] life: and I [you] will dwell in the house of the LORD for ever" (Psalm 23:6).

Prayer is an act of faith. Faith is a response to what we believe God has said in the promises of His Word. If we truly believed the promises of the Word of God, we would pray with confidence; "And this is the confidence that we have in him, that, if we ask any thing according to his will, he heareth us: And if we know that he hear us, whatsoever we ask, we know that we have the petitions that we desired of him" (1 John 5:14–15).

Faith is belief in what Jesus said in Mark 11:22, 24, "Have faith in God. Therefore I say unto you, What things soever ye desire, when ye pray, believe that ye receive them, and ye shall have them."

"And all things, whatsoever ye shall ask in prayer, believing, ye shall receive" (Matthew 21:22).

What could be more simple or direct? So what causes doubt? Many reasons may cause doubt, such as what we feel or do not feel, what we see or do not see, undeveloped faith and the principles that comprise faith; but also, impatience may cause us to doubt and think God has not heard us because, we may see no immediate evidence of an answer.

Do not doubt. A necessary condition of faith is not to doubt. "I will therefore that men pray every where, lifting up holy hands, without wrath and doubting" (1 Timothy 2:8).

Once you have prayed, the resolution, or the results, may not be immediate; however, "Cast not away therefore your confidence, which hath great recompence of reward. For ye have need of patience, that, after ye have done the will of God, ye might receive the promise" (Hebrews 10:35–36).

Patience is a quiet perseverance and endurance demonstrating *persistent courage in the face of delay.* "Be of good courage, and he shall strengthen your heart, all ye that hope in the LORD" (Psalm 31:24).

Be Patient. Patience is where our faithfulness to God is tested. Patience develops strength and character through experience, and this experience helps us to trust God more each time we use it until our hope and faith are strong and consistent. Scripture tells us, "That ye be not slothful [sluggish], but followers of them who through faith and patience inherit the promises" (Hebrews 6:12).

"... knowing that tribulation worketh patience; And patience, experience; and experience, hope: And hope maketh not ashamed; because the love of God is shed abroad in our hearts by the Holy Ghost which is given unto us" (Romans 5:3–5). "But let patience have her perfect work, that ye may be perfect and entire, wanting nothing" (James 1:4).

Endure under the pressure of tribulation and be devoted to persevering in prayer. Perseverant prayer goes along with being hopeful and patient; "Rejoicing in hope; patient in tribulation; continuing instant in prayer" (Romans 12:12). "And let us not be weary in well doing: for in due season we shall reap, if we faint not" (Galatians 6:9).

"Be careful [anxious] for nothing; but in every thing by prayer and supplication with thanksgiving let your requests be made known unto God. And the peace of God, which passeth all understanding, shall keep your hearts and minds through Christ Jesus" (Philippians 4:6–7). Christ tells us, "Let not your heart be troubled, neither let it be afraid" (John 14:27).

Learn to recognize the lie. The devil "is a liar, and the father of it" (John 8:44). Therefore, "Submit yourselves therefore to God. Resist the devil, and he will flee from you. Draw nigh to God, and he will draw nigh to you. Cleanse your hands, ye sinners; and purify your hearts, ye double minded. Humble yourselves in the sight of the Lord, and he shall lift you up" (James 4:7-8, 10). "For God hath not given us the spirit of fear; but of power, and of love, and of a sound mind" (2 Timothy 1:7).

Cast down every negative thought that is contrary to your prayer and renew your mind by thinking, "whatsoever things are true, whatsoever things are honest, whatsoever things are just, whatsoever things are pure, whatsoever things are lovely, whatsoever things are of good report; if there be any virtue, and if there be any praise, think on these things" (Philippians 4:8). You cannot always control your external circumstances but you can control your responses.

Memorizing and believing Scriptures will reinforce the positive, to counter the negative (the fear, the unbelief, the worry). Take authority over your negative thoughts with biblical truths of Scripture. Recalling a Scripture grounds and roots you to God's promises. Jesus declares in John 15:7, "If ye abide in me, and my words abide in you, ye shall ask what ye will, and it shall be done unto you." If we do not know what the Word says concerning a matter, there is a good chance, we will become doubtful and lose our faithfulness and sabotage our prayers.

Anchor God's Word in your thoughts, your spirit, your heart, your actions, your speech, and in your lifestyle. "Keep thy heart with all diligence; for out of it are the issues of life" (Proverbs 4:23). Stay focused, disciplined, committed, and patient in knowing that His way, His Word, and His principles cannot and will not fail. Recognize that they are the fundamental eternal truths, "for all the promises of God in him are yea, and in Him Amen" (2 Corinthians 1:20).

"Take heed what ye hear: with what measure ye mete, it shall be measured to you: and unto you that hear shall more be given" (Mark 4:24, emphasis added). We know that what you listen to have the ability to influence how you think, as well as how you feel. Words have the power to either encourage or discourage. What you hear will influence and affect how you think. The way you think will affect what you believe and what you believe will influence what you confess (say). Thinking and believing in alignment with the Word of God should become a mental discipline and will result in confessing the Word. "For by thy words thou shalt be justified, and by thy words thou shalt be condemned" (Matthew 12:37).

Speak in line with your confession; "Let us hold fast the profession of our faith without wavering; (for he is faithful that promised)" (Hebrews 10:23). Take control of what you say by confessing the relevant truths of the Word (speak faith), "The word is nigh thee, even in thy mouth, and in thy heart: that is, the word of faith, which we preach" (Romans 10:8). "Death and life are in the power of the tongue: and they that love it shall eat the fruit thereof" (Proverbs 18:21).

God acts independently, but through us, according to Genesis 1:26-27; and therefore, the activities in the Earth are affected by what we declare, speak, and execute by faith through prayer according to His Word.

"For we walk by faith, and not by sight" (2 Corinthians 5:7, emphasis added). "But without faith it is impossible to please him; for he that cometh to God must believe that he is, and that he is a rewarder of them that diligently seek him" (Hebrews 11:6).

Your   sanctification is, living by, the truth, knowledge, under-standing, wisdom, and revelation of the living Word.

Your   responsibility is to daily, "renew your mind."

Your   redemption and access is by the blood of Jesus.

Your   power is prayer through the communion and fellowship with the Holy Spirit.

Your   authority is by the name of Jesus.

Your   obligation is to love with the heart of God and to, "glorify God in your body, and in your spirit, which are God's."

Your   manifestation is, "as it is written, the just shall live by faith."

CHAPTER 7

Understanding the Power of Faith

What Is Faith?

"For I say [the Apostle Paul], through the grace given unto me, to every man that is among you, not to think of himself more highly than he ought to think; but to think soberly, according as God hath dealt to every man the measure of faith" (Romans 12:3).

Faith is defined many ways in the Bible. There are seven definitions in the Greek and sixteen variations of definitions in the Hebrew for faith. By faith, we come to salvation accepting Christ as Lord and Savior, which is saving faith. There are spiritual gifts of faith, imparted by the Holy Spirit, where "the manifestation of the Spirit is given to every man to profit withal...To another faith by the same Spirit" (1 Corinthians 12:7, 9). And then, there is an operational or a functional faith where we, "walk by faith and not by sight." All faiths are principled in belief and trust in respecting man's relationship to God and divine things.

Faith, defined in Random House Dictionary: 1) Confidence or trust in a person or thing. 2) Belief that is not based on proof. 3) Belief in anything, as a code of ethics, or the occurrence of a future event.

The Greek translation for faith is *pistis,* which means, "respecting man's relationship to God and divine things, trust, conviction, belief, or assurance." *Pistis,* in turn, is a derivation of the ancient Greek root word *peitho,* which means, "to wax confident." The Bible defines faith as, "Faith is the substance of things hoped for, the evidence of things not seen" (Hebrews 11:1).

So what is the substance? Defined in the Random House Dictionary, substance is "the subject matter of thought [the way you think], the essential part of a thing, the essence ..." One of the Greek translations for substance is *hypostasis,* which means "the steadfastness of mind, firmness, courage, resolution." What is the evidence? The evidence is the "result—the proof [that by which a thing is proved or tested]—the manifestation" of what you have hoped for.

Remember, the power of the unseen realm (the spiritual) is the origin and the root of all that is seen and experienced in our physical realm, and is governed by God's principles. Faith, by its very nature, begins in the realm of the unseen (the spiritual) and ends in what is seen (the physical). It is conviction supported by evidence concerning things we hope for and things we don't know. By faith, we accept that the invisible things of God are behind the visible universe. "Through faith we understand that the worlds were framed by the Word of God, so that things which are seen were not made of things which do appear" (Hebrews 11:3).

The first body of evidence to support our faith is the world, the first and general revelation of God to man. The very existence of the universe, its power, order, and complexity, illustrate that a power of omnificence sufficient to create it, in other words, God, must be behind it. "For the invisible things of him from the creation of the world are clearly seen, being understood by the things that are made, even his eternal power and Godhead; so that they are without excuse" (Romans 1:20).

Faith is our creative ability and a key factor to obtain results in any aspect of prayer. Faith is the foundation for a powerful prayer life. We live by faith every day consciously and subconsciously in various degrees. For example, just in the mere fact that we expect something to grow when it's planted, or we expect to be paid for a job performed, and on the list goes.

Faith operates within the spiritual laws. "For we know that the law is spiritual" (Romans 7:14), and the (spiritual) laws of faith that work in the unseen supersede the physical, for they are the results of the unseen that manifest in the physical. "While we look not at the things which are seen, but at the things which are not seen: for the things which are seen are temporal; but the things which are not seen are eternal" (2 Corinthians 4:18).

Faith releases the power for God to work in your life and the power of God in your life. Faith is a practical expression of your trust, your confidence, and your expectation in God's Word and your ability to believe that your prayers will be answered. Scripture states that we are to believe on the name of the Son of God, and to be so confident in our prayers that, "Whatsoever ye shall ask the Father in my name, he will give it you" (John 16:23) and "... if we ask any thing according to his will, he heareth us: And if we know that he hear us whatsoever we ask, we know that we have the petitions that we desired of him" (1 John 5:14–15).

In Matthew 17:20 Jesus said, "...If ye have faith as a grain of mustard seed, ye shall say unto this mountain, Remove hence to yonder place; and it shall remove; and nothing shall be impossible unto you." The majority of opinion in understanding this verse is, often misunderstood, in thinking that you only need a *tiny* amount of faith. However, in Matthew 13:31-32 Jesus makes it clear, "The kingdom of heaven is like to a grain of mustard seed, which a man took, and sowed in his field: Which indeed is the least of all seeds: but when it is grown, it is the greatest among herbs, and becometh a tree..." Faith is progressive and faith is active belief, which is merited on growth and the steadfastness of mind.

As stated in Romans 12:3, "God hath dealt to every man the measure of faith." However, there are varying degrees of faith that are revelatory in our abilities to believe as follows: no faith (unbelief), little faith, great faith, vacillating faith and Holy Spirit-led faith. These various degrees of faith were illustrated in the following Scriptures:

No Faith (Unbelief):
- "And he [Jesus] did not many mighty works there because of their unbelief" (Matthew 13:58).
- "Because of unbelief they were broken off, and thou standest by faith" (Romans 11:20).

Little Faith:
- "And he saith unto them, Why are ye fearful, O ye of little faith?" (Matthew 8:26)

Vacillating (Wavering) Faith:
- "If any of you lack wisdom, let him ask of God, that giveth to all men liberally, and upbraideth not; and it shall be given him. But let him ask in faith, nothing wavering. For he that wavereth is like a wave of the sea driven with the wind and tossed. For let not that man think that he shall receive any thing of the Lord. A double minded man is unstable in all his ways" (James 1:5–8).

Great Faith:
- "When Jesus heard it, he marvelled, and said to them that followed, Verily I say unto you, I have not found so great faith, no, not in Israel" (Matthew 8:10).

Holy Spirit-Led Faith:
- "They chose Stephen, a man full of faith and of the Holy Ghost, And Stephen, full of faith and power, did great wonders and miracles among the people" (Acts 6:5, 8).
- Jesus said, "I can of mine own self do nothing: as I hear, I judge: and my judgment is just; because I seek not

mine own will, but the will of the Father which hath sent me" (John 5:30).

Faith starts with human belief, which usually vacillates based on circumstance, but must quickly move to the real faith of Christ, which enters a person at the moment of baptism and conversion with the receiving of God's Holy Spirit. In Acts 2:38, "Peter said unto them, Repent, and be baptized every one of you in the name of Jesus Christ for the remission of sins, and ye shall receive the gift of the Holy Ghost."

Holy Spirit-led faith *is a process of development, and is truly powerful and is not moved by circumstance.* As your *faith is developed,* it becomes a Christ-like faith. It is this growth FROM human faith TO the faith of Christ that Paul referred to when he said, "For therein is the righteousness of God revealed from faith to faith: as it is written, the just shall live by faith" (Romans 1:17).

The Christ kind of faith is faithfulness to the relationship with God that is profoundly transformative. If we are, intentionally and consciously, seeking a deepening relationship and intimacy with God—which means, very simply, seeking and making God first, study, worship, prayer with thanksgiving, obedience to the living Word, confession, and reminding ourselves of the reality of God in our daily lives—if we are faithful to that relationship, we will be led in the Spirit. "For if ye live after the flesh, ye shall die: but if ye through the Spirit do mortify the deeds of the body, ye shall live. For as many as are led by the Spirit of God, they are the sons of God" (Romans 8:13–14).

The Christ kind of faith is not moved by what the circumstance is or by what may be seen, or is not seen, in the physical it is only moved by the WORD of God. This is how you resolve peace in knowing that no matter what, you will be okay. "Thou wilt keep him in perfect peace, whose mind is stayed on thee: because he trusteth in thee" (Isaiah 26:3). The Holy Spirit kind of faith operates in the principles of kingdom authority.

"Unto you it is given to know the mysteries of the kingdom of God" (Luke 8:10):

A sower went out to sow his seed: and as he sowed, some fell by the way side; and it was trodden down, and the fowls of the air devoured it. And some fell upon a rock; and as soon as it was sprung up, it withered away, because it lacked mois-ture. And some fell among thorns; and the thorns sprang up with it, and choked it. And other fell on good ground, and sprang up, and bare fruit an hundredfold. And when he had said these things, he cried, He that hath ears to hear, let him hear. (Luke 8:5–8)

What does this mean? The answer:

Now the parable is this: The seed is the word of God. Those by the way side are they that hear; then cometh the devil, and taketh away the word out of their hearts, lest they should believe and be saved. They on the rock are they, which, when they hear, receive the word with joy; and these have no root, which for a while believe, and in time of temptation fall away. And that which fell among thorns are they, which, when they have heard, go forth, and are choked with cares and riches and pleasures of this life, and bring no fruit to perfection. But that on the good ground are they, which in an honest and good heart, having heard the word, keep it, and bring forth fruit with patience (Luke 8:11–15).

"While the earth remaineth, seedtime and harvest...shall not cease" (Genesis 8:22). Our entire planet operates in "seed" form and every seed reproduces after its own kind. As we see in Genesis 1:12, "the earth brought forth grass, and herb yielding seed after his kind, and the tree yielding fruit, whose seed was in itself, after his kind." God told Abraham in Genesis 13:16, "I will make thy seed as the dust of the earth: so that if a man can number the dust of the earth, then shall thy seed also be numbered."

A seed is the germ or propagative source of anything. Seeds are planted or deposited either in the ground, in the womb, in your spirit or in your thoughts. The planted seed germinates. In order, for a seed to reproduce when it germinates it is nurtured from the source that gives it life, it then grows; and, "To every thing there is a season, and a time to every purpose under the heaven" (Ecclesiastes 3:1). And then, it gives birth to a manifestation or a result of the seed.

> For a good tree bringeth not forth corrupt fruit; neither doth a corrupt tree bring forth good fruit. For every tree is known by his own fruit … A good man out of the good treasure of his heart bringeth forth that which is good; and an evil man out of the evil treasure of his heart bringeth forth that which is evil: for of the abundance of the heart his mouth speaketh. (Luke 6:43–45)

The way a seed reproduces in the natural realm is symbolic of the way God's Word and faith operates in the spiritual realm and manifests, in our lives. The Word of God is the seed that produces faith; it is our spiritual food and nutrition. As Matthew 4:4 illustrates, Jesus said, "It is written, Man shall not live by bread alone, but by every word that proceedeth out of the mouth of God." "Being born again, not of corruptible seed, but of incorruptible, by the word of God, which liveth and abideth for ever. For all flesh is as grass, and all the glory of man as the flower of grass. The grass withereth, and the flower thereof falleth away: But the word of the Lord endureth for ever. And this is the word which by the gospel is preached unto you" (1 Peter 1:23-25).

Faith encompasses various functions to complete its creative manifestation. It is predicated on what you *hear*, how you *think*, your *belief*, what you *do* and what you *say*, your connection with *the Holy Spirit*, your *relationship* with *Christ* Jesus and *patience*.

God has ordained words to have influence and power over our life. Our life circumstances are influenced by the words that we speak; the natural man calls this affirmation; Scripture calls it confession. Speaking acts as a form of confessing, (declaring or admitting a thing as being true), "for with the heart man believeth unto righteousness; and with the mouth confession is made unto salvation" (Romans 10:10).

187

Faith also involves claiming and confessing specific promises made by God relative to your situation in correlation to what you are praying for. No promise of God can be claimed unless you have learned what the promise is. For, "The word is nigh thee, even in thy mouth, and in thy heart: that is, the word of faith, which we preach" (Romans 10:8).

When your faith is challenged, speak the Word of God over your circumstance. The power and the Spirit of God's Word are released when spoken. This is why Christ said, "It is the spirit that quickeneth; the flesh profiteth nothing: the words that I speak unto you, they are spirit, and they are life" (John 6:63).

What you *believe* and what you *say* go together. "We having the same spirit of faith, according as it is written, I believed, and therefore have I spoken; we also believe, and therefore speak" (2 Corinthians 4:13).

Living faith must be nurtured, spiritually fed, and developed; "So then faith cometh by hearing, and hearing by the word of God" (Romans 10:17). This is why hearers become believers and believers become receivers. "Take heed what ye hear: with what measure ye mete, it shall be measured to you: and unto you that hear shall more be given" (Mark 4:24). Hearing the ministry of the Word of God and being obedient to the Word of God develops faith; as noted in Acts 6:7, "the word of God increased; and the number of the disciples multiplied in Jerusalem greatly; and a great company of the priests were obedient to the faith."

Therefore, we know faith cometh by hearing and hearing by the Word of God; and Christ-like faith cometh from hearing and *hearing a Word (from) God*. Throughout Scripture, holy men and the prophets were sensitive to the voice of the Holy Spirit. After *hearing the voice from the Holy Spirit*, they acted in obedience to the Holy Spirit. This is the source of your power and true impartation of hearing and hearing by the Word of God.

The gift of wisdom involves having a sense of divine direction, being led by the Holy Spirit to act appropriately in a given set of circumstances, understanding of circumstances, situations, problems, or a body of facts by revelation and rightly applying knowledge; whereas, "ye have an unction from the Holy One, and ye know all things" (1John 2:20).

We are instructed in Matthew 6:33, "to first seek the kingdom of God and his righteousness; and all these things shall be added unto you." This is seeking the will of God, to hear from God, and then in obedience, to be led in the Spirit of God as Galatians 5:25 states, "If we live in the Spirit, let us also walk in the Spirit."

God calls for us to *believe* and *trust* Him—to know, beyond all doubt, with complete conviction, confidence, and assurance in Him that you are an integral, divine aspect and channel of expression of Him, to co-effect by and through Him; prayer executes this manifestation.

Prayer is an act of faith. Faith is predicated in our divine ability to manifest our prayers based on our beliefs, our trust, and confidence in God's promises in the physical realm. Throughout Scripture Christ states consistently, "your faith has made you whole." We also see throughout Scripture that the Son of God tells us to, "speak to the mountain, not to doubt, and calls us to believe." This pretense shifts the responsibility to us. Some would say how audacious to think that we have this authority and power, we do not in and of ourselves, but the power of God in us, does! "Know ye not that ye are the temple of God, and that the Spirit of God dwelleth in you" (1 Corinthians 3:16).

We must do our part in order for God to do His part as illustrated in Ephesians 3:20, "Now unto him that is able to do exceeding abundantly above all that we ask or think, according to the power that worketh in us." The *"power that worketh in us"* is our responsibility to believe, to act in obedience, and to trust God based on His Word.

Interestingly, the opposite of faith as trust is doubt, fear, unbelief, worry, and anxiety. Jesus stated that worry accomplishes nothing. "Which of you by taking thought can add one cubit unto his stature" (Matthew 6:27)?

So the degree of how much faith as trust there is in your life, is how much anxiety and worry there is in your life. "And he that doubteth is damned if he eat, because he eateth not of faith: for whatsoever is not of faith is sin" (Romans 14:23).

Human undeveloped faith waivers continually and goes up and down according to how one feels at any given moment in time. This does not mean, however, we cannot give thought to a doubt or ponder, but it does mean that we should seek God and His wisdom, and pray when tempted with doubt, worry, or fear. Replace the thoughts of doubt with what Scripture promises, resolve a plan of action, apply the appropriate course of action, and then execute patience. Because you may battle thoughts of doubt or fear, does not mean that you have to possess or own the thoughts. The degree of our faith determines how we perceive a thing and how we react to a thing.

Christ-like faith is permanent and does not waiver. God requires that all who come to Him in prayer with requests do "not waiver." He considers all who waiver to be unstable in everything they do, and says that they will receive nothing from Him. According to James 1:5–8, "If any of you lack wisdom, let him ask of God, that giveth to all men liberally, and upbraideth not; and it shall be given him. But let him ask in faith, nothing wavering. For he that wavereth is like a wave of the sea driven with the wind and tossed. For let not that man think that he shall receive any thing of the Lord. A double minded man is unstable in all his ways."

Radical trust in God is what can free us from that self-preoccupation of worry and anxiety that hinders, depresses, oppresses, restricts, limits, and confines our lives. When we become radical with our faith, our results will be radical. For, "He shall cover thee with his feathers, and under his wings shalt thou trust: his truth shall be thy shield and buckler" (Psalm 91:4). "There is no respect of persons with God" (Romans 2:11) *but God is a respecter of faith.*

It is our responsibility to be faithful. It should be a lifestyle for us as stewards on Earth to be faithful. "Moreover it is required in stewards, that a man be found faithful" (1 Corinthians 4:2) and to that end, "A faithful man shall abound with blessings" (Proverbs 28:20).

God works in and through us according to our faith. "Unto him that is able to do exceeding abundantly above all that we ask or think, according to the power that worketh in us" (Ephesians 3:20); for "the just shall live by faith: but if any man draw back, my soul shall have no pleasure in him" (Hebrews 10:38).

We have to accept the Word of God before we see anything that confirms it, for faith positions our thoughts from the reality of what is seen to the reality of the evidence of the Word of God. Faith empowers us to see and believe in the spiritual realm before we see it in the physical realm, and empowers us to see what you can't see. "What things soever ye desire, when ye pray, believe that ye receive them, and ye shall have them" (Mark 11:24).

When you exercise your faith, all the promises of God are executed, "For all the promises of God in him are yea, and in him Amen" (2 Corinthians 1:20), and what makes them a reality in our life is our faith.

What Is the Purpose of Faith?

To Trust God in Everything—That He Is Your Source

- "But without faith it is impossible to please him; for he that cometh to God must believe that he is, and that he is a rewarder of them that diligently seek him" (Hebrews 11:6).
- "That your faith should not stand in the wisdom of men, but in the power of God" (1 Corinthians 2:5).

Empower You to Fight Sinful Thinking

- "Above all, taking the shield of faith, wherewith ye shall be able to quench all the fiery darts of the wicked" (Ephesians 6:16).
- "And he that doubteth is damned if he eat, because he eateth not of faith: for whatsoever is not of faith is sin" (Romans 14:23).

To Have a Vision—To Hope

- "Where there is no vision, the people perish: but he that keepeth the law, happy is he" (Proverbs 29:18).

- "For we are saved by hope: but hope that is seen is not hope: for what a man seeth, why doth he yet hope for? But if we hope for that we see not, then do we with patience wait for it" (Romans 8:24–25).
- "Rejoicing in hope; patient in tribulation; continuing instant in prayer" (Romans 12:12).

To Be Good Stewards
- "Moreover it is required in stewards, that a man be found faithful" (1 Corinthians 4:2).

The Results of Faith
- "A faithful man shall abound with blessings" (Proverbs 28:20).

How Do You Acquire Faith?
Read, Study, Listen, and Learn about God Daily
- "Study to shew thyself approved unto God, a workman that needeth not to be ashamed, rightly dividing the word of truth" (2 Timothy 2:15).
- "So then faith cometh by hearing, and hearing by the word of God" (Romans 10:17).
- "Take heed what ye hear: with what measure ye mete, it shall be measured to you: and unto you that hear shall more be given" (Mark 4:24).
- "It is written, Man shall not live by bread alone, but by every word that proceedeth out of the mouth of God" (Matthew 4:4).

Listen and Obey the Voice of the Holy Spirit
- "Wherefore (as the Holy Ghost saith, To day if ye will hear his voice)" (Hebrews 3:7).
- "But ye have an unction from the Holy One, and ye know all things" (1 John 2:20).
- "If we live in the Spirit, let us also walk in the Spirit" (Galatians 5:25).

It Is an Inherited Birth Right

- "For I say, through the grace given unto me, to every man that is among you, not to think of himself more highly than he ought to think; but to think soberly, according as God hath dealt to every man the measure of faith" (Romans 12:3).

Believe

- "But the scripture hath concluded all under sin, that the promise by faith of Jesus Christ might be given to them that believe ... For ye are all the children of God by faith in Christ Jesus" (Galatians 3:22–26).
- "He staggered not at the promise of God through unbelief; but was strong in faith, giving glory to God; And being fully persuaded that, what he had promised, he was able also to perform. And therefore it was imputed to him for righteousness. Now it was not written for his sake alone, that it was imputed to him; But for us also, to whom it shall be imputed, if we believe on him that raised up Jesus our Lord from the dead" (Romans 4:20–24).
- "For the promise, that he should be the heir of the world, was not to Abraham, or to his seed, through the law, but through the righteousness of faith. For if they which are of the law be heirs, faith is made void, and the promise made of none effect" (Romans 4:13–14).

Corresponding Actions

- "What doth it profit, my brethren, though a man say he hath faith, and have not works? can faith save him?" (James 2:14)
- "Even so faith, if it hath not works, is dead, being alone" (James 2:17).
- "Ye see then how that by works a man is justified, and not by faith only" (James 2:24).
- "For as the body without the spirit is dead, so faith without works is dead also" (James 2:26).

Trust God

- "Trust in the LORD with all thine heart; and lean not unto thine own understanding. In all thy ways acknowledge him, and he shall direct thy paths" (Proverbs 3:5–6).
- "For whatsoever is born of God overcometh the world: and this is the victory that overcometh the world, even our faith" (1 John 5:4).

How Do You Stay Faithful?

Jesus

- "Looking unto Jesus the author and finisher of our faith" (Hebrews 12:2).

The Holy Spirit

- "Now the God of hope fill you with all joy and peace in believing, that ye may abound in hope, through the power of the Holy Ghost" (Romans 15:13).
- "For we through the Spirit wait for the hope of righteousness by faith" (Galatians 5:5).

Righteous Thinking

- "Let this mind be in you, which was also in Christ Jesus" (Philippians 2:5).
- "And be not conformed to this world: but be ye transformed by the renewing of your mind, that ye may prove what is that good, and acceptable, and perfect, will of God" (Romans 12:2).
- "For to be carnally minded is death; but to be spiritually minded is life and peace" (Romans 8:6).
- "For therein is the righteousness of God revealed from faith to faith: as it is written, The just shall live by faith" (Romans 1:17).

Do Not Doubt (Guard Your Thoughts)

- "For though we walk in the flesh, we do not war after the flesh: (For the weapons of our warfare are not carnal, but mighty through God to the pulling down of strong holds;) Casting down imaginations, and every high thing that exalteth itself against the knowledge of God, and bringing into captivity every thought to the obedience of Christ" (2 Corinthians 10:3–5).

- "And he that doubteth is damned if he eat, because he eateth not of faith: for whatsoever is not of faith is sin" (Romans 14:23).

Believe and Trust God

- "That your faith should not stand in the wisdom of men, but in the power of God" (1 Corinthians 2:5).
- "And all things, whatsoever ye shall ask in prayer, believing, ye shall receive" (Matthew 21:22).
- "Have faith in God" (Mark 11:22).
- "It is better to trust in the LORD than to put confidence in man. It is better to trust in the LORD than to put confidence in princes" (Psalm 118:8-9).

Believing and Speaking in Faith

- "We having the same spirit of faith, according as it is written, I believed, and therefore have I spoken; we also believe, and therefore speak" (2 Corinthians 4:13).
- "Then came the disciples to Jesus apart, and said, Why could not we cast him out? And Jesus said unto them, Because of your unbelief: for verily I say unto you, If ye have faith as a grain of mustard seed, ye shall say unto this mountain, Remove hence to yonder place; and it shall remove; and nothing shall be impossible unto you" (Matthew 17:19–20).
- "The word is nigh thee, even in thy mouth, and in thy heart: that is, the word of faith, which we preach" (Romans 10:8).
- "He that keepeth his mouth keepeth his life: but he that openeth wide his lips shall have destruction" (Proverbs 13:3).
- "And call those things which be not as though they were" (Romans 4:17).

Hope

- "For we are saved by hope: but hope that is seen is not hope: for what a man seeth, why doth he yet hope for? But if we hope for that we see not, then do we with patience wait for it" (Romans 8:24–25).
- "Rejoicing in hope; patient in tribulation; continuing instant in prayer" (Romans 12:12).

Patience

- "Knowing this, that the trying of your faith worketh patience. But let patience have her perfect work, that ye may be perfect and entire, wanting nothing" (James 1:3–4).
- "Therefore being justified by faith, we have peace with God through our Lord Jesus Christ: By whom also we have access by faith into this grace wherein we stand, and rejoice in hope of the glory of God. And not only so, but we glory in tribulations also: knowing that tribulation worketh patience; And patience, experience; and experience, hope: And hope maketh not ashamed; because the love of God is shed abroad in our hearts by the Holy Ghost which is given unto us" (Romans 5:1–5).
- "Cast not away therefore your confidence, which hath great recompence of reward. For ye have need of patience, that, after ye have done the will of God, ye might receive the promise" (Hebrews 10:35–36).
- "That ye be not slothful, but followers of them who through faith and patience inherit the promises" (Hebrews 6:12).

Biblical Meditation

- "Thou wilt keep him in perfect peace, whose mind is stayed on thee: because he trusteth in thee. Trust ye in the LORD for ever: for in the LORD JEHOVAH is everlasting strength" (Isaiah 26:3–4).
- "My son, attend to my words; incline thine ear unto my sayings. Let them not depart from thine eyes; keep them in the midst of thine heart. For they are life unto those that find them, and health to all their flesh. Keep thy heart with

all diligence; for out of it are the issues of life" (Proverbs 4:20-23).

- "Meditate on these things; give yourself entirely to them, that your progress may be evident to all. Take heed to yourself and to the doctrine. Continue in them, for in doing this you will save both yourself and those who hear you" (1 Timothy 4:15-16).

Be Unwavering—Steadfast

- "Fight the good fight of faith, lay hold on eternal life, whereunto thou art also called, and hast professed a good profession before many witnesses" (1 Timothy 6:12).
- "Humble yourselves therefore under the mighty hand of God, that he may exalt you in due time: Casting all your care upon him; for he careth for you. Be sober, be vigilant; because your adversary the devil, as a roaring lion, walketh about, seeking whom he may devour: Whom resist stedfast in the faith, knowing that the same afflictions are accomplished in your brethren that are in the world. But the God of all grace, who hath called us unto his eternal glory by Christ Jesus, after that ye have suffered a while, make you perfect, stablish, strengthen, settle you" (1 Peter 5:6–10).
- "Let us hold fast the profession of our faith without wavering; (for he is faithful that promised)" (Hebrews 10:23).

Staying in the Word (Scripture)

- "But be ye doers of the word, and not hearers only, deceiving your own selves" (James 1:22).
- "The sower soweth the word" (Mark 4:14).
- "It is written, Man shall not live by bread alone, but by every word that proceedeth out of the mouth of God" (Matthew 4:4).
- "So then faith cometh by hearing, and hearing by the word of God" (Romans 10:17).

Praying

- "And the Lord said, Simon, Simon, behold, Satan hath desired to have you, that he may sift you as wheat But I have prayed for thee, that thy faith fail not and when thou art converted, strengthen thy brethren" (Luke 22:31–32).

Lifestyle

- "Now the just shall live by faith: but if any man draw back, my soul shall have no pleasure in him" (Hebrews 10:38).
- "But that no man is justified by the law in the sight of God, it is evident: for, The just shall live by faith. And the law is not of faith: but, The man that doeth them shall live in them" (Galatians 3:11–12).
- "For therein is the righteousness of God revealed from faith to faith: as it is written, The just shall live by faith" (Romans 1:17).
- "A faithful man shall abound with blessings" (Proverbs 28:20).
- "Moreover it is required in stewards, that a man be found faithful" (1 Corinthians 4:2).

CHAPTER 8

Summary–Developing Your Faith

"So then faith cometh by hearing, and hearing by the word of God" (Romans 10:17). "But that no man is justified by the law in the sight of God, it is evident: for, The just shall live by faith. And the law is not of faith: but, The man that doeth them shall live in them" (Galatians 3:11–12).

Prayer is an action of faith. In order for prayer to work, to be effective, to be powerful, and to get results, you must be *Faithful* … God will not do it alone. He has given us knowledge of kingdom authority, spiritual keys (principles), wisdom and power through the Holy Spirit, and the authority in the name of Jesus Christ. The living Word teaches us to, "Be not conformed to this world: but be ye transformed by the renewing of your mind…and to think soberly, according as God hath dealt to every man the measure of faith" (Romans 12:2, 3); and "That your faith should not stand in the wisdom of men, but in the power of God" (1 Corinthians 2:5).

It is a common postulate that prayers change God. However, prayers do not change God, God always remains the same. The Word of God tells us that there is no variation of change in Him, for "Every good gift and every perfect gift is from above, and cometh down from the Father of lights, with whom is no variableness, neither shadow of turning" (James 1:17). The truth is, God has already moved on our behalf by the promises conveyed in Scripture that are avilable to us, by faith.

Circumstances, however, can change and prayer has been given to us to accomplish the changes in circumstances. It is our faith, spiritual gifts, and the glory of God, that bring those things that have already been accomplished in the spiritual realm to manifest them in the natural realm.

"Now faith is the substance of things hoped for, the evidence of things not seen" (Hebrews 11:1). *Since the subject matter of thought* (the way you think, in other words, your thoughts) should be predicated on hearing from God, which is the *substance* of things hoped for, then it is apparent to say that our faith is our divine creative ability and a key factor to obtain results in any aspect of prayer. For "**the law is not of faith**: but, **The man that doeth them shall live in them**" (Galatians 3:12, emphasis added).

You will never experience God beyond your level of expectations and your level of belief. It is so principled that Hebrews 11:6 states, "But without faith it is impossible to please him; for he that cometh to God must believe that he is, and that he is a rewarder of them that diligently seek him."

"For by grace are ye saved through faith" (Ephesians 2:8). There is a balance of grace and faith; we are saved by the combination of the two! Grace is God's part and FAITH is our part.

Grace is what God has provided for us, independent of us. However, grace alone does not save you unless there is the response of faith, trust, and confidence on our part to believe and receive it. There is a responsibility on our part to walk in the provision of what has already been given in the promises' of God. Faith appropriates what God has already done. "God is able to make all grace abound toward you; that ye, always having all sufficiency in all things, may abound to every good work" (2 Corinthians 9:8).

Your faith is a positive response to what God has provided by grace. We release the power of the promises by the "renewing of our minds" by believing, speaking and cooperating with the Word of God. All we need is a *renewed mind* to BELIEVE, and the Holy Spirit to ignite the indwelling power that resides and dwells within us.

2 Peter 1:3-4 makes this clear as stated, "According as his divine power hath given unto us all things that pertain unto life and godliness, through the knowledge of him that hath called us to glory and virtue: Whereby are given unto us exceeding great and precious promises: that by these ye might be partakers of the divine nature." "Blessed be the God and Father of our Lord Jesus Christ, who hath blessed us with all spiritual blessings in heavenly places in Christ" (Ephesians 1:3).

There are things you can do to release the power of God and things you can do to block the power of God. Fear, worry, doubt, unbelief and undeveloped faith are the contradictions of faith, which will sabotage your prayers. The results of these contradictions are:

- "Hast thou faith? have it to thyself before God. Happy is he that condemneth not himself in that thing which he alloweth. And he that doubteth is damned if he eat, because he eateth not of faith: for whatsoever is not of faith is sin" (Romans 14:22–23).
- "Now the just shall live by faith: but if any man draw back, my soul shall have no pleasure in him" (Hebrews 10:38).

We are to seek God for spiritual wisdom, engage and execute the Word, execute corresponding actions, and then trust God to do what we can't do. God works in and through us according to our faith. "Now unto him that is able to do exceeding abundantly above all that we ask or think, **according to the power that worketh in us**" (Ephesians 3:20, emphasis added).

(The power that worketh in us)—IS YOUR CONNECTION TO THE HOLY SPIRIT—YOUR OBEDIENCE TO THE WORD OF

GOD—YOUR RELATIONSHIP WITH CHRIST JESUS—YOUR LOVE WALK-YOUR FAITH—YOUR BELIEF—THE WAY YOU THINK, WHAT YOU SAY, AND WHAT YOU DO!

Faith is predicated in our innate ability to manifest our prayers *based on our beliefs, our trust,* and *our confidence in God's promises* in the physical realm. Christ tells us in Matthew 21:22, emphasis added, "And all things, whatsoever ye shall ask **in prayer, believing, ye shall receive.**"

Faith is active, which requires the execution of correct thinking and corresponding actions. The *works of faith* are prayer with belief, hope, trust, confidence, expectation, action, and patience. Without these principles and corresponding actions, your faith is powerless and without results—or perhaps not the results that you want. Scripture states, "What doth it profit, my brethren, though a man say he hath faith, and have not works? can faith save him?" (James 2:14)

Faith with works is our participation and our responsibility in the manifestation of effective prayer for results. "Ye see then how that by works a man is justified, and not by faith only" (James 2:24).

The following are key principles to develop your faith:
Your connection to the Holy Spirit is an awareness and sensitivity to the presence of the Holy Spirit. Hearing the voice of the Holy Spirit is an impartation of instruction on what to say or guidance on what to do. "Howbeit when he, the Spirit of truth, is come, he will guide you into all truth: for he shall not speak of himself; but whatsoever he shall hear, that shall he speak: and he will shew you things to come" (John 16:13).

We know faith cometh by hearing and hearing by the Word of God; and Christ-like faith cometh from hearing and hearing a Word (from) God. This is the source of your power and true impartation from the Holy Spirit. Jesus also operated within these principles and lived this lifestyle as he stated in John 5:30, "I can of mine own self do nothing: as I hear, I judge: and my judgment is just; because I seek not mine own will, but the will of the Father which hath sent me."

The power of and the relationship with the Father are not reserved for Jesus only, but for all who receive the gift of the Holy Spirit and are obedient; and "we are his witnesses of these things; and so is also the Holy Ghost, whom God hath given to them that obey him" (Acts 5:32). Peter is recorded telling the Jews and the Gentiles in Acts 2:38-39, "Repent, and be baptized every one of you in the name of Jesus Christ for the remission of sins, and ye shall receive the gift of the Holy Ghost. For the promise is unto you, and to your children, and to all that are afar off, even as many as the LORD our God shall call."

"Spoken by the prophet Joel; And it shall come to pass in the last days, saith God, I will pour out of my Spirit upon all flesh: and your sons and your daughters shall prophesy, and your young men shall see visions, and your old men shall dream dreams" (Acts 2:16-17).

Nothing is more invincible than a conscience that acknowledges the sovereignty of the Holy Spirit. "Ye shall receive power, after that the Holy Ghost is come upon you" (Acts 1:8).

- "If we live in the Spirit, let us also walk in the Spirit" (Galatians 5:25).
- "Know ye not that ye are the temple of God, and that the Spirit of God dwelleth in you" (1 Corinthians 3:16).

Your faith is part of a process in development operating within the universal law of God's laws that is impartial and impersonal. This is why Galatians 3:11–12 states, "But that no man is justified by the law in the sight of God, it is evident: for, The just shall live by faith. And the law is not of faith: but, The man that doeth them shall live in them."

God has woven this law into the very fabric of our life. It is a built in judgment of either curses or blessings. For if there is no belief, there are no results. If you sow unbelief, you will reap unbelief. "Be not deceived; God is not mocked: for whatsoever a man soweth, that shall he also reap" (Galatians 6:7).

The key principle in the following Scriptures is that *their faith in the power of Christ* made them whole:

> "And, behold, a woman, which was diseased with an issue of blood twelve years, came behind him, and touched the hem of his garment: For she said within herself, If I may but touch his garment, I shall be whole. But Jesus turned him about, and when he saw her, he said, Daughter, be of good comfort; thy faith hath made thee whole. And the woman was made whole from that hour" (Matthew 9:20–22).

> "And his name through faith in his name hath made this man strong" (Acts 3:16).

Your thinking is key. Whatever you focus on long enough will bring an effect. Your actions and your thoughts create reactions. Scripture teaches us what we should think about, and how to guard our thoughts to counteract negative thinking.

- "And be renewed in the spirit of your mind; And that ye put on the new man, which after God is created in righteousness and true holiness" (Ephesians 4:23–24).
- "Casting down imaginations, and every high thing that exalteth itself against the knowledge of God, and bringing into captivity every thought to the obedience of Christ" (2 Corinthians 10:5).

Your attitude is a culmination of your thinking and your beliefs. Your attitude reflects your disposition resulting from what you think and the corresponding actions and reactions to what you think. Proverbs 4:20-23 instructs us to, "attend to my words; incline thine ear unto my sayings. Let them not depart from thine eyes; keep them in the midst of thine heart. For they are life unto those that find them, and health to all their flesh. Keep thy heart with all diligence; for out of it are the issues of life."

Your belief is your power and conviction in faith. Believe your prayers will be answered, as Christ stated, "If thou canst believe, all things are possible to him that believeth" (Mark 9:23). A key principle in faith is to pray according to Mark 11:24, "What things soever ye desire, when ye pray, believe that ye receive them, and ye shall have them."

Trust and belief in and of itself incorporates confidence. Your confidence empowers you to be compensated. "Cast not away therefore your confidence, which hath great recompence of reward. For ye have need of patience, that, after ye have done the will of God, ye might receive the promise" (Hebrews 10:35–36).

"And when he was come into the house, the blind men came to him: and Jesus saith unto them, Believe ye that I am able to do this? They said unto him, Yea, Lord. Then touched he their eyes, saying, According to your faith be it unto you" (Matthew 9:28–29).

"It is better to trust in the LORD than to put confidence in man. It is better to trust in the LORD than to put confidence in princes" (Psalm 118:8-9).

Your faith must stand firm in the Word of God, for the Word of God is forever settled and it never changes. Luke 21:33 declares, "Heaven and earth shall pass away: but my words shall not pass away."

Faith is not being irresponsible or ignoring the condition or the situation; however, it is acknowledging and aligning the condition or the situation in agreement with God's Word of truths, percepts, and promises.

Your trust in God is an inner conviction in God's Word and promises. Scriptures tells us in Isaiah 12:2, "God is my salvation; I will trust, and not be afraid: for the LORD JEHOVAH is my strength and my song; he also is become my salvation." Jeremiah 17:7, "Blessed is the man that trusteth in the LORD, and whose hope the LORD is."

Remember that when you trust someone, you don't worry for there is no fear of consequence. Trust implies confidence and assurance; and total confidence comes with a peace of reassurance as reflected in 1 John 4:18-19, "There is no fear in love; but perfect love casteth out fear: because fear hath torment. He that feareth is not made perfect in love. We love him, because he first loved us," "by faith which worketh by love" (Galatians 5:6).

Your expectation is the seed for miracles. If you do not expect anything, what's the point in praying? To expect implies confidently believing and, therefore, anticipating in confidence your requested petition. We are in faith to expect God to answer prayer and thank Him before receiving our petition as illustrated in 1 John 5:14–15, "And this is the confidence that we have in him, that, if we ask any thing according to his will, he heareth us: And if we know that he hear us, whatsoever we ask, we know that we have the petitions that we desired of him."

Your hope is the perquisite for faith. "Where there is no vision, the people perish" (Proverbs 29:18). Hope generates enthusiasm. "For whatsoever things were written aforetime were written for our learning, that we through patience and comfort of the scriptures might have hope" (Romans 15:4). As long as you are still breathing, there is a hope.

Your praise should stem from knowing that as Christians we, "are a chosen generation, a royal priesthood, an holy nation, a peculiar people; that ye should shew forth the praises of him who called you out of darkness into his marvellous light" (1 Peter 2:9). In the most basic sense we can agree with, the Psalmist, David, "I will praise thee; for I am fearfully and wonderfully made: marvellous are thy works; and that my soul knoweth right well" (Psalm 139:14).

Your praise invites God's presence to invade your circumstance and is "the garment of praise for the spirit of heaviness" (Isaiah 61:3). Your praise mixed with faith produces an atmosphere to process the promises of God.

Your patience is a needed attribute for hope, and hope is a perquisite of faith. Patience is a quiet perseverance and endurance demonstrating persistent courage in the face of delay. Once you have prayed, the resolution or the results may not be immediate; however, "we are saved by hope: but hope that is seen is not hope: for what a man seeth, why doth he yet hope for? But if we hope for that we see not, then do we with patience wait for it" (Romans 8:24–25).

- "Knowing this, that the trying of your faith worketh patience" (James 1:3).
- "But that on the good ground are they, which in an honest and good heart, having heard the word, keep it, and bring forth fruit with patience" (Luke 8:15).

Your experience is the knowledge gained from what you have previously gone through, whereas your faith is strengthened by wisdom that is attained through maturity, skilled practices, and wise judgment. There are vital lessons to be learned in adversities, and the most mastered life lessons are how you respond to adversity. As Paul expressed in Philippians 4:11–12, "I have learned, in whatsoever state I am, therewith to be content ... I know both how to be abased, and I know how to abound."

Patience develops strength and character through experience, and this experience helps us to trust God more each time we use it until our hope and faith are strong and consistent.

Therefore being justified by faith, we have peace with God through our Lord Jesus Christ: By whom also we have access by faith into this grace wherein we stand, and rejoice in hope of the glory of God. And not only so, but we glory in tribulations also: knowing that tribulation worketh patience; And patience, experience; and experience, hope: And hope maketh not ashamed; because the love of God is shed abroad in our hearts by the Holy Ghost which is given unto us. (Romans 5:1–5)

Your words have creative power. Remember, God has ordained our words to have power over our life. Our life circumstances are influenced by the words that we speak. The natural man calls this affirmation; Scripture calls it confession. Speaking acts as a form of confessing, (declaring or admitting a thing as being true) "for with the heart man believeth unto righteousness; and with the mouth confession is made unto salvation" (Romans 10:10).

When your faith is challenged, speak the Word of God over your circumstance. What you believe and what you say go together. "We having the same spirit of faith, according as it is written, I believed, and therefore have I spoken; we also believe, and therefore speak" (2 Corinthians 4:13).

Speaking faith involves claiming specific promises made by God relative to your situation in correlation to what you are praying for. No promise of God can be claimed unless you have learned what the promise is. Scripture makes this clear as outlined:

- "For by thy words thou shalt be justified, and by thy words thou shalt be condemned" (Matthew 12:37).
- "Death and life are in the power of the tongue: and they that love it shall eat the fruit thereof" (Proverbs 18:21).
- "The word is nigh thee, even in thy mouth, and in thy heart: that is, the word of faith, which we preach" (Romans 10:8).
- "Out of the same mouth proceedeth blessing and cursing. My brethren, these things ought not so to be" (James 3:10).
- "He that keepeth his mouth keepeth his life: but he that openeth wide his lips shall have destruction" (Proverbs 13:3).
- "And Jesus answering saith unto them, Have faith in God. For verily I say unto you, That whosoever shall say unto this mountain, Be thou removed, and be thou cast into the sea; and shall not doubt in his heart, but shall believe that those things which he saith shall come to pass; he shall have whatsoever he saith" (Mark 11:22–23).

The (spiritual) laws of faith that work in the unseen supersede the physical, for they are the results of the unseen that manifest in the physical. "While we look not at the things which are seen, but at the things which are not seen: for the things which are seen are temporal; but the things which are not seen are eternal" (2 Corinthians 4:18). For just as there are physical laws of the universe, there are spiritual laws, as well. Some may equate this level of faith with the (laws of attraction). That may be debatable; however, there is a level of divine order of law working within this principle. These principles are operating in one form or another relative to faith (the matter of thought): Belief, Hope, Victory (the positive), or Fear, Worry, Doubt, Hopelessness, Unbelief ... (the negative).

Faith Is of God
"For God hath not given us the spirit of fear; but of power, and of love, and of a sound mind" (2 Timothy 1:7).

"Fear not, little flock; for it is your Father's good pleasure to give you the kingdom" (Luke 12:32).

Fear Is of the Adversary, the Devil
The devil cannot attack you physically; the attack is against your beliefs, your faith, your thoughts, and your hope. "Your adversary the devil, as a roaring lion, walketh about, seeking whom he may devour" (1 Peter 5:8). "For though we walk in the flesh, we do not war after the flesh: (For the weapons of our warfare are not carnal, but mighty through God to the pulling down of strong holds;) Casting down imaginations, and every high thing that exalteth itself against the knowledge of God, and bringing into captivity every thought to the obedience of Christ" (2 Corinthians 10:3–5).

Christ teaches us, "These things I have spoken unto you, that in me ye might have peace. In the world ye shall have tribulation: but be of good cheer; I have overcome the world" (John 16:33).

Worry is the inner fear that it will not work out and expectation is the inner confidence and trust that it will. Remain faithful, refuse to submit to worry, doubt, and fear; for in doing so, you have sabotaged and forfeited your power of belief in the principle thing that you are praying for. Do not yield to despair and hopelessness.

Kingdom Principles: "When any one heareth the word of the kingdom, and **understandeth it not,** then cometh the wicked one, and catcheth away that which was sown in his heart. This is he which received seed by the way side. But he that received the seed into stony places, the same is he that heareth the word, and anon with joy receiveth it; Yet hath he not root in himself, but dureth for a while: for when tribulation or persecution ariseth because of the word, by and by he is offended. He also that received seed among the thorns is he that heareth the word; and the care of this world, and the deceitfulness of riches, choke the word, and he becometh unfruitful.

But he that received seed into the good ground is he that **heareth the word, and understandeth it;** which also beareth fruit, and bringeth forth, some an hundredfold, some sixty, some thirty" (Matthew 13:19–23).

> "Every kingdom divided against itself is brought to desolation; and a house divided against a house falleth" (Luke 11:17).

Your Weapons of Warfare in Faith

If you do not know about your salvation, just being saved is not enough. The armor that we are to put on is the armor of the Spirit of truth, understanding of biblical knowledge, and spiritual wisdom. These truths consist of, righteousness, the gospel of peace, faith, salvation, the Word of God, intimacy with the Father, and praying in the Spirit.

- "Put on the whole armour of God, that ye may be able to stand against the wiles of the devil...Above all, taking the shield of faith, wherewith ye shall be able to quench all the fiery darts of the wicked. And take the helmet of salvation, and the sword of the Spirit, which is the word of God: Praying always with all prayer and supplication in the Spirit" (Ephesians 6:11,16-18).

- "Fight the good fight of faith" (1 Timothy 6:12).
- "Knowing this, that the trying of your faith worketh patience. But let patience have her perfect work, that ye may be perfect and entire, wanting nothing" (James 1:3–4).
- "The garment of praise for the spirit of heaviness" (Isaiah 61:3).
- "For the joy of the LORD is your strength" (Nehemiah 8:10).
- "God is our refuge and strength, a very present help in trouble" (Psalm 46:1).
- "Casting all your care upon him; for he careth for you" (1 Peter 5:7).
- "Thy words were found, and I did eat them; and thy word was unto me the joy and rejoicing of mine heart" (Jeremiah 15:16).
- "Prayer and fasting" (Matthew 17:21).

Your power is "The Kingdom of God within you." Recall, the Greek word for kingdom is *basileia* meaning, "royal power, kingship, dominion, and rule." *Basileia* is "not to be confused with an actual kingdom but rather the right or authority to rule over kingdom-of the royal power of Jesus...and of the royal power and dignity conferred on Christians in the Messiah's kingdom."

Your commitment to action requires taking responsibility for your choices, your actions, and your thoughts. Faith is an active belief, which requires tangible execution of exerting belief, correct thinking, hope, confidence, expectation, and trust in God. An example of "faith without works" is that you pray that you will receive good grades in school; however, you do not take any action to study (deposit the seed of knowledge) or do the required work. So it is with faith, faith must be accompanied with executable action on our part.

Knowing of knowledge does not entitle you to its rewards; you must apply, exercise, and commit to the principles to reap the results. Knowing is easy, but placing those beliefs into execution requires discipline, commitment, and strength. "Be ye doers of the word, and not hearers only, deceiving your own selves" (James 1:22) and "the sower soweth the word" (Mark 4:14).

Your revelation knows that you know that you know. Revelation means an unveiling of something that was once hidden, a disclosure or a realization that is not possible by our own natural minds. It implies the power of spiritual insight. Your revelation awakens your realization that you not only have knowledge of, but you're living it and demonstrating it with tangible results. To aid in this revelation, "gird up the loins of your mind, be sober, and hope to the end for the grace that is to be brought unto you at the revelation of Jesus Christ" (1 Peter 1:13).

Your development of faith is a process of your lifestyle, and it is achieved through your experience. It is further developed, as we grow closer and more aware of God's presence in our lives, as God is our Source and our Sustainer. The development of your faith will determine whether you have some faith, little faith, great faith, or Christ-like faith. To accomplish this, we must follow the examples set forth by Christ Jesus ... "Looking unto Jesus the author and finisher of our faith" (Hebrews 12:2). As your faith is developed, it becomes a Christ-like faith.

The Word of God is the seed that produces faith. In listening to ministry, your faith is strengthened and you are uplifted and encouraged. You feed your faith and starve your doubt. Hearers become believers, and believers, receivers. "Take heed what ye hear: with what measure ye mete, it shall be measured to you: and unto you that hear shall more be given" (Mark 4:24).

Recalling Scripture grounds and roots you to God's promises. Jesus said, "If ye abide in me, and my words abide in you, ye shall ask what ye will, and it shall be done unto you" (John 15:7).

We are not independent from God. "For in him we live, and move, and have our being" (Acts 17:28) and, "Not that we are sufficient of ourselves to think any thing as of ourselves; but our sufficiency is of God" (2 Corinthians 3:5).

Live a lifestyle of faith ..."For we walk by faith, and not by sight" (2 Corinthians 5:7). Faith is a mind-set of living in kingdom principles. The degree of our faith determines how we perceive a thing and how we react to a thing. Faith is not looking at the difficulties in life through the limitations of your human abilities, but to look at life and its challenges through God's ability and power to work through you. Faith is a diligence to duty of commitment of being tried and proven in standing on God's principles, truths, Word, and promises.

We are stewards on Earth with divine authority, as Scripture states in Hebrews 2:6–8, "But one in a certain place testified, saying, What is man, that thou art mindful of him? or the son of man that thou visitest him? Thou madest him a little lower than the angels; thou crownedst him with glory and honour, and didst set him over the works of thy hands: Thou hast put all things in subjection under his feet. For in that he put all in subjection under him, he left nothing that is not put under him."

As stewards we have been commissioned as our responsibility in 1 Corinthians 4:2 states, "it is required in stewards, that a man be found faithful"; and to that end, "A faithful man shall abound with blessings" (Proverbs 28:20). "For whatsoever is born of God overcometh the world: and this is the victory that overcometh the world, even our faith" (1 John 5:4).

The Word of God is powerful ... Scripture declares of God's thoughts, "For My thoughts are not your thoughts, Neither are your ways My ways," declares the LORD. "For as the heavens are higher than the earth, So are My ways higher than your ways, And My thoughts than your thoughts" (Isaiah 55:8–9).

The Scriptures of the Holy Bible outline wisdom, instructions on how to combat the adversary (Satan) and negativism, and how to empower yourself with the positive, the knowledge, the wisdom, and the know-how to overcome in victory.

We are to study Scripture, but for that to be effective, we also need to develop the art of biblical meditation.

To God Be the Glory!

CHAPTER 9

The Power of Biblical Meditation

"My mouth shall speak of wisdom; and the meditation of my heart shall be of understanding" (Psalm 49:3).

What Is Biblical Meditation?

Webster's Dictionary's definition of *meditation*: to think contemplatively, to reflect, to intend to do or achieve; a thinking over; thought.

There are at least seven Hebrew and two Greek words for the word *meditation*. Three of the seven Hebrew meanings are:

- *Hagah*: to murmur (in pleasure or anger), to ponder, imagine, meditate, mourn, mutter, roar, speak, study, talk, utter.
- *Siyach*: to ponder, converse (with oneself, and, hence, aloud), utter, commune, complain, declare, meditate, muse, pray, speak, or talk (with).
- *Siychah*: reflection, devotion, meditation, prayer.

As a generalized practice, meditation is a mental discipline by which one attempts to get beyond the reflexive, "thinking" mind into a deeper state of relaxation or awareness. Different meditative disciplines encompass a wide range of spiritual and psychophysics practices, which may emphasize different goals— from achievement of a higher state of consciousness, to greater focus, creativity, or self-awareness, or simply a more relaxed and peaceful frame of mind.

The biblical perspective of meditation employs the same function, but carries far more weight and purpose. Biblical meditation is the art of reflection in the Word, because meditating on the Word of God incorporates the presence and the works of the Holy Spirit. Biblical meditation begins with methodical reading, and rereading, of the Word and is followed by reflection on what has been read and committed to memory.

The key and most important element in biblical meditation is not just reading or even committing to memory what has been read, which is important; but more importantly, it is BELIEVING what you have read. Anyone may repeat a Scripture, but the source of power is in your belief and your faith of what is being read and what is being said.

Meditation is a process of continually thinking on a particular thought and involves turning your attention to a single point of reference. Scripture states that we should meditate on the things of God, "For to be carnally minded is death; but to be spiritually minded is life and peace" (Romans 8:6).

Biblical meditation does not mean to sit and ponder infinity or to empty the mind so some force can fill it by repeating some chant or mantra; however, meditation in the Bible means reflective thinking on biblical truth so that God is able to speak to us through Scripture and through the Holy Spirit that comes to us as we are reflecting on His Word. With the written Word comes the "Spirit of wisdom," the "spoken Word," or an utterance. This is what is considered as the *rhema* Word, an impartation of instruction on what to say, or guidance on what to do, or revelation in understanding. "You have an unction from the Holy One, and ye know all things" (1 John 2:20).

We all meditate in one form or another, whether consciously or subconsciously, negatively or positively. We may not sit down formally and cross our legs or remain silent in seeking our inner self, but even worry is a form of meditating.

Why Should We Meditate?

One of the reasons for meditating on the Word is to develop and build our faith. We must mix faith with what we read and hear. In other words, we must act and think by faith in what God has shown us from His Word. 1 Timothy 4:13, 15-16 tells us to, "Till I come, give attendance to reading, to exhortation, to doctrine. Meditate on these things; give yourself entirely to them, that your progress may be evident to all. Take heed to yourself and to the doctrine. Continue in them, for in doing this you will save both yourself and those who hear you." "Thou wilt keep him in perfect peace, whose mind is stayed on thee: because he trusteth in thee" (Isaiah 26:3).

The goal of biblical meditation is to internalize and personalize the Scriptures so that their truth can affect how we think, what we say, our attitudes, our actions, and how we live. Psalm 119:15–16 states, "I will meditate in thy precepts, and have respect unto thy ways. I will delight myself in thy statutes: I will not forget thy word."

When we meditate on God's Word, the Holy Spirit is motivated. When the Word of God is read and spoken, we are empowered and affected by the Holy Spirit. Moreover, the Holy Spirit employs the holy Word to work through God's Word to nurture, sustain, empower, and transform our spiritual life. The Word of God is our spiritual food; for "It is written, Man shall not live by bread alone, but by every *word* that proceedeth out of the mouth of God" (Matthew 4:4).

Meditating on the things of God is a process of renewing your mind to think like Christ. "Let this mind be in you, which was also in Christ Jesus" (Philippians 2:5). "And be not conformed to this world: but be ye transformed by the renewing of your mind, that ye may prove what is that good, and acceptable, and perfect, will of God" (Romans 12:2).

It is usually in stillness and quiet time when the Holy Spirit speaks, and the softness of the voice is so soft, that hurriedness, stress, and confusion oftentimes will overshadow the whisper. "Be still, and know that I am God" (Psalm 46:10).

The Word is also the sword of the Spirit that empowers us in spiritual warfare and temptation. Ephesians 6:11,17 tells us to, "Put on the whole armour of God, that ye may be able to stand against the wiles of the devil...And take the helmet of salvation, and the sword of the Spirit, which is the word of God."

Meditating on Scripture enables you to memorize Scripture to counteract contradictions to biblical truths, which is part of the process of, "Casting down imaginations, and every high thing that exalteth itself against the knowledge of God, and bringing into captivity every thought to the obedience of Christ" (2 Corinthians 10:5).

After Jesus was baptized, the Holy Spirit led Him into the wilderness, where He fasted forty days. At the end of His fast, Satan came to Him to tempt Him. Three times Satan tempted Him, and in each case, Jesus quoted to Satan Scripture.

This is the illustration and application of applying the principle of 2 Corinthians 10:5:

"Then was Jesus led up of the Spirit into the wilderness to be tempted of the devil. And when he had fasted forty days and forty nights, he was afterward and hungred. And when the tempter came to him, he said, If thou be the Son of God, command that these stones be made bread. But he answered and said, It is written, Man shall not live by bread alone, but by every word that proceedeth out of the mouth of God. Then the devil taketh him up into the holy city, and setteth him on a pinnacle of the temple, And saith unto him, If thou be the Son of God, cast thyself down: for it is written, He shall give his angels charge concerning thee: and in their hands they shall bear thee up, lest at any time thou dash thy foot against a stone. Jesus said unto him, It is written again, Thou shalt not tempt the Lord thy God.

Again, the devil taketh him up into an exceeding high mountain, and sheweth him all the kingdoms of the world, and the glory of them; And saith unto him, All these things will I give thee, if thou wilt fall down and worship me. Then saith Jesus unto him, Get thee hence, Satan: for it is written, Thou shalt worship the Lord thy God, and him only shalt thou serve. Then the devil leaveth him, and, behold, angels came and ministered unto him" (Matthew 4:1–11).

First, Jesus modeled for us the power of Scripture. Jesus quoted Scripture to rebuke Satan. Second, Jesus had memorized Scripture. To quote it, you need to memorize it; to memorize it, you need to meditate on it. So if Jesus used this method to rebuke the wiles and the deception of the devil and to flee from temptation, shouldn't we? The deception of the devil (Satan) is everything that goes against, and is in contradiction to, God's Word, His truth, principles, and promises.

What Should We Meditate On?

The Bible has outlined specific modalities that we should reflect, think, and meditate on as outlined in Philippians 4:8, "Finally, brethren, whatsoever things are true, whatsoever things are honest, whatsoever things are just, whatsoever things are pure, whatsoever things are lovely, whatsoever things are of good report; if there be any virtue, and if there be any praise, think on these things."

The process of "renewing your mind" by meditating on the Word of God changes your beliefs in alignment with God's Word, and once your beliefs are changed, this changes your attitude; your attitude changes your actions; your actions determine your habits; your habits determine your integrity; and your integrity determines your destiny. Scripture makes it clear, "For as [a person] he thinketh in his heart, so is he" (Proverbs 23:7).

Countless books and theories have been written on positive thinking and more recently, the law of attraction in the book *The Secret*. Think positive, for whatever you focus on gets stronger (the law of attraction). There is truth in all of these approaches, and some allude to the Bible, but why not just go straight to the source of our Creator?

There are four components that must go together in biblical meditation: reading, reflecting, revelation, and responding. Biblical wisdom has its foundation in knowledge and understanding, but it moves beyond that to discernment, revelation, and then the resulting action, to "be ye doers of the word, and not hearers only, deceiving your own selves" (James 1:22).

As a practical daily lifestyle, commit Scriptures to memory and in doing so, they will strengthen your faith, reinforce God's promises, and empower your spirit. The process of meditating on God's Word and His promises will bring illumination, and illumination will initiate action. Take responsibility for your role, and then God will do His role.

Manifestation of Biblical Meditation—The Results

- "Blessed is the man that walketh not in the counsel of the ungodly, nor standeth in the way of sinners, nor sitteth in the seat of the scornful, But his delight is in the law of the Lord; and in his law doth he meditate day and night. And he shall be like a tree planted by the rivers of water, that bringeth forth his fruit in his season; his leaf also shall not wither; and whatsoever he doeth shall prosper" (Psalm 1:1–3).
- "This book of the law shall not depart out of thy mouth; but thou shalt meditate therein day and night, that thou mayest observe to do according to all that is written therein: for then thou shalt make thy way prosperous, and then thou shalt have good success" (Joshua 1:8).
- "My son, attend to my words; incline thine ear unto my sayings. Let them not depart from thine eyes; keep them in the midst of thine heart. For they are life unto those that find them, and health to all their flesh. Keep thy heart with all diligence; for out of it are the issues of life" (Proverbs 4:20-23).

- "Meditate on these things; give yourself entirely to them, that your progress may be evident to all. Take heed to yourself and to the doctrine. Continue in them, for in doing this you will save both yourself and those who hear you" (1 Timothy 4:15-16).
- "Thou wilt keep him in perfect peace, whose mind is stayed on thee: because he trusteth in thee" (Isaiah 26:3).
- "The law of the LORD is perfect, converting the soul: the testimony of the LORD is sure, making wise the simple" (Psalm 19:7).
- "I have more understanding than all my teachers, For Your testimonies are my meditation" (Psalm 119:99).
- "The entrance of thy words giveth light; it giveth understanding unto the simple" (Psalm 119:130).

CHAPTER 10

The Power of Miracles

~

"Jesus... saith, With men it is impossible, but not with God: for with God all things are possible" (Mark 10:27).

Miracle as defined in *Random House Dictionary:* an event in the *physical* world that surpasses all known human or natural powers is ascribed to a divine or supernatural cause (a wonder marvel). *Webster's Dictionary*: An event that seems impossible to explain by natural laws and so is regarded as supernatural in origin or as an act of God.

The word miracle is defined in the Greek as *sēmeion*, which is "an unusual occurrence, transcending the common course of nature. A sign, mark, or token by which God authenticates the men sent by him, or by which men prove that the cause they are pleading is God's."

Further defined as miracle is the Greek word *dynamis*, which means "strength, power, ability – power for performing miracles and moral power and excellence of soul."

"The things which are impossible with men are possible with God" (Luke 18:27).

Miracles can be categorized in varying degrees; but one can agree in all instances, that a miracle is the contextually obvious intervention of God against the natural laws that we know of or against the probability of circumstance or chance.

Miracles are always astounding, unexplainable, and unprecedented events not understood, and they defy scientific explanation in the context of rational or perceived understanding. Miracles have been referred to as an event such as the survival of a disaster or escaping a life-threatening situation, survival of a fatal illness, conquering the odds, appearances of the unexplained, visions or sightings, and encounters with angels.

Some might say that miracles fall into the presumption of phenomenon. Others may debate that it is only our inability to have knowledge of the cause and effect working in and outside of the natural laws; but nonetheless, the obvious is that it is a law working within the supernatural order of law; and if that being the case, there is only one supreme source of supernatural power—and that is God.

To one who believes in a personal God, one who is omnipotent, omnipresent, omniscient, and omnificent, miracles are not impossible, nor are they incredible. For, "Jesus ... saith, With men it is impossible, but not with God: for with God all things are possible" (Mark 10:27).

How Are Miracles Manifested?

When a person is the source of origination of a miracle, the question arises, *why* some and not all. It is apparent throughout Scripture those that performed miracles in acts of healing, raising the dead, and casting out demons were men of God, men who were empowered with the Holy Spirit, and men of faith with the power of God working through them. Therefore, it can be affirmed that, "the Kingdom of God within us," incorporated with our faith and our spiritual gifts, along with the Holy Spirit's divine power, is how miracles are manifested.

By God, through the Holy Spirit and by the name of Jesus is the embodiment of God's power anointed on the Christian. Acts

1:8 declares, "But ye shall receive power, after that the Holy Ghost is come upon you." Therefore, the supernatural may be equated to God's "super" on our "natural," which equals the supernatural. Humanity's redemption through spiritual rebirth in Christ, allows us to have dominion and authority in Christ. "Herein is my Father glorified, that ye bear much fruit; so shall ye be my disciples" (John 15:8).

So how are miracles manifested?

Power Given to Believers

- "And now, Lord, behold their threatenings: and grant unto thy servants, that with all boldness they may speak thy word, By stretching forth thine hand to heal; and that signs and wonders may be done by the name of thy holy child Jesus. And when they had prayed, the place was shaken where they were assembled together; and they were all filled with the Holy Ghost, and they spake the word of God with boldness" (Acts 4:29–31).
- "...The Holy Ghost fell on all them which heard the word. And they of the circumcision which believed were astonished, as many as came with Peter, because that on the Gentiles also was poured out the gift of the Holy Ghost. For they heard them speak with tongues, and magnify God. Then answered Peter, Can any man forbid water, that these should not be baptized, which have received the Holy Ghost as well as we" (Acts 10:44-47)?
- "And the seventy returned again with joy, saying, Lord, even the devils are subject unto us through thy name. Behold, I give unto you power to tread on serpents and scorpions, and over all the power of the enemy: and nothing shall by any means hurt you. Notwithstanding in this rejoice not, that the spirits are subject unto you; but rather rejoice, because your names are written in heaven" (Luke 10:17, 19-20).
- "And these signs shall follow them that believe; In my name shall they cast out devils; they shall speak with new tongues; They shall take up serpents; and if they drink any

deadly thing, it shall not hurt them; they shall lay hands on the sick, and they shall recover" (Mark 16:17–18).

- "And John answered him, saying, Master, we saw one casting out devils in thy name, and he followeth not us: and we forbad him, because he followeth not us. But Jesus said, Forbid him not: for there is no man which shall do a miracle in my name, that can lightly speak evil of me" (Mark 9:38–39).

- "He that believeth on me, the works that I do shall he do also; and greater works than these shall he do; because I go unto my Father. And whatsoever ye shall ask in my name, that will I do, that the Father may be glorified in the Son. If ye shall ask any thing in my name, I will do it" (John 14:12–14).

- "But as many as received him, to them gave he power to become the sons of God, even to them that believe on his name" (John 1:12).

- "And when he had called unto him his twelve disciples, he gave them power against unclean spirits, to cast them out, and to heal all manner of sickness and all manner of disease" (Matthew 10:1).

By and through Faith

- He therefore that ministereth to you the Spirit, and worketh miracles among you, doeth he it by the works of the law, or by the hearing of faith? Even as Abraham believed God, and it was accounted to him for righteousness. Know ye therefore that they which are of faith, the same are the children of Abraham. And the scripture, foreseeing that God would justify the heathen through faith, preached before the gospel unto Abraham, saying, In thee shall all nations be blessed. So then they which be of faith are blessed with faithful Abraham. For as many as are of the works of the law are under the curse: for it is written, Cursed is every one that continueth not in all things which are written in the book of the law to do them. But that no man is justified by the law in the sight of God, it is evident:

for, The just shall live by faith. And the law is not of faith: but, The man that doeth them shall live in them. (Galatians 3:5–12)

- Recall, "The Hall of Faith" mentioned earlier, Hebrews 11:3–35, where people did extraordinary things through their faith.

By the Power of Prayer

- Now there was at Joppa a certain disciple named Tabitha, which by interpretation is called Dorcas: this woman was full of good works and almsdeeds which she did. And it came to pass in those days, that she was sick, and died: whom when they had washed, they laid her in an upper chamber... Peter put them all forth, and kneeled down, and prayed; and turning him to the body said, Tabitha, arise. And she opened her eyes: and when she saw Peter, she sat up. And he gave her his hand, and lifted her up, and when he had called the saints and widows, presented her alive. (Acts 9: 36-37, 40-41)

By the Power and Anointing of God

- "Ye men of Israel, hear these words; Jesus of Nazareth, a man approved of God among you by miracles and wonders and signs, which God did by him in the midst of you, as ye yourselves also know" (Acts 2:22).
- And it came to pass after these things, that the son of the woman, the mistress of the house, fell sick; and his sickness was so sore, that there was no breath left in him ... And he cried unto the LORD, and said, O LORD my God, hast thou also brought evil upon the widow with whom I sojourn, by slaying her son? And he stretched himself upon the child three times, and cried unto the LORD, and said, O LORD my God, I pray thee, let this child's soul come into him again.

  And the LORD heard the voice of Elijah; and the soul of the child came into him again, and he revived. And Elijah took the child, and brought him down out of the chamber into the house, and delivered him unto his mother: and Elijah said, See, thy son liveth. (1 Kings 17:17–23)

- "And God wrought special miracles by the hands of Paul: So that from his body were brought unto the sick handkerchiefs or aprons, and the diseases departed from them, and the evil spirits went out of them" (Acts 19:11–12).
- "And the people with one accord gave heed unto those things which Philip spake, hearing and seeing the miracles which he did. For unclean spirits, crying with loud voice, came out of many that were possessed with them: and many taken with palsies, and that were lame, were healed" (Acts 8:6–7).
- "And Moses stretched out his hand over the sea; and the LORD caused the sea to go back by a strong east wind all that night, and made the sea dry land, and the waters were divided" (Exodus 14:21).
- "God anointed Jesus of Nazareth with the Holy Ghost and with power: who went about doing good, and healing all that were oppressed of the devil; for God was with him" (Acts 10:38).

By the Power of the Holy Spirit
- "But ye shall receive power, after that the Holy Ghost is come upon you" (Acts 1:8).
- "They chose Stephen, a man full of faith and of the Holy Ghost, And Stephen, full of faith and power, did great wonders and miracles among the people" (Acts 6:5, 8).

By Spiritual Gifts
- Now there are diversities of gifts, but the same Spirit. And there are differences of administrations, but the same Lord. And there are diversities of operations, but it is the same God which worketh all in all. But the manifestation of the Spirit is given to every man to profit withal. For to one is given by the Spirit the word of wisdom; to another

the word of knowledge by the same Spirit; To another faith by the same Spirit; to another the gifts of healing by the same Spirit; To another the working of miracles; to another prophecy; to another discerning of spirits; to another divers kinds of tongues; to another the interpretation of tongues: But all these worketh that one and the selfsame Spirit, dividing to every man severally as he will. (1 Corinthians 12:4–11)

By the Power of Jesus

"And there are also many other things which Jesus did, the which, if they should be written every one, I suppose that even the world itself could not contain the books that should be written. Amen" (John 21:25).

Jesus said, "All power is given unto me in heaven and in earth" (Matthew 28:18). Jesus healed the sick, cast out demons, controlled nature, defied the laws of nature, walked on water, raised the dead, multiplied food, turn water into wine, and more ...

- **Raising the dead:** Jesus said, Take ye away the stone. Martha, the sister of him that was dead, saith unto him, Lord, by this time he stinketh: for he hath been dead four days. Jesus saith unto her, Said I not unto thee, that, if thou wouldest believe, thou shouldest see the glory of God? Then they took away the stone from the place where the dead was laid. And Jesus lifted up his eyes, and said, Father, I thank thee that thou hast heard me. And I knew that thou hearest me always: but because of the people which stand by I said it, that they may believe that thou hast sent me. And when he thus had spoken, he cried with a loud voice, Lazarus, come forth. And he that was dead came forth, bound hand and foot with graveclothes: and his face was bound about with a napkin. Jesus saith unto them, Loose him, and let him go. (John 11:38–44)
- **Walking on water:** "Jesus went unto them, walking on the sea ... And Peter answered him and said, Lord, if it be thou, bid me come unto thee on the water. And he said, Come.

And when Peter was come down out of the ship, he walked on the water, to go to Jesus" (Matthew 14:25–29).

- **Demonic spirits cast out:** And there was in their synagogue a man with an unclean spirit; and he cried out, Saying, Let us alone; what have we to do with thee, thou Jesus of Nazareth? art thou come to destroy us? I know thee who thou art, the Holy One of God. And Jesus rebuked him, saying, Hold thy peace, and come out of him. And when the unclean spirit had torn him, and cried with a loud voice, he came out of him. And they were all amazed, insomuch that they questioned among themselves, saying, What thing is this? what new doctrine is this? for with authority commandeth he even the unclean spirits, and they do obey him. (Mark 1:23–27)

CHAPTER 11

Why Jesus?

⌣

"He that committeth sin is of the devil; for the devil sinneth from the beginning. For this purpose the Son of God was manifested, that he might destroy the works of the devil" (1 John 3:8).

The Son of God

Scholars attest approximately four hundred Messianic prophecies were written centuries before the life of Jesus, which foretold a coming Messiah. Several, Old Testament, prophets wrote the Messianic prophecies over the span of a millennium. They spoke of a Messiah who would one day come to Earth and walk among humanity, namely to bring the world back to God, and make it a place of peace, justice and harmony.

These prophecies mentioned names, locations, and even the timing surrounding His appearance and events. The known date of completion for the Old Testament writings is 430 B.C., so these prophecies were in circulation at least 430 years before the birth of Christ. Therefore, these prophecies were not "conspired" or "manipulated" to be seen after-the-fact to conform to anyone. Statistically, the odds of these prophecies fulfilled by one man would be astronomical. The Messiah, Jesus Emmanuel, fulfilled Messianic prophecy. Jesus said, "These are the words which I spake unto you, while I was yet with you, that all things must be fulfilled, which were written in the law of Moses, and in the prophets, and in the psalms, concerning me" (Luke 24:44).

Jesus Christ: Jesus came to bring the Kingdom of God and restoration to the world. Jesus as recorded in Luke 4:18-19, "The Spirit of the Lord is upon me, because he hath anointed me to preach the gospel to the poor; he hath sent me to heal the brokenhearted, to preach deliverance to the captives, and recovering of sight to the blind, to set at liberty them that are bruised, To preach the acceptable year of the Lord."

"For God so loved the world, that he gave his only begotten Son, that whosoever believeth in him should not perish, but have everlasting life. For God sent not his Son into the world to condemn the world; but that the world through him might be saved" (John 3:16-17). "And the Word was made flesh, and dwelt among us, (and we beheld his glory, the glory as of the only begotten of the Father,) full of grace and truth" (John 1:14).

"Christ died for our sins according to the scriptures; And that he was buried, and that he rose again the third day according to the scriptures" (1 Corinthians 15:3-4). "To him give all the prophets witness, that through his name whosoever believeth in him shall receive remission of sins" (Acts 10:43).

Jesus declared in John 10:10, "I am come that they might have life, and that they might have it more abundantly." "I am the bread of life: he that cometh to me shall never hunger; and he that believeth on me shall never thirst" (John 6:35). "I am the living bread which came down from heaven: if any man eat of this bread, he shall live for ever: and the bread that I will give is my flesh, which I will give for the life of the world" (John 6:51).

The plan of salvation would be incomplete without the blood of His sacrifice, His intercession on our behalf, authority in His name, and fellowship with Him as our divine Mediator. Through His name, by and through His blood, and by the Holy Spirit, we have authority and power in the spiritual realm. "For in him dwelleth all the fulness of the Godhead bodily. And ye are complete in him, which is the head of all principality and power" (Colossians 2:9-10). The Holy Spirit intercedes through us, and Jesus intercedes for us.

The word for salvation in the Greek language is *soteria*, meaning "cure, recovery, and remedy." The word salvation in the Bible is used in many different ways. The basic meaning is "deliverance from danger."

Through the death, burial, Resurrection and Ascension of Jesus Christ He has brought about our salvation from the wrath of God, from sin, and from death. There are three kinds of death: physical death, spiritual death that is separation, from God in this life; and eternal death that is separation, from God forever.

Salvation, virtually synonymous with the overall concept of redemption, includes a past, present, and future sense. As Christians, we were saved from the penalty of sin when God brought us to faith in Christ; we are presently being saved from the power of sin as the Holy Spirit sanctifies us; and we will someday be saved from the presence of sin when we meet Christ face to face in glory. This salvation, however, is not merely a salvation from all these things; it is a salvation to something. We are saved to worship, glorify, and to serve God. Sin was disobedience to God and salvation brings about our obedience to God.

It was through the power of God's Spirit in Him that Christ accomplished *everything* that He did. He understood completely that it was only the presence of the Spirit of God in Him that allowed Him to perform miracles. He perfectly exercised the fruit of the anointing present in Him as evident in Acts 2:22, "...hear these words; Jesus of Nazareth, a man approved of God among you by miracles and wonders and signs, which God did by him in the midst of you..." John 14:9, "Jesus saith...he that hath seen me hath seen the Father..." Jesus exemplified the nature and the true essence of the Father.

This is he that came by **water** and **blood**, even Jesus Christ; not by water only, but by water and blood. And it is the Spirit that beareth witness, because the Spirit is truth. For there are three that bear record in heaven, the **Father**, the **Word**, and the **Holy Ghost**: and these three are one. And there are three that bear witness in earth, the **Spirit**, and the **water**, and the **blood**: and these three agree in one. (1 John 5:6–8, emphasis added)

Then cometh Jesus from Galilee to Jordan unto John, to be baptized of him. But John forbad him, saying, I have need to be baptized of thee, and comest thou to me? And Jesus answering said unto him, Suffer it to be so now: for thus it becometh us to fulfill all righteousness. Then he suffered him. And Jesus, when he was baptized, went up straightway out of the water: and, lo, the heavens were opened unto him, and he saw the Spirit of God descending like a dove, and lighting upon him: And lo a voice from heaven, saying, This is my beloved Son, in whom I am well pleased. (Matthew 3:13–17)

The Blood of Jesus

Many people normally understand this tenet—that God forgives our sins through Jesus Christ's blood, but not everyone understands how it occurs. Paul explained in Hebrews 9:22 that, "according to the Law ... And almost all things are by the law purged with blood; and without shedding of blood is no remission."

The Old Testament records God instructing the priesthood to perform certain duties that included a system of cleansing and purification using the blood of sacrificed animals, thus, foreshadowing the shedding of Christ's blood, the ultimate sacrifice for sin. He commanded the nation of Israel to follow this temporary system of the ritualistic cleansing of sin as described in Hebrews 9:6–7, "Now when these things were thus ordained, the priests went always into the first tabernacle, accomplishing the service *of God* ... But into the second went the high priest alone once every year, not without blood, which he offered for himself, and for the errors of the people."

The reason for blood is apparent in Leviticus 17:11, "For the life of the flesh is in the blood: and I have given it to you upon the altar to make an atonement for your souls: for it is the blood that maketh an atonement for the soul."

Animal sacrifices served and represented as a type of the one and only real and future sacrifice of Jesus Christ, who would pay the penalty for everyone's sins once and for all.

Hebrews 9:11–18 states,

But Christ being come an high priest of good things to come, by a greater and more perfect tabernacle, not made with hands, that is to say, not of this building; Neither by the blood of goats and calves, but by his own blood he entered in once into the holy place, having obtained eternal redemption for us. For if the blood of bulls and of goats, and the ashes of an heifer sprinkling the unclean, sanctifieth to the purifying of the flesh: How much more shall the blood of Christ, who through the eternal Spirit offered himself without spot to God, purge your conscience from dead works to serve the living God?

And for this cause he is the mediator of the new testament, that by means of death, for the redemption of the transgressions that were under the first testament, they which are called might receive the promise of eternal inheritance. For where a testament is, there must also of necessity be the death of the testator. For a testament is of force after men are dead: otherwise it is of no strength at all while the testator liveth. Whereupon neither the first testament was dedicated without blood.

The Blood Covenant of Jesus: The blood of Christ also signifies that He has entered into a covenant, or agreement, with us. When Jesus instituted wine for the New Testament Passover, He said in Matthew 26:27–28, "Drink ye all of it; For this is my blood of the New Testament, which is shed for many for the remission of sins."

The terms of this covenant are absolute, because it was sealed with the shed blood of Jesus Christ. We must understand that repentance, baptism, and the acceptance of Jesus Christ as our Lord and Savior, along with the belief that God raised Him from the dead, constitutes a covenant with God. Hebrews 10:16–17 states, "This is the covenant that I will make with them after those days, saith the Lord, I will put my laws into their hearts, and in their minds will I write them; And their sins and iniquities will I remember no more."

The unblemished male animals represented Jesus Christ as the perfect, sinless sacrifice for our sins. "For he hath made him to be sin for us, who knew no sin; that we might be made the righteousness of God in him" (2 Corinthians 5:21). "In whom we have redemption through his blood, the forgiveness of sins, according to the riches of his grace" (Ephesians 1:7).

Jesus Our Redeemer

The disobedience and Fall of the first man, Adam, and first woman, Eve, disconnected us from our divine nature and communion with God. Jesus was the firstborn of the new image of man for mankind, in the image of God. Colossians 1:15 states, "Who is the image of the invisible God, the firstborn of every creature."

Jesus was perfectly obedient and sinless, therefore, He was qualified to be the Son of God and to restore man's relationship with the Father by overcoming sin and death through His sacrifice on the cross. "Therefore as by the offence of one judgment came upon all men to condemnation; even so by the righteousness of one the free gift came upon all men unto justification of life. For as by one man's disobedience many were made sinners, so by the obedience of one shall many be made righteous" (Romans 5:18–19).

And so it is written, The first man Adam was made a living soul; the last Adam [Jesus] was made a quickening spirit. Howbeit that was not first which is spiritual, but that which is natural; and afterward that which is spiritual. The first man is of the earth, earthy; the second man is the Lord from heaven. As is the earthy, such are they also that are earthy: and as is the heavenly, such are they also that are heavenly. And as we have borne the image of the earthy, we shall also bear the image of the heavenly. (1 Corinthians 15:45–49)

Jesus Our Mediator and Intercessor

"For there is one God, and one mediator between God and men, the man Christ Jesus" (1 Timothy 2:5). Because the blood of Jesus Christ removes sin, making us pure before God, Christ's shed blood also makes it possible for our access to the very Throne of God, the Father. "...And he bare the sin of many, and made intercession for the transgressors" (Isaiah 53:12).

> "For Christ is not entered into the holy places made with hands, which are the figures of the true; but into heaven itself, now to appear in the presence of God for us" (Hebrews 9:24).

Under the Old Covenant, only the high priest could enter the area of the tabernacle known as the Holiest of Holy. By the sacrifice of Jesus Christ, we can now approach God the Father without hesitation or fear of rejection, but with confidence and assurance as Hebrews 10:19–22 declares, "Having therefore, brethren, boldness to enter into the holiest by the blood of Jesus, By a new and living way, which he hath consecrated for us, through the veil, that is to say, his flesh; And having an high priest over the house of God; Let us draw near with a true heart in full assurance of faith, having our hearts sprinkled from an evil conscience, and our bodies washed with pure water."

Hebrews 4:16, speaks of the confidence we can have when we approach God, "Let us therefore come boldly to the throne of grace, that we may obtain mercy and find grace to help in time of need." Jesus Christ makes it possible for us to experience this intimate relationship with our Father.

The Apostle Peter said, "There is no other name ... by which we must be saved" (Acts 4:12). God attaches great significance to names. His own names are powerful testimonials to His great glory and majesty: The All-Sufficient One (El-Shaddai), God of Peace (Yahweh Shalom), and God Our Provider (Jehovah Jireh) ...

In the same way, the name Jesus Christ tells us a great deal about His purpose and role in God's master plan, as well. It enlightens us about His character, purpose, love for humanity, and His love of God.

The Name of Jesus

The New Testament was written in Greek, and the name Jesus here means the same in Greek as the Hebrew name *Joshua*, which means literally "God is salvation." Jesus' Hebrew name is *Yeshua*, meaning "salvation." "Neither is there salvation in any other: for there is none other name under heaven given among men, whereby we must be saved" (Acts 4:12).

The Hebrew word for Christ is *Messiah.* Christ comes from the Greek word *Christos*, meaning "Anointed." What is the significance of being anointed? The act of anointing was used in the priesthood to consecrate as a means to dedicate or set something apart for holy use. This teaches us something about Jesus Christ, His purpose, and His mission, and why He is called the "Anointed One."

Christ dedicated Himself to the mission God had given Him. Simply put, Christ's entire life was set apart for God's holy use. As He stated, "And he that sent me is with me: the Father hath not left me alone; for I do always those things that please him" (John 8:29). "I can of mine own self do nothing: as I hear, I judge: and my judgment is just; because I seek not mine own will, but the will of the Father which hath sent me" (John 5:30). His entire life was an example of complete and total dedication to God's will.

"The angel of the LORD appeared unto Joseph in a dream, saying, Joseph, thou son of David, fear not to take unto thee Mary thy wife: for that which is conceived in her is of the Holy Ghost. And she shall bring forth a son, and thou shalt call his name JESUS: for he shall save his people from their sins ... Behold, a virgin shall be with child, and shall bring forth a son, and they shall call his name Emmanuel, which being interpreted is, God with us" (Matthew 1:20–21, 23).

Our names identify who we are, but more importantly in Scripture, they identified the person, as well as revealed the person's character. Throughout Scripture, names were given by divine inspiration and were symbolic of the essence of the person's nature and characteristics. The prophetic name of Jesus speaks to His mission on earth, "For unto us a child is born, unto us a son is given: and the government shall be upon his shoulder: and his name shall be called Wonderful, Counsellor, The mighty God, The everlasting Father, The Prince of Peace" (Isaiah 9:6).

This is why when a person's nature or purpose changed, God changed their name, as reflected in Genesis 17:4–5, "As for me, behold, my covenant is with thee, and thou shalt be a father of many nations. Neither shall thy name any more be called Abram, but thy name shall be Abraham; for a father of many nations have I made thee." Genesis 17:15, "And God said unto Abraham, As for Sarai thy wife, thou shalt not call her name Sarai, but Sarah shall her name be."

Know and Petition God by His Names: God is not without a name; He has a personal name by which He can, and is to, be worshiped and honored. The name of God ushers in the divine presence of God and Jesus Christ. The name is no mere label, but is significant of the real personality of Him to whom it belongs.

Like other Hebrew proper names, the name of God is more than a mere distinguishing title. It represents the Hebrew conception of the divine nature or character and of the relation of God to His people. It represents the deity as He is known to His worshipers, and stands for all those attributes which He bears in relation to them and which are revealed to them through His activity on their behalf. When God passed by before Moses, "the LORD descended in the cloud, and stood with him there..." God revealed and proclaimed Himself to be, "The LORD, The LORD

God, merciful and gracious, longsuffering, and abundant in good-ness and truth, Keeping mercy for thousands, forgiving iniquity and transgression and sin..." (Exodus 34:5-7). Exodus 6:3 states, "And I appeared unto Abraham, unto Isaac, and unto Jacob, by the name of God Almighty, but by my name JEHOVAH was I not known to them."

In Exodus 3:14 God said to Moses, "I AM THAT I AM." We can understand this as God is our All-Sufficiency, and His name dif-fers depending on what our need is at a particular time. In other words, God is saying to us, if you need health, pray, Jehovah Rapha, you are my healer. If you need peace, then pray, Jehovah Shalom.

We must not only take care to understand what is God's name; more importantly, we must understand the meaning and the significance of God's name. The significance of His name relates to the reality of His being. Since the name of God dis-closes aspects of His nature, that name carries with it the ele-ments of authority, power, and holiness, and this is why the name is treated with such reverence. This is why there are many names attributed to God in the Old Testament. The following are some of the names of God:

Adonai (Lord, Master)
El Elyon (The Most High God)
El Olam (The Everlasting God)
El Shaddai (The All-Sufficient One)
Elohim (God, The Creator)
Emmanuel (God With Us)
Jehovah Jireh (The Lord Will Provide)
Jehovah Nissi (The Lord My Banner)
Jehovah-Raah (The Lord My Shepherd)
Jehovah Rapha (The Lord That Heals)
Jehovah Sabaoth (The Lord of Hosts)
Jehovah Shalom (The Lord Is Peace)
Jehovah Shammah (The Lord Is There)
Jehovah Mekoddishkem (The Lord Who Sanctifies You)
Jehovah Tsidkenu (The Lord Our Righteousness)

Yahweh (Lord, Jehovah)
Yeshua (Jesus, Salvation)

Hallowed Be Your Name: To hallow is to make something holy or to set it apart to be exalted as being worthy of absolute devotion. To hallow the name of God is to regard Him with complete devotion and loving admiration, honor, respect, and reverence. God's name is of the utmost importance (Nehemiah 9:5); therefore, we should reserve grave significance, reverence, and respect in our minds and hearts when we think of God's name. We should never take His name lightly or use it in vain (Exodus 20:7; Leviticus 22:32), but always rejoice in it and think deeply upon its true meaning. The main reason we are commanded not to use the name of God in vain is that His name does not just represent who He is; but also, it is who He is.

Our Authority through the Name of Jesus: The authority we have in Jesus' name through prayer is based on a covenantal authority by the blood covenant relationship with God through Christ. Praying in the name and authority and power of Jesus is giving Him authority to intercede on our behalf when you make requests of the Father God. Jesus is the High Priest of our confession, and whenever we say what the Word says, Jesus releases His authority and blessings on the confession to accomplish the purposes of God. "... It is Christ that died, yea rather, that is risen again, who is even at the right hand of God, who also maketh intercession for us" (Romans 8:34).

Praying in the Name of Jesus. Many believers misunderstand what it means to pray in the name of Jesus. We are not guaranteed an answered prayer just by ending or beginning our prayer with "in the name of Jesus, amen." However, it is in the understanding the significance of who He is, our relationship with Christ, and appropriating His power through faith in His name that prayer is effective.

One of the fundamental teachings of Judaism and Christianity is that God has put us here on Earth to be bridges to bring His qualities, His characteristics, and His manifestation in the world. We are to pray in the name, as well as in the NATURE, of Jesus.

Praying in the name of Jesus isn't telling us to just use His name; rather, He is *also* calling on us to believe, to understand His nature, His attributes, His power, *and to develop in it to conform to His image*, and appropriate it in faith.

We are privileged to pray to God directly in Jesus' name because of His sacrifice and the authority He has given us, because Christ has redeemed us, "that we might be made the righteousness of God in Him" (2 Corinthians 5:21). His name is our spiritual authority in prayer-whether we are praying to God (Heaven), or dealing with men (Earth), or the rulers of darkness-under the earth (Satan). "That at the name of Jesus every knee should bow, of things in heaven, and things in earth, and things under the earth" (Philippians 2:10). We see clearly in the following Scriptures the power in Christ's name.

- "And his name through faith in his name hath made this man strong...yea, the faith which is by him hath given him this perfect soundness in the presence of you all" (Acts 3:16).
- "He that believeth on me, the works that I do shall he do also; and greater works than these shall he do; because I go unto my Father. And whatsoever ye shall ask in my name, that will I do, that the Father may be glorified in the Son. If ye shall ask any thing in my name, I will do it" (John 14:12–14).

Only through Christ do we have authority and power in prayer, and only through Christ and the Holy Spirit are we restored to our purpose in God. The Greek word for Christian is *Christianos* which means, "follower of Christ." To accept Jesus as "The Anointed" implies that we are willing to be anointed with the same Holy Spirit with which He was anointed. Basically, then, a Christian is one who not only believes that God anointed Jesus with the Holy Spirit, but also allows God to anoint him or her. "Whosoever shall confess that Jesus is the Son of God, God dwelleth in him, and he in God" (1 John 4:15).

The following Scriptures give further understanding and illumination in the purpose of Jesus and our fellowship with the Lord.

Salvation
- That if thou shalt confess with thy mouth the Lord Jesus, and shalt believe in thine heart that God hath raised him from the dead, thou shalt be saved. For with the heart man believeth unto righteousness; and with the mouth confession is made unto salvation. (Romans 10:9–10)
- "Neither is there salvation in any other: for there is none other name under heaven given among men, whereby we must be saved" (Acts 4:12).

Christ Is Our Example
- For even hereunto were ye called: because Christ also suffered for us, leaving us an example, that ye should follow his steps: Who did no sin, neither was guile found in his mouth: Who, when he was reviled, reviled not again; when he suffered, he threatened not; but committed himself to him that judgeth righteously: Who his own self bare our sins in his own body on the tree, that we, being dead to sins, should live unto righteousness: by whose stripes ye were healed. For ye were as sheep going astray; but are now returned unto the Shepherd and Bishop of your souls. (1 Peter 2:21–25)
- And we know that all things work together for good to them that love God, to them who are the called according to his purpose. For whom he did foreknow, he also did predestinate to be conformed to the image of his Son, that he might be the firstborn among many brethren. Moreover whom he did predestinate, them he also called: and whom he called, them he also justified: and whom he justified, them he also glorified. What shall we then say to these things? If God be for us, who can be against us? He that spared not his own Son, but delivered him up for us all,

how shall he not with him also freely give us all things? (Romans 8:28–32)

- I am the true vine, and my Father is the husbandman. Every branch in me that beareth not fruit he taketh away: and every branch that beareth fruit, he purgeth it, that it may bring forth more fruit. Now ye are clean through the word which I have spoken unto you. Abide in me, and I in you. As the branch cannot bear fruit of itself, except it abide in the vine; no more can ye, except ye abide in me. I am the vine, ye are the branches: He that abideth in me, and I in him, the same bringeth forth much fruit: for without me ye can do nothing. If a man abide not in me, he is cast forth as a branch, and is withered; and men gather them, and cast them into the fire, and they are burned. If ye abide in me, and my words abide in you, ye shall ask what ye will, and it shall be done unto you.

  Herein is my Father glorified, that ye bear much fruit; so shall ye be my disciples. As the Father hath loved me, so have I loved you: continue ye in my love. If ye keep my commandments, ye shall abide in my love; even as I have kept my Father's commandments, and abide in his love. These things have I spoken unto you, that my joy might remain in you, and that your joy might be full. This is my commandment, That ye love one another, as I have loved you. Greater love hath no man than this, that a man lay down his life for his friends. Ye are my friends, if ye do whatsoever I command you. (John 15:1–14)
- "Therefore if any man be in Christ, he is a new creature: old things are passed away; behold, all things are become new" (2 Corinthians 5:17).

Revelation

- Jesus cried and said, He that believeth on me, believeth not on me, but on him that sent me. And he that seeth me seeth him that sent me. I am come a light into the world, that whosoever believeth on me should not abide in darkness.

And if any man hear my words, and believe not, I judge him not: for I came not to judge the world, but to save the world. (John 12:44–47)

- Jesus saith unto him, I am the way, the truth, and the life: no man cometh unto the Father, but by me. If ye had known me, ye should have known my Father also: and from henceforth ye know him, and have seen him. (John 14:6–7)

- I am the door: by me if any man enter in, he shall be saved, and shall go in and out, and find pasture. The thief cometh not, but for to steal, and to kill, and to destroy: I am come that they might have life, and that they might have it more abundantly. I am the good shepherd: the good shepherd giveth his life for the sheep. (John 10:9–11)

- Then said Jesus to those Jews which believed on him, If ye continue in my word, then are ye my disciples indeed; And ye shall know the truth, and the truth shall make you free. (John 8:31–32)

Wisdom

- Therefore whosoever heareth these sayings of mine, and doeth them, I will liken him unto a wise man, which built his house upon a rock: And the rain descended, and the floods came, and the winds blew, and beat upon that house; and it fell not: for it was founded upon a rock. And every one that heareth these sayings of mine, and doeth them not, shall be likened unto a foolish man, which built his house upon the sand: And the rain descended, and the floods came, and the winds blew, and beat upon that house; and it fell: and great was the fall of it. (Matthew 7:24–27)

Redemption of Our Sins

- All we like sheep have gone astray; we have turned every one to his own way; and the LORD hath laid on him the iniquity of us all. He was oppressed, and he was afflicted, yet he opened not his mouth: he is brought as a lamb to the slaughter, and as a sheep before her shearers is dumb, so he openeth not his mouth. He was taken from prison

and from judgment: and who shall declare his generation? for he was cut off out of the land of the living: for the
transgression of my people was he stricken. And he made
his grave with the wicked, and with the rich in his death;
because he had done no violence, neither was any deceit
in his mouth.

Yet it pleased the LORD to bruise him; he hath put him to
grief: when thou shalt make his soul an offering for sin, he
shall see his seed, he shall prolong his days, and the pleasure of the LORD shall prosper in his hand. He shall see of
the travail of his soul, and shall be satisfied: by his knowledge shall my righteous servant justify many; for he shall
bear their iniquities. Therefore will I divide him a portion
with the great, and he shall divide the spoil with the strong;
because he hath poured out his soul unto death: and he
was numbered with the transgressors; and he bare the sin
of many, and made intercession for the transgressors.

In whom we have redemption through his blood, even
the forgiveness of sins: Who is the image of the invisible
God, the firstborn of every creature: For by him were all
things created, that are in heaven, and that are in earth,
visible and invisible, whether they be thrones, or domin-
ions, or principalities, or powers: all things were created
by him, and for him: And he is before all things, and by
him all things consist. And he is the head of the body, the
church: who is the beginning, the firstborn from the dead;
that in all things he might have the preeminence. (Isaiah
53:6–12)

Covered by the Blood

- For when Moses had spoken every precept to all the people
  according to the law, he took the blood of calves and of
  goats, with water, and scarlet wool, and hyssop, and sprinkled both the book, and all the people, Saying, This is the
  blood of the testament which God hath enjoined unto you.

Moreover he sprinkled with blood both the tabernacle, and all the vessels of the ministry. And almost all things are by the law purged with blood; and without shedding of blood is no remission.

It was therefore necessary that the patterns of things in the heavens should be purified with these; but the heavenly things themselves with better sacrifices than these. For Christ is not entered into the holy places made with hands, which are the figures of the true; but into heaven itself, now to appear in the presence of God for us: Nor yet that he should offer himself often, as the high priest entereth into the holy place every year with blood of others; For then must he often have suffered since the foundation of the world: but now once in the end of the world hath he appeared to put away sin by the sacrifice of himself. And as it is appointed unto men once to die, but after this the judgment: So Christ was once offered to bear the sins of many; and unto them that look for him shall he appear the second time without sin unto salvation. (Hebrews 9:19–28)

Atonement for Our Sins

- But God commendeth his love toward us, in that, while we were yet sinners, Christ died for us. Much more then, being now justified by his blood, we shall be saved from wrath through him. For if, when we were enemies, we were reconciled to God by the death of his Son, much more, being reconciled, we shall be saved by his life. And not only so, but we also joy in God through our Lord Jesus Christ, by whom we have now received the atonement.

Wherefore, as by one man sin entered into the world, and death by sin; and so death passed upon all men, for that all have sinned: (For until the law sin was in the world: but sin is not imputed when there is no law. Nevertheless death reigned from Adam to Moses, even over them that had not sinned after the similitude of Adam's transgression, who is the figure of him that was to come. But not as the offence, so also is the free gift. For if through the offence of one many be dead, much more the grace of God, and the gift by grace, which is by one man, Jesus Christ, hath abounded unto many. And not as it was by one that sinned, so is the gift: for the judgment was by one to condemnation, but the free gift is of many offences unto justification. For if by one man's offence death reigned by one; much more they which receive abundance of grace and of the gift of righteousness shall reign in life by one, Jesus Christ.)

Therefore as by the offence of one judgment came upon all men to condemnation; even so by the righteousness of one the free gift came upon all men unto justification of life. For as by one man's disobedience many were made sinners, so by the obedience of one shall many be made righteous. Moreover the law entered, that the offence might abound. But where sin abounded, grace did much more abound: That as sin hath reigned unto death, even so might grace reign through righteousness unto eternal life by Jesus Christ our Lord. (Romans 5:8-21)

- Herein is love, not that we loved God, but that he loved us, and sent his Son to be the propitiation for our sins. Beloved, if God so loved us, we ought also to love one another. No man hath seen God at any time. If we love one another, God dwelleth in us, and his love is perfected in us. (1 John 4:10–12)

Intercession on Our Behalf

- It is Christ that died, yea rather, that is risen again, who is even at the right hand of God, who also maketh intercession for us. Who shall separate us from the love of Christ? shall tribulation, or distress, or persecution, or famine, or nakedness, or peril, or sword? As it is written, For thy sake we are killed all the day long; we are accounted as sheep for the slaughter. Nay, in all these things we are more than conquerors through him that loved us. For I am persuaded, that neither death, nor life, nor angels, nor principalities, nor powers, nor things present, nor things to come, Nor height, nor depth, nor any other creature, shall be able to separate us from the love of God, which is in Christ Jesus our Lord. (Romans 8:34–39)

- Seeing then that we have a great high priest, that is passed into the heavens, Jesus the Son of God, let us hold fast our profession. For we have not an high priest which cannot be touched with the feeling of our infirmities; but was in all points tempted like as we are, yet without sin. Let us therefore come boldly unto the throne of grace, that we may obtain mercy, and find grace to help in time of need. (Hebrews 4:14–16)

Empowers Us to Overcome Sin

- Now if I do that I would not, it is no more I that do it, but sin that dwelleth in me. I find then a law, that, when I would do good, evil is present with me. For I delight in the law of God after the inward man: But I see another law in my members, warring against the law of my mind, and bringing me into captivity to the law of sin which is in my members. O wretched man that I am! who shall deliver me from the body of this death? I thank God through Jesus Christ our Lord. So then with the mind I myself serve the law of God; but with the flesh the law of sin. (Romans 7:20–25)

- "Ye are of God, little children, and have overcome them: because greater is he that is in you, than he that is in the world" (1 John 4:4).

Relationship with the Holy Spirit

- Jesus answered and said unto him, If a man love me, he will keep my words: and my Father will love him, and we will come unto him, and make our abode with him. He that loveth me not keepeth not my sayings: and the word which ye hear is not mine, but the Father's which sent me. These things have I spoken unto you, being yet present with you. But the Comforter, which is the Holy Ghost, whom the Father will send in my name, he shall teach you all things, and bring all things to your remembrance, whatsoever I have said unto you. Peace I leave with you, my peace I give unto you: not as the world giveth, give I unto you. Let not your heart be troubled, neither let it be afraid. (John 14:23–27)

- "He that hath my commandments, and keepeth them, he it is that loveth me: and he that loveth me shall be loved of my Father, and I will love him, and will manifest myself to him" (John 14:21).
- "For through him we both have access by one Spirit unto the Father" (Ephesians 2:18).

Reconciled to God

- Wherefore remember, that ye being in time past Gentiles in the flesh, who are called Uncircumcision by that which is called the Circumcision in the flesh made by hands; That at that time ye were without Christ, being aliens from the commonwealth of Israel, and strangers from the covenants of promise, having no hope, and without God in the world: But now in Christ Jesus ye who sometimes were far off are made nigh by the blood of Christ. For he is our peace, who hath made both one, and hath broken down the middle wall of partition between us; Having abolished in his flesh the enmity, even the law of commandments contained in ordinances; for to make in himself of twain one new man, so making peace; And that he might reconcile both unto God in one body by the cross, having slain the enmity thereby. (Ephesians 2:11–16)
- For it pleased the Father that in him should all fulness dwell; And, having made peace through the blood of his cross, by him to reconcile all things unto himself; by him, I say, whether they be things in earth, or things in heaven. And you, that were sometime alienated and enemies in your mind by wicked works, yet now hath he reconciled

in the body of his flesh through death, to present you holy and unblameable and unreproveable in his sight: If ye continue in the faith grounded and settled, and be not moved away from the hope of the gospel, which ye have heard, and which was preached to every creature which is under heaven. (Colossians 1:14–23)

Joint Heirs in the Abrahamic Covenant

- Christ hath redeemed us from the curse of the law, being made a curse for us: for it is written, Cursed is every one that hangeth on a tree: That the blessing of Abraham might come on the Gentiles through Jesus Christ; that we might receive the promise of the Spirit through faith. Brethren, I speak after the manner of men; Though it be but a man's covenant, yet if it be confirmed, no man disannulleth, or addeth thereto. Now to Abraham and his seed were the promises made. He saith not, And to seeds, as of many; but as of one, And to thy seed, which is Christ. (Galatians 3:13–16)
- "That the Gentiles should be fellow heirs, and of the same body, and partakers of his promise in Christ by the gospel" (Ephesians 3:6).
- "And if ye be Christ's, then are ye Abraham's seed, and heirs according to the promise" (Galatians 3:29).

We Are the Righteousness of God through Him

- As ye have therefore received Christ Jesus the Lord, so walk ye in him: Rooted and built up in him, and stablished in the faith, as ye have been taught, abounding therein with thanksgiving. Beware lest any man spoil you through philosophy and vain deceit, after the tradition of men, after the rudiments of the world, and not after Christ. For in him dwelleth all the fulness of the Godhead bodily. And ye are complete in him, which is the head of all principality and power: In whom also ye are circumcised with the circumcision made without hands, in putting off the body of the sins of the flesh by the circumcision of Christ: Buried with him in baptism, wherein also ye are risen with him through the faith of the operation of God, who hath raised him from the dead. And you, being dead in your sins and the uncircumcision of your flesh, hath he quickened together with him, having forgiven you all trespasses;

Blotting out the handwriting of ordinances that was against us, which was contrary to us, and took it out of the way, nailing it to his cross; And having spoiled principalities and powers, he made a shew of them openly, triumphing over them in it. Let no man therefore judge you in meat, or in drink, or in respect of an holyday, or of the new moon, or of the sabbath days: Which are a shadow of things to come; but the body is of Christ. Let no man beguile you of your reward in a voluntary humility and worshipping of angels, intruding into those things which he hath not seen, vainly puffed up by his fleshly mind, And not holding the Head, from which all the body by joints and bands having nourishment ministered, and knit together, increaseth with the increase of God.

Wherefore if ye be dead with Christ from the rudiments of the world, why, as though living in the world, are ye subject to ordinances, (Touch not; taste not; handle not; Which all are to perish with the using;) after the commandments and doctrines of men? Which things have indeed a shew of wisdom in will worship, and humility, and neglecting of the body: not in any honour to the satisfying of the flesh. (Colossians 2:6–23)

Blessings, Wealth, Increase, and Prosperity

- "The blessing of the LORD, it maketh rich, and he addeth no sorrow with it" (Proverbs 10:22).
- Praise ye the LORD. Blessed is the man that feareth the LORD, that delighteth greatly in his commandments. His seed shall be mighty upon earth: the generation of the upright shall be blessed. Wealth and riches shall be in his

house: and his righteousness endureth for ever. (Psalm 112:1–3)

- "But my God shall supply all your need according to his riches in glory by Christ Jesus" (Philippians 4:19).

Divine Healing

- But he was wounded for our transgressions, he was bruised for our iniquities: the chastisement of our peace was upon him; and with his stripes we are healed. (Isaiah 53:5)
- And these signs shall follow them that believe; In my name shall they cast out devils; they shall speak with new tongues. They shall take up serpents; and if they drink any deadly thing, it shall not hurt them; they shall lay hands on the sick, and they shall recover. (Mark 6:17–18)

Authority and Power in the Name of Jesus

- Who, being in the form of God, thought it not robbery to be equal with God: But made himself of no reputation, and took upon him the form of a servant, and was made in the likeness of men: And being found in fashion as a man, he humbled himself, and became obedient unto death, even the death of the cross. Wherefore God also hath highly exalted him, and given him a name which is above every name: That at the name of Jesus every knee should bow, of things in heaven, and things in earth, and things under the earth. And that every tongue should confess that Jesus Christ is Lord, to the glory of God the Father. (Philippians 2:6–11)
- And the seventy returned again with joy, saying, Lord, even the devils are subject unto us through thy name. And he said unto them, I beheld Satan as lightning fall from heaven. Behold, I give unto you power to tread on serpents and scorpions, and over all the power of the enemy: and nothing shall by any means hurt you. Notwithstanding in this rejoice not, that the spirits are subject unto you; but

rather rejoice, because your names are written in heaven. (Luke 10:17–20)

- "And Jesus came and spake unto them, saying, All power is given unto me in heaven and in earth" (Matthew 28:18).
- "Who is gone into heaven, and is on the right hand of God; angels and authorities and powers being made subject unto him" (I Peter 3:22).

Victory in All Things

- "I can do all things through Christ which strengtheneth me" (Philippians 4:13).
- "As it is written, For thy sake we are killed all the day long; we are accounted as sheep for the slaughter. Nay, in all these things we are more than conquerors through him that loved us" (Romans 8:36–37).
- "Then spake Jesus again unto them, saying, I am the light of the world: he that followeth me shall not walk in darkness, but shall have the light of life" (John 8:12).
- "Looking unto Jesus the author and finisher of our faith" (Hebrews 12:2).

Why Jesus? Let's reiterate, He is: Wonderful, Counsellor, The mighty God, The everlasting Father, The Miracle of the Ages, Prince of Peace, King of Kings, Lord of Lords, The Sinners' Savior, The Bread of Life, Deliverer of the Captives, Doorway to Deliverance, The Shepherd and Bishop of Our Souls, The True Vine, Our Healer, Our Mediator, Our Intercessor, The Author and Finisher of Our Faith, Our Salvation, Our Strength, Our Authority, Our Example...

"Come unto me, all ye that labour and are heavy laden, and I will give you rest. Take my yoke upon you, and learn of me; for I am meek and lowly in heart: and ye shall find rest unto your souls. For my yoke is easy, and my burden is light" (Matthew 11:28-30).

"And I, if I be lifted up from the earth, will draw all men unto me" (John 12:32). "Whosoever shall confess me before men, him shall the Son of man also confess before the angels of God: But he that denieth me before men shall be denied before the angels of God" (Luke 12:8-9).

- "That all men should honour the Son, even as they honour the Father. He that honoureth not the Son honoureth not the Father which hath sent him" (John 5:23).
- "If any man serve me, let him follow me; and where I am, there shall also my servant be: if any man serve me, him will my Father honour" (John 12:26).
- "Thou art worthy to take the book, and to open the seals thereof: for thou wast slain, and hast redeemed us to God by thy blood out of every kindred, and tongue, and people, and nation; Worthy is the Lamb that was slain to receive power, and riches, and wisdom, and strength, and honour, and glory, and blessing" (Revelation 5:9,12).

"Thank you Jesus (Yeshua) my Lord and my Savior"

CHAPTER 12

Humanity's Responsibility and Purpose

"In every thing give thanks: for this is the will of God in Christ Jesus concerning you" (1 Thessalonians 5:18).

Without an ability to understand and apply the truths of Scripture in a practical and meaningful way in our every day life believers miss out on the benefits, the anointing, the power, and the manifestation of the divine life God has ascribed for us. "If we say that we have fellowship with him, and walk in darkness, we lie, and do not the truth: But if we walk in the light, as he is in the light, we have fellowship one with another, and the blood of Jesus Christ his Son cleanseth us from all sin" (1 John 1:6-7).

"For this is the love of God, that we keep his commandments: and his commandments are not grievous. For whatsoever is born of God overcometh the world: and this is the victory that overcometh the world, even our faith. Who is he that overcometh the world, but he that believeth that Jesus is the Son of God" (1 John 5:3-5)?

Agape love, defined in Greek as "brotherly love, affection, good will, love, benevolence and charity" is the cornerstone of Christianity, as it is exemplified in Christ's sacrificial love on the Cross of Calvary. Christianity is a personal and intimate love relationship with God. Christians should be characterized by love not only in words, but also in deeds. Love is what love does.

As followers of Christ, we should be accountable when we hear the Word of God, accountable to share the Word of God, and accountable to walk it out. Our accoutablity is to God and to each other. "...Be thou an example of the believers, in word, in conversation, in charity, in spirit, in faith, in purity" (1 Timothy 4:12). "Herein is my Father glorified, that ye bear much fruit; so shall ye be my disciples" (John 15:8).

The absolutes of God's Word provide spiritual wisdom for a sure foundation that promotes right thinking and right attitudes, right direction and right choices, core values and ethical priorities, power and freedom.

Yes, Christ has redeemed us and paid for our sins. However, the more we justify sin the more we "grieve" and "quench" the Holy Spirit; and, therefore, the less we see impossible things made possible because our anointing, power, and victory is only made possible by our faith, through our renewed mind, our love walk, relationship with the Holy Spirit, and our obedience to the living Word.

You choose ... Man was made as a free moral agent. God provides opportunity to know His will, but He will never impose His will on us. Therefore, Scripture records, "I have set before you life and death, blessing and cursing: therefore choose life, that both thou and thy seed may live" (Deuteronomy 30:19).

When you have faith in God's truth, there should be a definite conviction of certainty-not that He may but that He will and has kept His promises to those whom are obedient to His covenants.

Renew Your Mind to Glorify God

- But unto every one of us is given grace according to the measure of the gift of Christ. Wherefore he saith, When he ascended up on high, he led captivity captive, and gave gifts unto men. (Now that he ascended, what is it but that he also descended first into the lower parts of the earth? He that descended is the same also that ascended up far above all heavens, that he might fill all things.)

And he gave some, apostles; and some, prophets; and some, evangelists; and some, pastors and teachers; For the perfecting of the saints, for the work of the ministry, for the edifying of the body of Christ: Till we all come in the unity of the faith, and of the knowledge of the Son of God, unto a perfect man, unto the measure of the stature of the fulness of Christ: That we henceforth be no more children, tossed to and fro, and carried about with every wind of doctrine, by the sleight of men, and cunning craftiness, whereby they lie in wait to deceive;

But speaking the truth in love, may grow up into him in all things, which is the head, even Christ: From whom the whole body fitly joined together and compacted by that which every joint supplieth, according to the effectual working in the measure of every part, maketh increase of the body unto the edifying of itself in love.

This I say therefore, and testify in the Lord, that ye henceforth walk not as other Gentiles walk, in the vanity of their mind, Having the understanding darkened, being alienated from the life of God through the ignorance that is in them, because of the blindness of their heart: Who being past feeling have given themselves over unto lasciviousness, to work all uncleanness with greediness. But ye have not so learned Christ; If so be that ye have heard him, and have been taught by him, as the truth is in Jesus: That ye put off concerning the former conversation the old man, which is corrupt according to the deceitful lusts; And be renewed in the spirit of your mind; (Ephesians 4:7-23)

- That ye present your bodies a living sacrifice, holy, acceptable unto God, which is your reasonable service. And be not conformed to this world: but be ye transformed by the renewing of your mind, that ye may prove what is that good, and acceptable, and perfect, will of God. (Romans 12:1-2)
- Thou shalt love the Lord thy God with all thy heart, and with all thy soul, and with all thy mind. This is the first and great commandment. And the second is like unto it, Thou shalt love thy neighbour as thyself. On these two commandments hang all the law and the prophets. (Matthew 22:36–40)

Desire and Seek to Know God

- God that made the world and all things therein, seeing that he is Lord of heaven and earth, dwelleth not in temples made with hands; Neither is worshipped with men's hands, as though he needed any thing, seeing he giveth to all life, and breath, and all things; And hath made of one blood all nations of men for to dwell on all the face of the earth, and hath determined the times before appointed, and the bounds of their habitation; That they should seek the Lord, if haply they might feel after him, and find him, though he be not far from every one of us: For in him we live, and move, and have our being; as certain also of your own poets have said, For we are also his offspring. (Acts 17:24–28)
- "What doth the LORD require of thee, but to do justly, and to love mercy, and to walk humbly with thy God?" (Micah 6:8)

Be Reconciled to God

- For we must all appear before the judgment seat of Christ; that every one may receive the things done in his body, according to that he hath done, whether it be good or bad. Knowing therefore the terror of the Lord, we persuade men; but we are made manifest unto God; and I trust also are made manifest in your consciences...For the love of Christ constraineth us; because we thus judge, that **if one died for all, then were all dead: And that he died for all, that they which live should not henceforth live unto themselves, but unto him which died for them, and rose again.**

- Wherefore henceforth know we no man after the flesh: yea, though we have known Christ after the flesh, yet now henceforth know we him no more. Therefore if any man be in Christ, he is a new creature: old things are passed away; behold, all things are become new. And all things are of God, who hath reconciled us to himself by Jesus Christ, and hath given to us the ministry of reconciliation; To wit, that God was in Christ, reconciling the world unto himself, not imputing their trespasses unto them; and hath committed unto us the word of reconciliation... we pray you in Christ's stead, be ye reconciled to God. (2 Corinthians 5:10-11,14–20)

Believers Are Called to Be Examples of Christ on Earth

- Do all things without murmurings and disputings: That ye may be blameless and harmless, the sons of God, without rebuke, in the midst of a crooked and perverse nation, among whom ye shine as lights in the world; Holding forth the word of life; that I may rejoice in the day of Christ, that I have not run in vain, neither laboured in vain. (Philippians 2:14-16)

Christians Are Called to Share the Gospel – "The Good News"

- Take heed unto thyself, and unto the doctrine; continue in them: for in doing this thou shalt both save thyself, and them that hear thee. (1 Timothy 4:16)
- And Jesus came and spake unto them, saying, All power is given unto me in heaven and in earth. Go ye therefore, and teach all nations, baptizing them in the name of the Father, and of the Son, and of the Holy Ghost: Teaching them to observe all things whatsoever I have commanded

you: and, lo, I am with you always, even unto the end of the world. Amen. (Matthew 28:18–20)

We pray ...

"Beloved, I wish above all things that thou mayest prosper and be in health, even as thy soul prospereth" (3 John 1:2).

CHAPTER 13

Pulling It All Together

Making Prayer Powerful—Lifestyle Principles for Empowerment

Examine the greatest self-help book ever written, the *Holy Bible* ..."**If ye continue in my word, then are ye my disciples** indeed; And ye shall know the truth, and the truth shall make you free...If the Son therefore shall make you free, ye shall be free indeed" (John 8:31-32, 36 emphasis added).

We have God's promises ... "For all the promises of God in him are yea, and in him Amen" (2 Corinthians 1:20). "My covenant will I not break, nor alter the thing that is gone out of my lips. It shall be established for ever as the moon, and as a faithful witness in heaven. Selah" (Psalm 89:34, 37).

We have the truths ... "God is not a man, that he should lie" (Numbers 23:19). We have the fundamental elements and the wisdom to awaken, encourage, and empower ourselves to have a powerful, faith-filled, and result-orientated prayer life as outlined in Scripture.

Spiritual wisdom is the Word of God. The Word of God is the Seed that produces Faith; Prayer is an act of Faith, The Works of Faith are your belief, trust, confidence, patience, experience, what you say, what you think, what you do, and your obedience to God's Word. Faith is the Seed for Miracles; and Miracles are the execution of Spiritual Wisdom through Faith and the Godhead: God, Jesus Emmanuel and the Holy Spirit.

The heart of prayer is love; the posture of prayer is humility; the focus of prayer is worship; the power of prayer is the Holy Spirit; the authority of prayer is Christ; the principle of prayer is faith; the manifestation of prayer is change, by the glory of God.

We are to deploy prayer as our arsenal in spiritual warfare: to combat worry, fear, anxiety, doubt, lust, jealousy, envy, pride, and everything that is in contradiction to God's Word. Prayer is used to enable us to reform and realign our thinking in the process of renewing our minds. Prayer is used to resist temptation when confronted with sin, to encourage when hopeless, to heal when sick, to petition God for our personal needs and desires, to seek wisdom and discern God's will, to pray for the salvation of others, and to intercede for someone or something (a ministry, a community, a nation, a world) that is in need of prayer. Above all, prayer is used to fellowship, worship, give thanks and have intimacy with God.

There is no magic formula. Walking in kingdom principles is a consistent lifestyle, not religion. The following are not formulas to obtain the blessings; however, they are principles and the foundational ways that affect the results that expresses and manifests our faith in God. These principles of faith flow through us and empower our relationship with God that grows from a relationship with God. All of these practices are inclusive of the whole. Powerful, effective prayer is a process and has everything to do with being united with God through Christ. "For through him we both have access by one Spirit unto the Father" (Ephesians 2:18).

The divine science of prayer is developed by engaging the Word of God, exercising faith in God's Word, renewing our mind, living in His will, being led by the Holy Spirit, and a right relationship with Christ. The following are key points for your spiritual reformation in the development of your ability to get results for a powerful prayer life.

Prioritize and make God first. In order to do this, Scripture states, "Seek ye first the kingdom of God, and his righteousness; and all these things shall be added unto you" (Matthew 6:33).

Operate by kingdom principles. The Kingdom of God is His law and Word that governs and operates in our life. "For the kingdom of God is not in word, [not in word only] but in power" (1 Corinthians 4:20). God is ALPHA and OMEGA, the beginning and the ending. God is ALL-knowing, ALL-powerful and has ALL authority. He is our Source and our Sustainer.

There are two systems of operation: God's way (our spiritual, divine nature) and the earthy way (unspiritual, the natural and the carnal man). We operate in kingdom authority when we live according to God's principles, His code of ethics, His statues, and His laws.

The Word of God is the seed that produces faith. When you engage the Word of God, you meditate in it, you confess it (speak it), you *believe* it, you *obey* it—this is sowing the Word of God. "The sower soweth the word" (Mark 4:14). Regarding the Word of God, "they are spirit, and they are life" (John 6:63).

Anchor God's Word in your thoughts, your spirit, your heart, your actions, your speech, and in your lifestyle. Stay focused, disciplined, committed, and patient in knowing that His way, His Word, and His principles cannot and will not fail. Recognize that they are the fundamental eternal truths, "for the things which are seen are temporal; but the things which are not seen are eternal" (2 Corinthians 4:18).

Join a church. The church represents God in this world. Seek out a local ministry for fellowship in an assembly that is Bible-taught and uncompromised in teaching the Word of God. Hebrews 10:25 tells us, "Not forsaking the assembling of ourselves together, as the manner of some is; but exhorting one another: and so much the more, as ye see the day approaching."

The practice of hearing ministry is similar to that of a coach; whereas both the minister and coach instructs with an end means to train, develop discipline, encourage, and inspire, with the hope of achieving empowerment. Scriptures tell us in Romans 10:14–17, "How then shall they call on him in whom they have not believed? and how shall they believe in him of whom they have not heard? and how shall they hear without a preacher? ... So then faith cometh by hearing, and hearing by the word of God."

"Repent, and be baptized every one of you in the name of Jesus Christ for the remission of sins, and ye shall receive the gift of the Holy Ghost" (Acts 2:38, emphasis added). Baptisms are commands that Jesus instructs for His followers recorded in John 3: 5, "Except a man be born of water and of the Spirit, he cannot enter into the kingdom of God." "He that believeth and is baptized shall be saved; but he that believeth not shall be damned" (Mark 16:16).

Listen to and watch gospel media broadcasts. A once-a-week assembly in a church is a start, but it is not enough. You eat more than once a week, therefore, feed your spiritual man more than once a week. In listening to ministry, your faith is strengthened and you are uplifted and encouraged. You feed your faith and starve your doubt. Mark 4:24 instructs us to, "Take heed what ye hear: with what measure ye mete, it shall be measured to you: and unto you that hear shall more be given."

Seek the truth. It is our nature to be inquisitive and curious. Is it not prudent to search the intent, the knowledge, and the how-to from our Creator? "Put on the new man, which is renewed in knowledge after the image of him that created him" (Colossians 3:10). Developing a powerful effective prayer life requires discipline to grow in spiritual knowledge and understanding, along with sanctification.

Feed your spiritual man. The Word of God is our spiritual nutrition. "It is written, Man shall not live by bread alone, but by every word that proceedeth out of the mouth of God" (Matthew 4:4).

Study, learn and become a disciple. Invest in a practical study Bible, with a Greek and Hebrew Lexicon, and a concordance. Scripture tells us in 2 Timothy 2:15, "Study to shew thyself approved unto God, a workman that needeth not to be ashamed, rightly dividing the word of truth." "For every one that asketh receiveth; and he that seeketh findeth; and to him that knocketh it shall be opened" (Luke 11:10).

Develop and maintain a relationship with God. The issues of confession, repentance, and being born-again are very important to one's relationship with God. Relationship means we are to let His Spirit, statutes, and principles govern our life.

Pursue spiritual wisdom. "For the LORD giveth wisdom: out of his mouth cometh knowledge and understanding" (Proverbs 2:6). Spiritual wisdom is a Word from God and the Word of God. "Give instruction to a wise man, and he will be yet wiser: teach a just man, and he will increase in learning. The fear of the LORD is the beginning of wisdom: and the knowledge of the holy is understanding" (Proverbs 9:9–10).

"So shall the knowledge of wisdom be unto thy soul: when thou hast found it, then there shall be a reward, and thy expectation shall not be cut off" (Proverbs 24:14).

Acquire understanding. It is of the utmost importance that you read, learn, and understand for yourself. "Wisdom is the principal thing; therefore get wisdom: and with all thy getting get understanding" (Proverbs 4:7).

This will enable you to use discernment, which will safeguard you from false doctrines, as Scriptures teach, "many false prophets shall rise, and shall deceive many" (Matthew 24:11). "Beloved, believe not every spirit, but try the spirits whether they are of God: because many false prophets are gone out into the world" (1 John 4:1).

Ask for spiritual discernment. Before you start to read your Bible or meditate, ask the Holy Spirit to reveal Himself in your inner man, your spirit, and your mind ... Jesus taught, "If ye then, being evil, know how to give good gifts unto your children: how much more shall your heavenly Father give the Holy Spirit to them that ask him?" (Luke 11:13)

Commit and set aside time daily with God. The degree of time spent in seeking God will determine the degree of God's intervention in our lives. No time, no knowledge, no knowledge, no manifestation. Jeremiah 29:13 tells us, "And ye shall seek me, and find me, when ye shall search for me with all your heart."

Set aside quiet time. Stillness is usually when the Holy Spirit speaks, and the softness of the voice is so soft that hurriedness, stress, and confusion oftentimes will overshadow the whisper. "Be still, and know that I am God" (Psalm 46:10).

Become aware and sensitive to the presence of the Holy Spirit. The Holy Spirit empowers us to hear from God, to receive guidance with a Word of knowledge and the Spirit of truth, discern spiritual wisdom, to conquer spiritual warfare, to fight sin, to pray, and lead us to redemption.

The Creator's holy nature is revealed to every person through his or her spirit. This powerful presence is key to our revelation, unwavering faith, and power in our spiritual transformation, in spiritual wisdom, in our right relationship with God, a powerful prayer life, and the power in the manifestation of miracles. *Our spirit and the Holy Spirit* is the vehicle by which we are meant to commune with God. It is the medium through which our spirit is intended to affect and be affected by God.

"Howbeit when he, the Spirit of truth, is come, he will guide you into all truth: for he shall not speak of himself; but whatsoever he shall hear, that shall he speak: and he will shew you things to come" (John 16:13).

"For the Holy Ghost shall teach you in the same hour what ye ought to say" (Luke 12:12). Some may call this intuition or a hunch and, "you have an unction from the Holy One, and ye know all things" (1 John 2:20).

Seeking God is also discerning His will and purpose in our daily lives that affects our intentions, choices, and decisions. "Trust in the LORD with all thine heart; and lean not unto thine own understanding. In all thy ways acknowledge him, and he shall direct thy paths" (Proverbs 3:5–6).

Pray in the Holy Spirit. "Ye shall receive power, after that the Holy Ghost is come upon you" (Acts 1:8). The Holy Spirit is the author of prayer. "Likewise the Spirit also helpeth our infirmities: for we know not what we should pray for as we ought:

but the Spirit itself maketh intercession for us with groanings which cannot be uttered" (Romans 8:26).

The speaking of "tongues" is supernatural, spiritual gifts. "For he that speaketh in an unknown tongue speaketh not unto men, but unto God...He that speaketh in an unknown tongue edifieth himself..." (1 Corinthians 14:2, 4).

"Earnestly desire the best gifts' (I Corinthians 12:31, emphasis added). "Now ye are the body of Christ, and members in particular. And God hath set some in the church, first apostles, secondarily prophets, thirdly teachers, after that miracles, then gifts of healings, helps, governments, diversities of tongues" (1 Corinthians 12:27-28).

Avoid prayer hindrances. "Grieve not the holy Spirit of God, whereby ye are sealed unto the day of redemption" (Ephesians 4:30). The barriers to answered prayer are ignorance to the Word of God, unbelief, worry, fear, doubt, self condemnation (guilt), unconfessed sin, unforgiveness, wrong motives, involvement in the occult, undeveloped faith, and rejection of spiritual authority and spiritual principles. You cannot violate the principles of God without consequence. These violations include natural and spiritual, as well as eternal, consequences.

Strive to live a holy and righteous life. The power and manifestation of prayer is conditional as Jesus stated in John 15:7, "If ye abide in me, and my words abide in you, ye shall ask what ye will, and it shall be done unto you." In order to walk in kingdom authority and to exercise our divine authority, we must be born-again of the Spirit.

Forgive yourself and others. Forgiveness is one of the deepest parts of love because it is probably one of the most difficult to give. In some instances it is only by the presiding power of the Holy Spirit that we are able to forgive and love with the heart of God. It was by the sovereignty of the Holy Spirit that Jesus while on the Cross was able to say, "Father, forgive them; for they know not what they do" (Luke 23:34).

Confess and repent of your sins. Unrepentance separates us from God. When we repent and confess our sins, condemnation goes away. "There is therefore now no condemnation to them which are in Christ Jesus, who walk not after the flesh, but after the Spirit" (Romans 8:1).

Be thankful for your past, your present, and your future blessings. Every blessing received should prompt us to praise God in prayer. How can God give us greater blessings if we do not appreciate those already given? Being thankful opens a gateway for additional blessings to flow to you and expands your capacity to receive more. It also validates your appreciation for what you do have, and it acknowledges your belief, faith, and confidence in God to manifest what you are praying for. "In every thing give thanks: for this is the will of God in Christ Jesus concerning you" (1 Thessalonians 5:18).

- "Bless the LORD, O my soul, and forget not all his benefits" (Psalm 103:2).
- "By him therefore let us offer the sacrifice of praise to God continually, that is, the fruit of our lips giving thanks to his name" (Hebrews 13:15).

Worship and praise God in Spirit and in Truth. *Worship* is the reverent honor, respect, humility, sincerity, and love with which we acknowledge God and live a submitted life in obedience according to His Word.

Praise comes out of worship from a rooted personal and intimate experience with God and a deep, heartfelt release of who God is and what He has done for you.

- "Let every thing that hath breath praise the LORD. Praise ye the LORD" (Psalm 150:6).
- "I will bless the LORD at all times: his praise shall continually be in my mouth" (Psalm 34:1).
- "I will praise thee; for I am fearfully and wonderfully made: marvellous are thy works; and that my soul knoweth right well" (Psalm 139:14).

Listen to worship and praise music. "Speaking to your-selves in psalms and hymns and spiritual songs, singing and making melody in your heart to the Lord" (Ephesians 5:19).

- "For the LORD taketh pleasure in his people: he will beau-tify the meek with salvation. Let the saints be joyful in glory: let them sing aloud upon their beds. Let the high praises of God be in their mouth…" (Psalm 149:4–6).
- "Make a joyful noise unto the LORD, all ye lands. Serve the LORD with gladness: come before his presence with singing. Know ye that the LORD he is God: it is he that hath made us, and not we ourselves; we are his people, and the sheep of his pasture. Enter into his gates with thanks-giving, and into his courts with praise: be thankful unto him, and bless his name" (Psalm 100:1–4).

Pray as a lifestyle, not to be performed only in times of the crisis but every day. Jesus stated in Luke 18:1, "that men ought always to pray, and not to faint." The Apostle Paul stated in Colossians 4:2, "Continue earnestly in prayer, being vigilant in it with thanksgiving." Prayerlessness will eventually lead to *spiritual* suicide.

We are to "come boldly unto the throne of grace, that we may obtain mercy and find grace to help in time of need" (Hebrews 4:16, emphasis added). We are not to pray as victims, "Nay, in all these things we are more than conquerors through him that loved us" (Romans 8:37).

Pray the solution, not the problem. God knows what we have need of before we ask; however, it is in the act of praying that we need to ask. As we pray, it is important to speak the Word of God and believe His Word and the fact that His power is moving through you as you speak. "Ye have not, because ye ask not" (James 4:2).

As we know "faith comes by hearing and hearing by the Word of God." Speaking your prayers out loud also has the effect of increasing your faith. In the same way, when reading your Bible, read it out loud and turn what you're reading into prayer.

Agreeing with God and His Word is a powerful act of intercession. As we declare the Word, we are *prophesying* into our circumstance according to God's Word.

Pray in the name and authority of Jesus. The authority we have in Jesus' name through prayer is based on a covenantal authority by the blood covenant relationship with God through Christ. All Christians have blood bought, promised, redemptive, legal and family rights to use the name of Jesus.

There is power in agreement and power in numbers. Christ has commissioned and released into the life of every Christian according to John 17:15-23 the ability to affect divine activity by cooperating and agreeing with the Word of God.

There is *power in agreement* and *power in numbers* in united prayer. The principal governing the prayer of agreement illustrates the power of unity, praying "in one accord [one mind]." Jesus declared in Matthew 8:19-20, "I say unto you, That if two of you shall agree on earth as touching any thing that they shall ask, it shall be done for them of my Father which is in heaven. For where two or three are gathered together in my name, there am I in the midst of them."

Pray blessings for your enemies. It has been said, whatever you curse will curse you, and whatever you bless will bless you. "Therewith bless we God, even the Father; and therewith curse we men, which are made after the similitude of God. Out of the same mouth proceedeth blessing and cursing. My brethren, these things ought not so to be" (James 3:9-11).

Pray with fasting. When these are combined, they are a powerful method that empowers us to discipline our physical body so that we become more in tune with our spiritual body. It allows us to hear and receive guidance, wisdom, instruction, and knowledge from God through the Holy Spirit. Together, they make up the most critical weapons of spiritual warfare and deliverance in our lives. Only through prayer and fasting can some hindrances, yokes of oppression, and spiritual warfare be conquered. As Jesus said in Mark 9:29, "this kind can come forth by nothing, but by prayer and fasting."

Pray with faith. Faith, by its very nature, begins in the realm of the unseen (the spiritual) and ends in what is seen (the physical). Faith encompasses various functions to complete its creative manifestation. The "prayer of faith" secures the manifestation. Every prayer should be prayed in *faith* with an expected manifestation; and if there is no manifestation, Scripture instructs us to, "Examine yourselves, whether ye be in the faith; prove your own selves. Know ye not your own selves, how that Jesus Christ is in you, except ye be reprobates" (2 Corinthians 13:5)?

Faith is active, which requires the execution of correct thinking. The works of faith is prayer with belief, hope, trust, confidence, and expectation in God, patience, what you think, what you say, and what you do. Without these principles and corresponding actions, your faith is powerless and without results; or perhaps it may not produce the results that you want. "... Faith without works is dead" (James 2:20).

Live a lifestyle of faith ... Your faith must stand firm in the Word of God, for the Word of God is forever settled and it never changes. Luke 21:33 declares, "Heaven and earth shall pass away: but my words shall not pass away" (Luke 21:33). It is a mind-set of thinking and acting in kingdom principles. Faith is not looking at the difficulties in life through the limitations of your human abilities, but it is looking at life and its challenges through God's ability and power to work through you. Refuse to submit to worry, doubt, and fear, for in doing so, you have forfeited your power of belief in the principle thing that you are praying for.

Persevere. Let us hold fast the profession of our faith without wavering; (for he is faithful that promised)" (Hebrews 10:23) and "Fight the good fight of faith" (1 Timothy 6:12).

- "(For we walk by faith, and not by sight)" (2 Corinthians 5:7).
- "But that no man is justified by the law in the sight of God, it is evident: for, The just shall live by faith. And the law

is not of faith: but, The man that doeth them shall live in them" (Galatians 3:11–12).

Be Hopeful. Hope is a perquisite for faith; hope generates enthusiasm. "Where there is no vision, the people perish" (Proverbs 29:18).

- "For we are saved by hope: but hope that is seen is not hope: for what a man seeth, why doth he yet hope for? But if we hope for that we see not, then do we with patience wait for it" (Romans 8:24–25).
- "Rejoicing in hope; patient in tribulation; continuing instant in prayer" (Romans 12:12).

Be Patient. Patience is a needed attribute. Once you have prayed, the resolution or the results may not be immediate, but Hebrews 10:35–36 tells us, "Cast not away therefore your confidence, which hath great recompence of reward. For ye have need of patience, that, after ye have done the will of God, ye might receive the promise." "...Knowing that tribulation worketh patience; And patience, experience; and experience, hope: And hope maketh not ashamed; because the love of God is shed abroad in our hearts by the Holy Ghost which is given unto us" (Romans 5:3–5).

Learn from your experiences. Experience is the knowledge gained from what you have previously gone through, whereas your faith is strengthened by wisdom that is attained through maturity, skilled practices, and wise judgment. There are vital lessons to be learned in adversities, and the most mastered life lessons are how you respond to adversity. As the Apostle Paul expressed in Philippians 4:11–12, "I have learned, in whatsoever state I am, therewith to be content ... I know both how to be abased, and I know how to abound."

Spiritual maturity is growth and development in perfecting our weakness in alignment with God's precepts that are cultivated by trust, relationship, and intimacy with God.

Developing your faith is a process, a lifestyle, and is achieved through your experience. It is further developed, as we grow closer and more aware of God's presence in our lives as God is our source. With each experience, we have in victory defeating the wiles of the devil, resisting temptation, and walking in the Spirit, we are empowered and further developed in spiritual wisdom, in the process of sanctification, to be Christ-like.

Believe your prayers will be answered. Your BELIEF is your POWER. Jesus taught in Matthew 21:22, "And all things, whatsoever ye shall ask in prayer, believing, ye shall receive." Again, Jesus said, "If thou canst believe, all things are possible to him that believeth" (Mark 9:23).

Trust in God. Trust is an inner conviction in God's Word and promises. Scriptures tells us in Isaiah 12:2, "God is my salvation; I will trust, and not be afraid: for the LORD JEHOVAH is my strength and my song; he also is become my salvation."

Remember, when you trust someone, you don't worry for there is no fear of consequence. Trust implies confidence and assurance; and total confidence comes with a peace of reassurance as reflected in 1 John 4:18-19, "There is no fear in love; but perfect love casteth out fear: because fear hath torment. He that feareth is not made perfect in love. We love him, because he first loved us," "by faith which worketh by love" (Galatians 5:6).

Expect that yours prayers will be answered. Expectation is the seed for miracles. Expectation is your confidence of belief. Worry is the inner fear that it will not work out and expectation is the inner confidence and trust that it will. Expect God to answer your prayers and thank Him before receiving your petition. If you do not expect anything, what's the point in praying? What you expect moves toward you, and what you do not expect moves away from you. Trust and belief, in and of itself, incorporates confidence. Your confidence empowers you to be compensated. "And this is the confidence that we have in him, that, if we ask any thing according to his will, he heareth us: And if we know that he hear us, whatsoever we ask, we know that we have the petitions that we desired of him" (1 John 5:14–15).

Guard your thoughts. The psychological warfare of the enemy is the war zone of the mind; faith and belief, or fear, worry, doubt, and unbelief. It is a war against good and evil, obedience and disobedience, the spirit and the flesh. "For though we walk in the flesh, we do not war after the flesh" (2 Corinthians 10:3).

So the degree of how much faith as trust there is in your life is how much anxiety and worry there is in your life. "And he that doubteth is damned if he eat, because he eateth not of faith: for whatsoever is not of faith is sin" (Romans 14:23).

Deploy your weapons of warfare. Prayer is used to enable us to realign our thinking in accordance to what Scripture says when our faith is challenged. Christ models this example in Luke 22:31-32, "And the Lord said, Simon, Simon, behold, Satan hath desired to have you, that he may sift you as wheat: But I have prayed for thee, that thy faith fail not: and when thou art converted, strengthen thy brethren."

"For the weapons of our warfare are not carnal, but mighty through God to the pulling down of strong holds; Casting down imaginations, and every high thing that exalteth itself against the knowledge of God, and bringing into captivity every thought to the obedience of Christ" (2 Corinthians 10:4–5).

Your Weapons: If you do not know about your salvation, just being saved is not enough. The armor that we are to put on is the armor of the Spirit of truth, understanding of biblical knowledge, and spiritual wisdom. These truths consist of, righteousness, the gospel of peace, faith, salvation, the Word of God, intimacy with the Father, and praying in the Spirit.

- "Put on the whole armour of God, that ye may be able to stand against the wiles of the devil... Above all, taking the shield of faith, wherewith ye shall be able to quench all the fiery darts of the wicked. And take the helmet of salvation, and the sword of the Spirit, which is the word of God: Praying always with all prayer and supplication in the Spirit" (Ephesians 6:11, 16-18).
- "Rejoicing in hope; patient in tribulation; continuing instant in prayer" (Romans 12:12).

- "Fight the good fight of faith" (1 Timothy 6:12).
- "The garment of praise for the spirit of heaviness" (Isaiah 61:3).
- "God is our refuge and strength, a very present help in trouble" (Psalm 46:1).
- "And let us not be weary in well doing: for in due season we shall reap, if we faint not" (Galatians 6:9).
- "Casting all your care upon him; for he careth for you" (1 Peter 5:7).
- "Submit yourselves therefore to God. Resist the devil, and he will flee from you. Draw nigh to God, and he will draw nigh to you. Cleanse your hands, ye sinners; and purify your hearts, ye double minded. Humble yourselves in the sight of the Lord, and he shall lift you up" (James 4:7–8, 10).
- "Thy words were found, and I did eat them; and thy word was unto me the joy and rejoicing of mine heart" (Jeremiah 15:16).

Replace the thoughts of fear with what Scripture says. Fear is the contradiction of faith. Your mental state is critical in conquering fear. "For God hath not given us the spirit of fear; but of power, and of love, and of a sound mind" (2 Timothy 1:7).

Renew your mind ... The Word tells us in Philippians 2:5, "Let this mind be in you, which was also in Christ Jesus." "Be not conformed to this world: but be ye transformed by the renewing of your mind, that ye may prove what is that good, and acceptable, and perfect, will of God" (Romans 12:2).

Think positive, for whatever you focus on gets stronger (the law of attraction) ... The Bible has outlined specific modalities that we should reflect, think, and meditate on. "Finally, brethren, whatsoever things are true, whatsoever things are honest, whatsoever things are just, whatsoever things are pure, whatsoever things are lovely, whatsoever things are of good report; if there be any virtue, and if there be any praise, think on these things" (Philippians 4:8).

Meditate on biblical Scriptures. The goal of biblical meditation is to *internalize and personalize the Scriptures* so that their truth can affect how we think, our attitudes, our actions, and how we live. Reflect and meditate on key points of Scriptures that apply to your circumstance.

Meditating on Scripture enables you to memorize Scripture, which is part of the process of, "Casting down imaginations, and every high thing that exalteth itself against the knowledge of God, and bringing into captivity every thought to the obedience of Christ" (2 Corinthians 10:5).

Speak the Word (Faith). To quote it, you need to memorize it; to memorize it, you need to meditate on it. "For the word of God is quick, and powerful, and sharper than any two edged sword..." (Hebrews 4:12).

When you pray, incorporate Scriptures, verses, and the promises of God in your prayers, for angels hear, obey, and act on your behalf when you speak God's Word. "Bless the LORD, ye his angels, that excel in strength, that do his commandments, hearkening unto the voice of his word" (Psalm 103:20).

Your words have creative power. Remember, God has ordained our words to have influence and power over our life. "Death and life are in the power of the tongue: and they that love it shall eat the fruit thereof" (Proverbs 18:21).

When your faith is challenged, speak the Word of God over your circumstance. What you believe and what you say go together. "We having the same spirit of faith, according as it is written, I believed, and therefore have I spoken; we also believe, and therefore speak" (2 Corinthians 4:13).

- "For by thy words thou shalt be justified, and by thy words thou shalt be condemned" (Matthew 12:37).

Walk in the Spirit of spiritual wisdom. Man needs God's Spirit to see things from God's perspective. The key indicator of spiritual maturity is one's ability to love in a godly way. How do we know this? To be spiritually mature is to be like Christ. We have been called to imitate Christ. It is the Holy Spirit that gives us the capacity to love as God loves.

> Thus saith the LORD, Let not the wise man glory in his wisdom, neither let the mighty man glory in his might, let not the rich man glory in his riches: But let him that glorieth glory in this, that he understandeth and knoweth me, that I am the LORD which exercise lovingkindness, judgment, and righteousness, in the earth: for in these things I delight, saith the LORD. (Jeremiah 9:23-24)

Walk in the Spirit of giving and watch God wonderfully supply all things you really need. "Give, and it shall be given unto you; good measure, pressed down, and shaken together, and running over, shall men give into your bosom. For with the same measure that ye mete withal it shall be measured to you again" (Luke 6:38).

- "He that hath pity upon the poor lendeth unto the LORD; and that which he hath given will he pay him again" (Proverbs 19:17).
- "Therefore all things whatsoever ye would that men should do to you, do ye even so to them: for this is the law and the prophets" (Matthew 7:12).
- "But this I say, He which soweth sparingly shall reap also sparingly; and he which soweth bountifully shall reap also bountifully" (2 Corinthians 9:6).

The Spirit of giving is not necessarily material; in fact, the most powerful forms of giving are nonmaterial. The gifts of giving of your time, appreciation, love, caring, affection, and prayers are precious gifts you can give, and they don't cost you anything. Whatever you are standing in need of, give to someone. As long as you are giving, you will be receiving. "Be not deceived; God is not mocked: for whatsoever a man soweth, that shall he also reap" (Galatians 6:7).

If you give grudgingly, there is no gift. It is the intention behind your giving that is the most important thing. 2 Corinthians 9:7 teaches, "Every man according as he purposeth in his heart, so let him give; not grudgingly, or of necessity: for God loveth a cheerful giver."

Walk in the Spirit of tithing. We give out of an acknowledgment of God's ownership as an act of love, gratefulness, and thanksgiving. For it is by Him that we are able to give. Tithing is also an act of obedience that connects you to the protection and the blessings of God. Believers should realize that God is their source and is the owner of everything that we possess. For, "thou shalt remember the LORD thy God: for it is he that giveth thee power to get wealth that he may establish his covenant which he sware unto thy fathers, as it is this day" (Deuteronomy 8:18). Tithing is a biblical ordinance and principle of giving to God a tenth of all of your first increase to support God's work and the ministry on Earth.

Walk in the Spirit of charity. When we remember the needs of our fellow man and give generously, we reflect the true essence of the heart of God. "And now abideth faith, hope, charity, these three; but the greatest of these is charity" (1 Corinthians 13:13).

- "And though I have the gift of prophecy, and understand all mysteries, and all knowledge; and though I have all faith, so that I could remove mountains, and have not charity, I am nothing" (1 Corinthians 13:2).
- "Now the end of the commandment is charity out of a pure heart, and of a good conscience, and of faith unfeigned" (1 Timothy 1:5).

Walk in the Spirit of love. Real Christianity recognizes as Jesus Himself said in Matthew 22:36–40, "Thou shalt love the Lord thy God with all thy heart, and with all thy soul, and with all thy mind. This is the first and great commandment. And the second is like unto it, Thou shalt love thy neighbour as thyself. On these two commandments hang all the law and the prophets."

Your commitment and call to action. Having knowledge does not entitle you to its rewards; you must apply, exercise, and commit to the principles to reap the results. Knowing is easy, but placing those beliefs into execution requires discipline, commitment, and strength.

"But be ye doers of the word, and not hearers only, deceiving your own selves" (James 1:22). "For not the hearers of the law are just before God, but the doers of the law shall be justified" (Romans 2:13).

"Keep thy heart with all diligence; for out of it are the issues of life" (Proverbs 4:23).

The result is a partnership. God works in and through us according to our faith. "Now unto him that is able to do exceeding abundantly above all that we ask or think, according to the power that worketh is us" (Ephesians 3:20).

(The power that worketh in us) IS KEY, AND IS WORTH REITERATING: IT IS YOUR RELATIONSHIP AND OBEDIENCE TO THE GODHEAD: GOD–CHRIST JESUS–HOLY SPIRIT–YOUR LOVE WALK-YOUR FAITH–YOUR BELIEF–YOUR PATIENCE–THE WAY YOU THINK, WHAT YOU SAY, AND WHAT YOU DO!

Elevate your consciousness ... "And be renewed in the spirit of your mind; And that ye put on the new man, which after God is created in righteousness and true holiness" (Ephesians 4:23–24).

Develop and execute your redeemed authority ... As we develop confidence in truth, knowledge, understanding and wisdom of Him, we will walk in greater courage, peace, trust, victory and authority. The authority you exercise is the result of divine exchange in operation, in your life.

- "He that believeth on me, the works that I do shall he do also; and greater works than these shall he do; because I go unto my Father. And whatsoever ye shall ask in my name, that will I do, that the Father may be glorified in the

Son. If ye shall ask any thing in my name, I will do it" (John 14:12–14).

- "But be ye doers of the word, and not hearers only, deceiving your own selves ... But whoso looketh into the perfect law of liberty, and continueth therein, he being not a forgetful hearer, but a doer of the work, this man shall be blessed in his deed" (James 1:22–25).
- "For as many as are led by the Spirit of God, they are the sons of God" (Romans 8:14).

This authority was declared by Christ in Matthew 16:18, "I will give unto thee the keys of the kingdom of heaven: and whatsoever thou shalt bind on earth shall be bound in heaven: and whatsoever thou shalt loose on earth shall be loosed in heaven." The "keys" are spiritual principles and insight that have been disclosed to live a powerful and liberated life in Christ; for "the Lord is that Spirit: and where the Spirit of the Lord is, there is liberty" (2 Corinthians 3:17).

Execute your divine power. "You shall receive power, after that the Holy Ghost is come upon you" (Acts 1:8). The power of the Holy Spirit must be combined with our obedience, faith, belief, trust, conviction, confidence, patience, our spiritual gifts and our relationship with Christ. "For in him dwelleth all the fulness of the Godhead bodily. And ye are complete in him, which is the head of all principality and power" (Colossians 2:9-10). "The kingdom of God cometh not with observation: ...behold, the kingdom of God is within you" (Luke 17:20-21).

"Know ye not that ye are the temple of God, and that the Spirit of God dwelleth in you" (1 Corinthians 3:16). Sanctify yourself through the living Word-God's truth. Keep from the evil; that you may become one with the Father so that the glory that Jesus conferred on the Body of Christ may be manifested through you. (John 17:17, 21-23) If we hear from Heaven, then Heaven will hear from us.

Awaken to your higher purpose. "That ye might walk worthy of the Lord unto all pleasing, being fruitful in every good work, and increasing in the knowledge of God; Strengthened with all might, according to his glorious power, unto all patience and longsuffering with joyfulness" (Colossians 1:10–11).

Evolve to be Christ-like. It is man's destiny and purpose to be conformed to the image of Jesus. As Jesus was the first-born (among many brethren), that means that there should be many more following in His steps. "And we know that all things work together for good to them that love God, to them who are the called according to his purpose. For whom he did foreknow, he also did predestinate to be conformed to the image of his Son, that he might be the firstborn among many brethren" (Romans 8:28–29). "But we all, with unveiled face, beholding as in a mirror the glory of the Lord, are being transformed into the same image from glory to glory, just as by the Spirit of the Lord" (2 Corinthians 3:18).

Our lifestyle should be a reflection of the characteristics and attributes of Christ. "A new commandment I give unto you, That ye love one another; as I have loved you, that ye also love one another. By this shall all men know that ye are my disciples, if ye have love one to another" (John 13:34–35).

Jesus, our example ... "For even hereunto were ye called: because Christ also suffered for us, leaving us an example, that ye should follow his steps" (1 Peter 2:21). "According as his divine power hath given unto us all things that pertain unto life and godliness, through the knowledge of him that hath called us to glory and virtue: Whereby are given unto us exceeding great and precious promises: that by these ye might be partakers of the divine nature" (2 Peter 1:3-4). "Blessed be the God and Father of our Lord Jesus Christ, who hath blessed us with all spiritual blessings in heavenly places in Christ" (Ephesians 1:3).

"Looking unto Jesus the author and finisher of our faith" (Hebrews 12:2).

Jesus, our model for living ... Jesus modeled who He is in God and who we are in Him. He came to show us who we are in His image as the power, the purpose, and the authority as, "sons and daughters of God." "Then spake Jesus again unto them, saying, I am the light of the world: he that followeth me shall not walk in darkness, but shall have the light of life" (John 8:12).

- "He that believeth on me, as the scripture hath said, out of his belly shall flow rivers of living water" (John 7:38).

We Have an Advocate. "For he hath said, I will never leave thee, nor forsake thee" (Hebrews 13:5). God is our Source. Admitting you can't do it all yourself is not a weakness, it is a strength. The Apostle Paul sought the Lord in his infirmities and the Lord said to him, "My grace is sufficient for thee: for my strength is made perfect in weakness. Most gladly therefore will I rather glory in my infirmities, that the power of Christ may rest upon me. Therefore I take pleasure in infirmities, in reproaches, in necessities, in persecutions, in distresses for Christ's sake: for when I am weak, then am I strong" (2 Corinthians 12:9–10).

"I am the vine, ye are the branches: He that abideth in me, and I in him, the same bringeth forth much fruit: for without me ye can do nothing" (John 15:5). "And we can do all things through Christ which strengtheneth us" (Philippians 4:13).

The Holy Spirit intercedes through us. We are not in this alone; we have resources to tap into the realm of the spiritual and connect with the Holy Spirit. "The Comforter, which is the Holy Ghost, whom the Father will send in my name, he shall teach you all things" (John 14:27). "I am with you always, even unto the end of the world. Amen" (Matthew 28:20). Only through a spiritual rebirth are we redeemed, conformed, transformed, sanctified, and regenerated. "Quench not the Spirit" (1 Thessalonians 5:18–19).

Jesus intercedes for us. "For there is one God, and one mediator between God and men, the man Christ Jesus" (1 Timothy 2:5).

- "Jesus saith unto him, I am the way, the truth, and the life: no man cometh unto the Father, but by me" (John 14:6).

Our authority in the name of Christ Jesus. Only through Christ are we restored to our purpose in God. Christ delegated and commissioned believers with the spiritual authority (influence) and the right of (privilege) to act in the authority of His name.

"And these signs shall follow them that believe; In my name shall they cast out devils; they shall speak with new tongues; They shall take up serpents; and if they drink any deadly thing, it shall not hurt them; they shall lay hands on the sick, and they shall recover" (Mark 16:17–18).

- "That at the name of Jesus every knee should bow, of things in heaven, and things in earth, and things under the earth" (Philippians 2:10).

Honor God... Your honor of God takes place in truth, in obedience, and in action.

- "Let us hear the conclusion of the whole matter: Fear God, and keep his commandments: for this is the whole duty of man" (Ecclesiastes 12:13).
- "Honour the LORD with thy substance, and with the first-fruits of all thine increase: So shall thy barns be filled with plenty, and thy presses shall burst out with new wine" (Proverbs 3:9–10).
- "The LORD saith, Be it far from me; for them that honour me I will honour" (1 Samuel 2:30).
- Jesus states, "If any man serve me, let him follow me; and where I am, there shall also my servant be: if any man serve me, him will my Father honour" (John 12:26).
- "That all men should honour the Son, even as they honour the Father. He that honoureth not the Son honoureth not the Father which hath sent him" (John 5:23).

Praise, Worship and Glorify God ... "But he that is joined unto the Lord is one spirit. What? know ye not that your body is the temple of the Holy Ghost which is in you, which ye have of

God, and ye are not your own? For ye are bought with a price: therefore glorify God in your body, and in your spirit, which are God's" (1 Corinthians 6:17,19–20).

"Thine, O LORD is the greatness, and the power, and the glory, and the victory, and the majesty: for all that is in the heaven and in the earth is thine; thine is the kingdom, O LORD, and thou art exalted as head above all" (1 Chronicles 29:11).

CHAPTER 14

A Relationship, Not Religion

"And this is life eternal, that they might know thee the only true God, and Jesus Christ, whom thou has sent" (John 17:3).

"God is love" and because of God's *agapē* love for humanity He sacrificed His Son. John the Apostle wrote, "For God so loved the world, that he gave his only begotten Son, that whosoever believeth in him should not perish, but have everlasting life" (John 3:16). "But God commendeth his love toward us, in that, while we were yet sinners, Christ died for us" (Romans 5:8).

Sin separates us from God by "grieving" and "quenching" our relationship with the Holy Spirit. In the New Testament, one of the words for sin in Greek, *hamartia*, literally means, "to miss the mark, to be without a share in, a violation of the divine law in thought or in act." **Salvation saves us from sin.** The Greek root word of salvation is *sozo* meaning, "to save, deliver or protect; heal, preserve, be (or make) whole."

No human works can result in salvation, "For by grace you are saved through faith, and this is not of yourselves, it is the gift of God; it is not of works, so that no one can boast. For we are his workmanship, created in Christ Jesus unto good works, which God hath before ordained that we should walk in them" (Ephesians 2:8-10). "Not by works of righteousness which we have done, but according to his mercy he saved us, by the washing of regeneration, and renewing of the Holy Ghost; Which he shed on us abundantly through Jesus Christ our Saviour; That being justified by his grace, we should be made heirs according to the hope of eternal life" (Titus 3:5-7).

No matter how hard you might try, you can never live a perfect life *in your own power*. "This is a faithful saying, and these things I will that thou affirm constantly, that they which have believed in God might be careful to maintain good works. These things are good and profitable unto men" (Titus 3:8).

Just as a loving parent loves his or her child in spite of their imperfect behavior, God loves us in spite of our imperfect lives; and because He loves us, He wants to be in a relationship with us. As the Apostle Peter wrote, "The Lord is not slack concerning His promise, as some count slackness, but is longsuffering toward us, not willing that any should perish but that all should come to repentance" (2 Peter 3:9).

The major pillars of the Christian faith are: there is only one true living God, the Bible is the inspired Word of God, Jesus is "the Son of the living God" and He died and rose the third day and, "He that believeth on the Son hath everlasting life: and he that believeth not the Son shall not see life; but the wrath of God abideth on him" (John 3:36).

God has provided this amazing solution to the problem of sin and our separation from Him: the Living Word, the Holy Spirit and the Word made flesh, Jesus. The execution of the Word and the results that it produces allow us to operate in kingdom authority through God's principles in kingdom law. "For the kingdom of God is not in word, [not in word only] but in power" (1 Corinthians 4:20). Everything we need to know and the know-how to resolve effective powerful prayer, to the glory of God, is depicted, taught, and lived out in the teachings and doctrine of the living Word.

It was through the power of the Holy Spirit in the disciples, and the followers of Christ, that they accomplished everything that they did. Christ makes it clear in John 3:5 that, "Except a man be born of water and of the Spirit, he cannot enter into the kingdom of God."

It was the relationship with the Father that Christ performed miracles and the relationship with, and the power of, the Holy Spirit that the disciples, and the followers of Christ, walked in the glory, the anointing, and the power to perform miracles. The same anointing, glory, and power is available to the Christian today. God's desire is that we would become united with Him. We are to dwell in Him and He in us. "...truly our fellowship is with the Father and with His Son Jesus Christ" (1 John 1:3). Fellowship is the Greek word *koinonia*, which literally means "partnership and communion."

If there is no spiritual connection, there is no intervention, and if there is no intervention, there is no revelation, and if there is no revelation there is no kingdom authority or power.

Simplistically speaking, our kingdom authority and our power in and of it is predicated in a walk of love, a walk of obedience, a walk of humility, and a walk of faith in honor and reverence to God in His Word and His supreme order. "Let us hear the conclusion of the whole matter: Fear God, and keep his commandments: for this is the whole duty of man" (Ecclesiastes 12:13). Jesus tells us, "If a man love me, he will keep my words: and my Father will love him, and we will come unto him, and make our abode with him" (John 14:23). "And whatsoever we ask, we receive of him, because we keep his commandments, and do those things that are pleasing in his sight" (1 John 3:22).

The continuing progression on our path of spiritual enlightenment, spiritual maturity, and spiritual development determines the degree of interaction, the degree of power, and the degree of results between the realm of Heaven and Earth, the spiritual and the physical, between our prayers and our answers.

Our aspired lifestyle should be one that has been reformed, refined, and regenerated by way of our thinking, speaking, and acting that is guided by the Holy Spirit through relationship with the Father, our love walk, spiritual wisdom, knowledge, understanding, and revelation in truth. For, "godliness is profitable unto all things, having promise of the life that now is, and of that which is to come" (1 Timothy 4:8).

Recorded as one of the eight Beatitudes during the Sermon on the Mount, Jesus tells us in Matthew 5:5, "Blessed are the meek: for they shall inherit the earth." The original word for meek in Greek is *praus,* defined as "gentle and caring, *yet* with characteristics of *self-control and moral strength.*" Isaiah, the great Messianic Prophet, preached in Isaiah 29:19, "The meek also shall increase their joy in the LORD." Anything worth mastering requires commitment and discipline.

To live in the precepts of the Word and a virtuous life is no exception, especially when society is so opposite of the moral ethics that are taught in the Bible. The visual, physical, emotional, and mental stimuli of our societies are geared to affect psychologically the pleasure center of the brain which has powerful effects on human behavior, profoundly influencing our choices and even our priorities. We can, however, make the right choices and keep our priorities in order and still experience a successful, prosperous, fun, happy, fulfilling, and blessed life. We are blessed to be a blessing.

The relationship and the connection to our heavenly Father in the success and power of our prayer life depend on it as does what happens to us in the Day of Judgment. "As it is appointed unto men once to die, but after this the judgment" (Hebrews 9:27). "For we must all appear before the judgment seat of Christ; that every one may receive the things done in his body, according to that he hath done, whether it be good or bad" (2 Corinthians 5:10). There is a heaven and there is a hell.

Revelation 20:12–15 states,

And I saw the dead, small and great, stand before God; and the books were opened: and another book was opened, which is the book of life: and the dead were judged out of those things which were written in the books, according to their works. And the sea gave up the dead which were in it; and death and hell delivered up the dead which were in them: and they were judged every man according to their works. And death and hell were cast into the lake of fire. This is the second death. And whosoever was not found written in the book of life was cast into the lake of fire.

"But the fearful, and unbelieving, and the abominable, and murderers, and whoremongers, and sorcerers, and idolaters, and all liars, shall have their part in the lake which burneth with fire and brimstone: which is the second death" (Revelation 21:8).

For the saved Christ tells us in John 14:1-4, "Let not your heart be troubled: ye believe in God, believe also in me. In my Father's house are many mansions: if it were not so, I would have told you. I go to prepare a place for you. And if I go and prepare a place for you, I will come again, and receive you unto myself; that where I am, there ye may be also. And whither I go ye know, and the way ye know." Hear the Word of the Lord, "a new Heaven and a new Earth":

1 Corinthians 15:49-58,

And as we have borne the image of the earthy, we shall also bear the image of the heavenly. Now this I say, brethren, that flesh and blood cannot inherit the kingdom of God; neither doth corruption inherit incorruption.

Behold, I shew you a mystery; We shall not all sleep, but we shall all be changed, In a moment, in the twinkling of an eye, at the last trump: for the trumpet shall sound, and the dead shall be raised incorruptible, and we shall be changed. For this corruptible must put on incorruption, and this mortal must put on immortality. So when this corruptible shall have put on incorruption, and this mortal shall have put on immortality, then shall be brought to pass the saying that is written, Death is swallowed up in victory. O death, where is thy sting? O grave, where is thy victory? The sting of death is sin; and the strength of sin is the law.

But thanks be to God, which giveth us the victory through our Lord Jesus Christ. Therefore, my beloved brethren, be ye stedfast, unmoveable, always abounding in the work of the Lord, forasmuch as ye know that your labour is not in vain in the Lord.

Some think that the ministry of the Bible is a yoke of bondage and that it's just too hard to do what's right. Others think that the godly are weak, are misconstrued as doormats, and are not prosperous or successful in society's mainstream viewpoint of success. The vast majority of people feel that Christians or faith-based believers should be infallible, and when they "miss the mark," they are perceived as hypocritical. Observers then become disillusioned by the faith when people professing the faith do not walk in perfection. The outright sinful wonder how God could forgive and accept them because of all the sin and wrong they have done. And, "The fool hath said in his heart, There is no God" (Psalm 53:1).

All of these mind-sets, and more, keep people from the Word of God. Truth be told, we are all a work in progress. Scripture says, "If we say that we have no sin, we deceive ourselves, and the truth is not in us... If we say that we have not sinned, we make him a liar, and his word is not in us" (1 John 1:8, 10). "But we are all as an unclean thing, and all our righteousnesses are as filthy rags; and we all do fade as a leaf; and our iniquities, like the wind, have taken us away ... But now, O LORD, thou art our father; we are the clay, and thou our potter; and we all are the work of thy hand" (Isaiah 64:6–8).

"For all have sinned, and come short of the glory of God; Being justified freely by his grace through the redemption that is in Christ Jesus: Whom God hath set forth to be a propitiation through faith in his blood, to declare his righteousness for the remission of sins that are past, through the forbearance of God" (Romans 3:23–25).

The Apostle Paul said it like this, "Not as though I had already attained, either were already perfect: but I follow after, if that I may apprehend that for which also I am apprehended of Christ

Jesus. Brethren, I count not myself to have apprehended: but this one thing I do, forgetting those things which are behind, and reaching forth unto those things which are before, I press toward the mark for the prize of the high calling of God in Christ Jesus" (Philippians 3:12–14).

"What shall it profit a man, if he shall gain the whole world, and lose his own soul? or what shall a man give in exchange for his soul" (Mark 8:36)? It's never too late to do right. Becoming a Christian, a follower of Christ, does not exempt you from trials and tribulations, but what it should do by your faithfulness and through prayer is, empower you. Our power lies in the Source of the power, which is God, through the authority in Christ and by the power and fellowship of the Holy Spirit. "No weapon that is formed against thee shall prosper; and every tongue that shall rise against thee in judgment thou shalt condemn. This is the heritage of the servants of the LORD, and their righteousness is of me, saith the LORD" (Isaiah 54:17).

"Who shall separate us from the love of Christ? shall tribulation, or distress, or persecution, or famine, or nakedness, or peril, or sword? As it is written, For thy sake we are killed all the day long; we are accounted as sheep for the slaughter. Nay, in all these things we are more than conquerors through him that loved us. For I am persuaded, that neither death, nor life, nor angels, nor principalities, nor powers, nor things present, nor things to come, Nor height, nor depth, nor any other creature, shall be able to separate us from the love of God, which is in Christ Jesus our Lord" (Romans 8:35–39).

The Apostle Paul writes, "And we know that all things work together for good to them that love God, to them who are the called according to his purpose" (Romans 8:28).

Scripture says, "For whosoever shall call upon the name of the Lord shall be saved" (Romans 10:13). "That if thou shalt confess with thy mouth the Lord Jesus, and shalt believe in thine heart that God hath raised him from the dead, thou shalt be saved. For with the heart man believeth unto righteousness; and with the mouth confession is made unto salvation. For the scripture saith, Whosoever believeth on him shall not be ashamed. For there is no difference between the Jew and the Greek: for the same Lord over all is rich unto all that call upon him" (Romans 10:9–12).

"How then shall they call on him in whom they have not believed? and how shall they believe in him of whom they have not heard? and how shall they hear without a preacher? And how shall they preach, except they be sent? as it is written, How beautiful are the feet of them that preach the gospel of peace, and bring glad tidings of good things! But they have not all obeyed the gospel. For Esaias saith, Lord, who hath believed our report? So then faith cometh by hearing, and hearing by the word of God" (Romans 10:14–17).

Beloved, God, our Creator loves us and beckons us to come, not as a religion, but a way of life, not as a denomination or ritualistic formalities, but to seek Him and to know His will in an intimate and personal relationship, and as a doer of the Word. Some would call this obtaining your higher consciousness, we as Christians call it Jesus. For Jesus declares, "I am the way, the truth, and the life: no man cometh unto the Father, but by me" (John 14:6).

The continuing progression on our path of spiritual enlightenment, spiritual maturity, and spiritual development in realizing deeper truths is that we need to learn how to live deeper within the truths, and values, of who we are in Christ. "Therefore if any man be in Christ, he is a new creature: old things are passed away; behold, all things are become new" (2 Corinthians 5:17).

Humanity was intended to be a reflection of the nature of God on Earth. It is, sinful fallen, humanity that has deviated from the standard of perfection that God set for us when He created us in His image and likeness. God's plan to restore humanity to His intended divine nature was perfected in Christ Jesus. Only through Christ are we restored to our purpose in God. Only through a spiritual rebirth are we redeemed, conformed, transformed, sanctified, and regenerated.

"Wherefore, as by one man sin entered into the world, and death by sin; and so death passed upon all men, for that all have sinned: (For until the law sin was in the world: but sin is not imputed when there is no law. Nevertheless death reigned from

Adam to Moses, even over them that had not sinned after the similitude of Adam's transgression, who is the figure of him that was to come. But not as the offence, so also is the free gift. For if through the offence of one many be dead, much more the grace of God, and the gift by grace, which is by one man, Jesus Christ, hath abounded unto many. And not as it was by one that sinned, so is the gift: for the judgment was by one to condemnation, but the free gift is of many offences unto justification. For if by one man's offence death reigned by one; much more they which receive abundance of grace and of the gift of righteousness shall reign in life by one, Jesus Christ.)

Therefore as by the offence of one judgment came upon all men to condemnation; even so by the righteousness of one the free gift came upon all men unto justification of life. For as by one man's disobedience many were made sinners, so by the obedience of one shall many be made righteous. Moreover the law entered, that the offence might abound. But where sin abounded, grace did much more abound" (Romans 5:12–20). "Neither is there salvation in any other: for there is none other name under heaven given among men, whereby we must be saved" (Acts 4:12).

You can enter into His presence just as you are, and if you have not accepted Jesus Emmanuel, the Christ, as your personal Lord and Savior, then say this prayer aloud, "Our Father, which are in heaven, hallow be thy name, please forgive me of my sins, come into my life, I believe that Jesus is the Son of God and that God raised Him from the dead. I accept Jesus Christ as my personal Lord and Savior and surrender to the Holy Spirit. Help me, teach me, and lead me in your path of righteousness."

If you are a born-again Christian and have strayed off the path, Scriptures states, "If we confess our sins, he is faithful and just to forgive us our sins, and to cleanse us from all unrighteousness" (1 John 1:9). "Being confident of this very thing, that he which hath begun a good work in you will perform it until the day of Jesus Christ" (Philippians 1:6).

"There is joy in the presence of the angels of God over one sinner that repenteth" (Luke 15:10).

We pray ...

"The LORD bless thee, and keep thee: The LORD make his face shine upon thee, and be gracious unto thee: The LORD lift up his countenance upon thee, and give thee peace" (Numbers 6:24-26).

Acknowledgments

Thank you heavenly Father, Christ Jesus, and the Holy Spirit; blessed are your holy names. I thank my loving husband, Arthur, for his patience, understanding, and help in the critiquing of this work. I am thankful for the love of my mother, father, and brother; and prayers and love of family and friends.

We are the sum total of all the people we learn from. This work is a result of the promptings of the Holy Spirit, a prayerful study, as well as hearing the living Word of the Holy Bible taught by teachers, and preachers that have also given me insight into a greater knowledge, and understanding, that I have written in this book.

Breinigsville, PA USA
21 February 2011
255965BV00003B/2/P